THE WORLD OF NUMISMATICS

GENERAL EDITOR: PETER A. CLAYTON, F.S.A.

Roman Coins

by C.H.V. SUTHERLAND
Keeper, Heberden Coin Room,
Ashmolean Museum, Oxford

G.P. PUTNAM'S SONS
New York

First published in the United States of
America in 1974 by G.P. Putnam's Sons,
New York, N.Y. 10016

Copyright © 1974 by Office du Livre,
Fribourg.

Published simultaneously in Canada
by Longmans Canada Limited, Toronto.
Library of Congress Catalog Card Number:
73-81400
SBN 399-11239-1

Printed in Switzerland

CONTENTS

INTRODUCTION

A short, clear history of Roman coinage is, almost by definition, impossible. The span of time itself is long—nearly eight centuries. This, however, would present no insuperable difficulties if it were not for the actual nature of the coinage. It is in the first place remarkably complex, not so much in its own internal development as in its relationship with those many other coinages—regal, provincial, and civic—with which for a long time it co-existed before it finally absorbed them. Then again, it was extraordinarily varied in its type content. So too in many ways were the coinages of the city-states of Greece, already described in this series by Mr G. K. Jenkins in his *Ancient Greek Coins*. But the Roman idiom, unlike the Greek, for long periods showed variety followed, if not for variety's sake, at least as the result of often firm policy, backed by deliberate purpose. Thirdly, as a matter of historical circumstance, most periods of Roman coinage are capable of being more or less closely dated. Greek coins, by and large, bore no visible indications of date for a long time, and their types are pre-eminent for beauty rather than for topicality. Roman coinage, by contrast, was not long in reflecting that annalistic turn of mind for which the Roman

character, with all its instinct for commemorative order, was famous. Under the Republic the moneyers soon came to add their names to the coins which they produced; and, although absolute dating for the moneyers is usually conjectural, their relative sequence is reasonably clear so that, with the topicality of some types as an additional help, most of the Republican series can be given a fairly firm (and detailed) chronology. For the Empire chronological definition is much greater: an emperor's titles and dated offices, combined with type-topicality, enable most sections of the imperial coinage to be arranged, observed, and studied within a surprisingly exact chronological framework.

From this it has resulted that a mass of research has taken place on the detailed implications of what can be so exactly studied. Many questions which originally seemed simple have been subjected to critical re-examination, and those questions which originally seemed to be of special difficulty are in many cases no easier now, simply because they must be viewed in the strict chronological context of the history of the time. The study of Roman coinage, in short, has become a severely critical discipline; and every decade, even if it brings remarkable discoveries, adds to that severity.

For these reasons a short history of Roman coinage must inevitably be very selective, and the plan of selection must obviously be personal and arbitrary. The most recent attempt to produce a short and comprehensive history was the *Roman Coins* written and later revised by Harold Mattingly, that undisputed master upon whom others will for so long depend. In the present volume no such degree of detail can be attempted, for it is much shorter. On the other hand, its more essentially narrative form, and the range and refinement of its illustrations, may contrive to give, more in miniature, a clearer and more integrated picture, supported as it is where necessary by critical foot-notes. It must, however, be emphasized that not every ephemeral emperor, not every successful usurper, and not every even temporarily busy mint could be recorded in so short a survey.

The earliest technique of Roman coins was, so to say, local, and of the simplest kind—the casting of bronze, at first into rough lumps, and then into bars and, ultimately, into circular coins. Early Roman contacts with the coinages of the Greeks in Italy led to the adoption of Greek methods of striking (as distinct from casting) coins, with the unsophisticated apparatus of engraved dies and hammer described in Mr Jenkins's volume for Greece. As time went on, Roman techniques acquired improvements of their own. The dies, at first 'paired' in no fixed physical relationship, came to be fixed in certain positions relative to each other. The 'flans' or blanks used for striking coins came to be more regularly rounded than many of the Greek coins of an earlier period. The organization of mints, originally simple, was administratively elaborated to a point, finally, where a coin of the Roman State bore a visible indication not only of the mint which produced it but also of the responsible subsection of that mint. This was one result of the powerful bureaucratic control which the Roman empire bred as a method of keeping that empire an integral unity. It was a similar degree of control that assured the imperial government an absolute power over the production and supply of the coinage metals.

The two great contributions made by Rome to the coinage of antiquity were, first, the principle of varying types, and secondly the development of portraiture. Type-variation was astonishing. Sometimes, perhaps, the degree of variation has stimulated too much subtlety in the explanations of modern scholars. But it remains a fact (which historians of Rome will neglect at their own and very serious risk) that for long periods during both the Republic and also the Empire this variation was perennial and intense—and therefore presumably a matter of deliberate policy, the purpose of which can only have been informative, that is to say, in the interests of the central and ultimately the imperial government. This was the imperial achievement as the imperial government wished it to be seen (in quick and small-scale form, and widely variable) by those to whom new issues were first circulated and by those, more remote, whose immediate reactions were of less importance as those issues spread slowly outwards.

8

As regards coin portraiture, this began late during the Republic. Throughout the Empire it was constant : occasionally poor, usually very good indeed, and not infrequently superb. The imperial portraits form a series of magnificent skill and perception, all the more splendid when it is remembered that portrait-dies had to be produced in large numbers—and also in repetitive sequence, which can so easily kill an artist's creative gifts. It is curious that we do not know the name of a single engraver. Greek coins had in some few cases borne the artist's name, in shorter or longer form : Roman coins never did. Perhaps this was due to some stricter aspect of organization under the Romans. Our loss today, however, is great, for, while it is easy to detect the rise and fall of particular artistic schools of portraiture, we know virtually nothing of the personal influences which individually great artists must have exerted in the formation of those varying schools.

The Roman territories under the Republic came to possess a great span, won by hard fighting and often shrewd diplomacy. Under the emperors that span was greatly increased, to a point at which the empire comprised the major part of the then civilized world. It was this huge administrative and economic unit that had to be supplied with an unfaltering coinage. Much has been written in recent years of the social classes and sectional interests for which coinage-supply was primarily designed, and of the possibly small coinage-needs of lesser and more remote rural communities. It is certainly true that coinage was required primarily so that the state might pay the army and civil service and also defray the cost of state-contracts. But money, once diffused, continues to be diffused outwards in payment for goods and services; and although the ripples grow less as they spread outwards the outward spread goes on. Moreover, the very circumstances of communication and supply in the ancient world meant that the great expanse of Roman territory was covered by a vast number of market towns each with its surrounding economic area, reciprocally supporting and supported. The maintenance of a loyal army and civil service, the stimulus to production and trade, and the preservation of strong economic links between town and country all depended upon the flow of coinage. At most times that flow was very great; and, in the light of the huge quantity of Roman coinage that has survived to the present day (the result, merely, of the discovery of coin-hoards and of coins that were casually lost), it is a sobering thought to reflect that what survives is only the tiniest percentage of what originally existed. Regarded in this way the planned variability of informative coin-types and the general insistence upon a high standard in representing the imperial features—the *sacri vultus*—were of clear and overwhelming importance. The Roman coinage, Republican as well as Imperial, acquired and developed an actuality and realism which is almost totally lacking in many another period.

These are qualities which are most clearly felt when the coins themselves are handled, and indeed handled in series. And in fact there is no true substitute for this. However, the illustrations in the pages that follow are designed to suggest the greatest possible degree of reality. Coin-photography is an art as subtle as it is difficult : the mean of clarity lies between the extremes of softness on the one hand and harshness on the other. The discriminating skill of Mr R. Gardner's photographs is immediately self-evident : so, too, the fine techniques by which his photographs have been transformed into the subsequent series of plates.

To this it must be added, and in deep gratitude, that neither photographer nor printer could have produced such fine illustrations without the author's ability to draw upon the superb series of Roman coins in the British Museum. Nearly every coin here shown is in that great collection. Finally, warm thanks must be expressed to Mr Peter Clayton, for his encouragement in the work of the book as a whole.

I.   THE EARLIEST COINAGE OF THE ROMAN REPUBLIC

The birth of coinage at Rome came late in comparison with that of the great Mediterranean basin as a whole. What is now conveniently, if rather loosely, called Greek coinage had originated in the early seventh century B.C. in and around Ionia, in Asia Minor; and from this early stage of currency, where electrum pieces of fairly regular weight were prevented by their variation in alloy from satisfying the requirements of a true coinage, namely, a predictable intrinsic value guaranteed by authority, Greek coinage had developed with remarkable speed. During the sixth century B.C., while gold still retained an importance in lands east of the Aegean sea, owing to its natural distribution in that area, cities and peoples of Greece proper (including the north and the Aegean islands) turned increasingly to the use of silver, of which their local supplies were often good. The convenience of silver coinage soon came to be widely appreciated. Intrinsically silver was valuable: free from the high-value risks of gold, but worth much more than copper or bronze. It was not difficult to refine, and, once refined, it was fairly malleable (if not so malleable as gold) and thus easy to strike into the form of coin. With the development of industry and commerce, therefore, the various Greek communities— if they were of any size and vigour—were quick to adopt coinage of pure silver as a means of exchange. Their individual coinages varied in respect of the weight of their basic units : the drachma in use at Aegina, for example, was heavier than the Athenian, and the Athenian was heavier than the Corinthian. However, as each city or community marked its coins with a clearly distinguishing type, often accompanied later on by its actual name, convertibility would have been no more difficult in inter-city transactions than is the case with the varying currency-units of the modern world.[1] Apart from the eastern shores of the Aegean, gold was seldom used for coinage except in case of emergency until the later fourth century : bronze (or copper) was slowly introduced to provide fractional values below the silver unit.

By about 300 B.C. coinage was a normal phenomenon in the lands comprising the Mediterranean basin. It was, principally, of silver, though the establishment of Macedonian power by Philip II and Alexander, together with their exploitation of rich Macedonian gold deposits, had led also to a familiarity with their abundantly issued gold 'philippeioi'. Alexander's powerful successors—Lysimachus of Thrace, Seleucus of Syria, and Ptolemy of Egypt—consolidated a systematized coinage in their own kingdoms; but elsewhere cities that were still free from these new kingdoms were also coining profusely, even as far west as Massalia in Gaul and Rhode in Spain. As early as the late sixth century Greek colonies in Italy and Sicily were beginning to strike their own silver issues: silver of Etruscan mintage was also to appear; and by the end of the fourth century Tarentum, Metapontum, and Neapolis had shown themselves pre-eminently as mints of great output and vigour. Across the narrow waist of the Mediterranean, moreover, a Carthaginian coinage was well established in North Africa. To all intents and purposes, therefore, the Greek monetary tradition flourished from the easternmost limits of the legacy of Alexander's conquests westward to busy colonial sites in Gaul and Spain.

Rome itself, about 300 B.C., was a community which, if small, had developed a remarkably precise political and military system—the early flowering of that genius for organization for which Rome became and long remained so famous. The expulsion of the early monarchy, and the successful repulse of the threat of Etruscan domination, had been followed by the need to consolidate a position in central Italy. This was a laborious process, even if it served to sharpen the cutting-edge of the Roman citizen-army; and it was not until 290 B.C. that Samnium and Latium, straddling the whole Italian peninsula below Rome, were conquered. It was at this juncture—and

1 ▶

2 ▶

1 Republic. *Obv., head of Janus, bearded.* c. *240-225 B.C., Rome (cast As, 240 gm., diam. 63 mm., BMCRR Rome 1). (For rev. see No. 3.)*

2 Republic. *Obv., elephant advancing.* c. *285-275 B.C., Rome (cast bronze bar, 1745 gm., 162 by 92 mm., BM). (For rev. see No. 4.)*

3

4

not before—that the true coinage of Rome was begun.

Currency, indeed, as distinct from coinage, had existed in central Italy from a much earlier date. Tradition, unsurprisingly anxious to seek respectable antiquity and continuity in state institutions, assigned coinage to the period of the Roman kings Servius Tullius and Numa.[2] Such a view, lacking any evidence to support it, is untenable. What is, however, certain is that early Rome recognized two major media of exchange, cattle and bronze. Ancient historians are at one in recording the derivation *pecus* (cattle)– **5, 6** *pecunia* (money); and there is equally strong evidence that in the course of the fifth century bronze was taking the place of cattle at specified equivalences of value (e.g. 100 lbs. bronze = 1 ox).[3] This bronze consisted of rough pieces—shapeless and unstamped—of an infinitely varying weight, so that in the payment of a given sum it had necessarily to be weighed out (*expendere*). According to the Elder Pliny, whose account of early Roman coinage is equally long and confusing,[4] this unworked bronze (*aes rude*) preceded the regal coinage of Servius Tullius. In fact (and with all possibility of regal coinage rejected), it is evident that *aes rude* had constituted the currency of central Italy for a long time, and that it certainly continued throughout the fourth century B.C., being doubtless produced at many a local centre by the local smith.[5]

As time went on, the inconvenience of a currency-medium made up in a form of such varying weight must have been more and more deeply felt. A change therefore came about, probably in the later fourth century, when the bronze was cast into the

3 Republic. *Rev., ship's prow to r. ;* l. c. *240-225 B.C., Rome (cast As, 240 gm., diam. 68 mm., BMCRR Rome 1). (For obv. see No. 1.)*

4 Republic. *Rev., sow standing.* c. *285-275 B.C., Rome (cast bronze bar, 1745 gm., 162 by 92 mm., BM). (For obv. see No. 2.)*

form of flat bars. These, too, must have been made in various centres : their weights fluctuated considerably, above and below a usual focus of five Roman pounds. Known today for convenience as *aes signatum*—a term without ancient authority [6]— these oblong bricks of bronze sometimes bore a design moulded on one side only : later, each side bore a design, of which one at least might be of a kind that facilitated chopping the bar into roughly even sections. They have been found widely distributed over north-central and south-central Italy, the earlier specimens in association with *aes rude*, the later with the first true bronze coins of Italy. Their original function has been variously interpreted.[7] It is enough to say here that, owing to weight-variation, they did not constitute coinage. But they were certainly a medium of exchange, like *aes rude,* though (unlike *aes rude*) made up into a form that could more easily be carried, packed, and subdivided. The designs which they bore were, for some time, those which a metal-smith could personally select. Only later, as we shall show, can local or political significance be seen in them.

The widespread use of bronze as an exchange-medium in central Italy was natural enough. Even if the central Italic peoples had, during the fifth and fourth centuries B.C., advanced to an economic point at which the high intrinsic value of silver would have been appropriate or acceptable, supplies of silver were not available to them. Etruria might get silver from the north, and also from further afield by sea; if southern Italy had any at all,[8] it was extremely little. By contrast, the ores needed for bronze were abundant in central and north-central Italy; and when the peoples of the centre exploited bronze as a heavy-weight exchange-medium they were doing no more than had been done with copper, bronze, and iron in earlier times elsewhere.[9] These were dual-purpose metals—vital for manufactured goods (including weapons), and thus valuable in exchange.

Rome in due course produced its own bronze bars. The earliest cannot be positively identified. About 300 B.C., however, among a range of double-type bars,[10] two varieties of special importance appeared. One broken bar survives with Branch, ROM.../Incuse tendril. Four others are known with Eagle/Pegasus, ROMANOM ('of the Romans').[11] The association of the latter (Eagle = Rome; Pegasus = (?) Carthage) with the Rome-Carthage treaty of 280 B.C. is impossible, for the legend ROMANOM would hardly have been associated directly with the Carthaginian device. What is fairly certain is that Rome continued to produce bronze bars during the first quarter of the third century B.C., and even longer. Those (uninscribed) with Indian elephant/Sow must surely reflect Aelian's reference to the war in Italy against Pyrrhus of Epirus in the 280s : others (also uninscribed) with Hens/Rostra may commemorate one of Rome's naval victories in the 260s or just after.[12] It seems certain, in any case, that round about 300 B.C. Rome was producing bronze bars as a state-currency, as witnessed by the explicit inscriptions ROM... and ROMANOM.

None of these, however, amounted to coinage proper; and for the beginnings of

7, 8

2', 4

21, 2

this we must consider the conjunction of events whereby, with the Samnite wars concluded in 290, and with Pyrrhus of Epirus in the ascendant and casting eyes upon south Italy (leading Rome to ally with Carthage in 280), monetary arrangements were put on a regular and fully public footing at Rome *c.* 289. This last date is given by Pomponius, a lawyer of the second century A.D., who wrote explicitly [13] that at that time the *triumviri monetales* were established as *aeris, argenti, auri flatores* : these are plainly the junior officials, aspirants to a senatorial career, who are found with the later and continuous title of *IIIviri aere argento auro flando feriundo,* i.e. the *collegium* of three responsible for the melting and striking of bronze, silver, and gold. The physical choice of a site for the actual mint is recorded by Suidas :[14] it was set up in the time of the Pyrrhic wars within the temple of Juno Moneta, which lay on the Capitol. Pliny, in his elaborate and difficult summary of early Roman coinage,[15] emphasized the following points : (i) the Roman people coined no silver before Pyrrhus' failure (275 B.C.); (ii) the currency unit being used at that time was a bronze As weighing one pound; (iii) earlier bronze had consisted of *aes rude* or stamped bars; (iv) silver was coined—i.e. for the first time—in 269 B.C.;[16] and (v), by implication, this silver consisted of denarii each worth 10 bronze one-pound Asses.

From Pliny's comments there has arisen a long and deep dispute, recently analysed with great patience in R. Thomsen's masterly work.[17] Briefly expressed, the problem is this. Was the earliest Roman denarius (marked x, = 10 bronze Asses) first struck by the *IIIviri* in 269, as Pliny appears to state ? If so, how did it relate at various later periods in the third century B.C. with (a) silver Greek-style didrachms in the Roman name, (b) Roman silver 'quadrigati' [18] and their halves, (c) Roman gold pieces and their fractions, and (d) a long series of bronze coins with Roman types, some struck, some cast, in which an original one-pound weight standard sank by a half ? The importance of these questions can be underlined by asking two more. First, if the earliest Roman mint was officially systematized only in 289 B.C., is it conceivable that within 20 years Rome would have been able, with the Pyrrhic war only just finished and the First Punic War imminent, to give silver a fixed and visible value (x) in terms of bronze, bearing in mind the greatly increased use for bronze that armament production would bring ? Secondly, and more to the point, is there any evidence apart from Pliny that the denarius was introduced in 269 B.C. ?

For nearly all scholars [19] the answer to this last question is negative, and decisive. Literary evidence places the first denarius at about the end of the third century.[20] The evidence of archaeology proper assigns it to about 211 B.C.[21] From the comparative analysis of coin-hoards—an instrument of great power—a similar date emerges.[22] The whole complex story may be read in Thomsen's great work, from which it should be decisively clear that the first x-denarius was struck at Rome, not in 269 B.C., but *c.* 211 B.C., and that it reflected the great economic strain suffered by Rome during the Hannibalic wars in Italy.

It remains, then, to determine for what practical purpose Rome established a board of moneyers *c.* 289, with a mint upon the Capitol : an organization implies a product. Rome was by then perfectly familiar with the concept of coinage, i.e. pieces of metal (normally circular) of predictable weight, and bearing a device—usually by now with an inscription—indicating the community which issued and guaranteed it. The Greek colonies of south Italy had been producing coinage for a long time past : so too the cities of Sicily. Naples (Neapolis) lay in Campania only a little more than 100 miles away to the south of Rome; and its coinage of silver, and later of bronze, bearing the characteristic type of a man-headed bull with the legend *ΝΕΟΠΟΛΙΤΩΝ,* must have been readily available in that region to any who journeyed thither by land or by sea. In 326 B.C., in fact, Rome made a treaty with Naples; and it will have been at some time after that date (and not necessarily at once) that bronze coins were struck, closely similar in type and weight to those of Naples itself, but bearing the legend *ΡΩΜΑΙΩΝ.* The issue was small—only some half-dozen examples now survive; but they must certainly reflect the closer ties which the treaty encouraged. And if they contained any reciprocal element of compliment, it is likely that they were struck at Naples itself on behalf of Rome. They were followed by a bronze issue now known only from a single coin. The obverse of this shows a Minerva-head instead of Apollo: the reverse, still with the Neapolitan man-headed bull, now reads ROMANO[*m*], 'of the Romans'. It is probable that this derivative coinage was struck at Rome

5, 6 Republic. *Obv., bull r., head facing. Rev., bull. l., head facing. c. 300 B.C., Rome (?) (cast bronze bar, 1790. 23 gm., 170 by 94 mm., BMCRR Rome 1).*

7, 8 Republic. *Obv., eagle, wings spread, holding thunderbolt. Rev., Pegasus prancing, wings spread;* ROMANOM. *c. 300-275 B.C., Rome (cast bronze bar, 1389.64 gm., 167 by 99 mm., BMCRR Rome 2).*

9, 10 Republic. *Obv., head of young Janus, beardless and diademed ;* l. *Rev., head of Mercury wearing winged petasus ;* l. *c. 289-280 B.C., Rome (cast As, 340 gm., diam. 36 mm., BM).*

11, 12 Republic. *Obv., head of young Mars, beardless and helmeted ;* S. *Rev., head of Venus, diademed ; sickle behind ;* S. *c. 260-240 B.C., Italy (cast semis, 173.40 gm., diam. 28 mm., BM).*

5

6

7

8

9

10

11

12

13

14

15

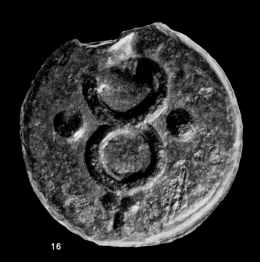

16

17

18

19

20

itself as the polite counterpart (made by Greek workmen) of the *PΩMAIΩN* pieces.[23]

By 290 B.C., therefore, Rome had emerged victorious over a large 'Italic' area of central Italy, with great spoils of bronze,[24] and had begun her contacts with Campania, the gateway to the Greek south. It was at this point that the decision was made to establish an orthodox monetary system. Bronze bars, indeed, still continued for a little, as we have seen—perhaps for ceremonial or votive purposes. For normal purposes, however, they were superseded by true coinage : the impressive and even formidable progress now just made by Rome as a military power brought the certainty of contact, friendly or otherwise, with the south. The monetary system devised *c.* 289 therefore showed a highly interesting dualism. In the Italic centre, long accustomed to heavy weights of bronze, a heavy coinage of bronze was instituted, based upon an As of one pound containing 12 unciae (ounces), with the following range :[25]

As (*c.* 322 g.)	Young Janus-head, I (= 1 As)/Mercury-head, I	9, 10
Semis (6 unciae)	Young Mars-head, s(emis) /Venus-head, s(emis)	11, 12
Triens (4 unciae)	Thunderbolt, 4 dots /Dolphin, 4 dots	13, 14
Quadrans (3 unciae)	Two barley grains, 3 dots /Open hand, 3 dots	
Sextans (2 unciae)	Shell, 2 dots/Caduceus, 2 dots	15, 16
Uncia	Knucklebone, 1 dot/1 dot	
Semuncia (1/2 uncia)	Acorn/Value mark	

All these denominations were cast in moulds—their points of junction in the mould are visible—for they were too large and too thick, and with relief too high, to

13, 14 Republic. *Obv., thunderbolt ; · · · ·. Rev., dolphin ; sickle above ; · · · ·.c. 245 B.C., Rome (cast triens, 91.23 gm., diam. 25 mm., BM).*

15, 16 Republic. *Obv., scallop-shell ; · ·. Rev., caduceus ; · ·. c. 289-280 B.C., Rome (cast sextans, 47.4 gm., diam. 19 mm., BM).*

17, 18 Republic. *Obv., diademed head of Apollo. Rev., diademed head of Apollo. c. 280-260 B.C., Rome (cast As, 300 gm., diam. 36 mm., BM).*

19 Republic. *Obv., Pegasus prancing ; S. c. 280-260 B.C., Rome (cast semis, 175.24 gm., diam. 30 mm., BM).*

20 Republic. *Obv., horse's head ; · · · ·. c. 280-260 B.C., Rome (cast triens, 103.43 gm., diam. 26 mm., BM).*

allow striking from dies. Cumbrous though they may seem, however (and they were far less cumbrous than bronze bars), they furnished a suddenly complete coinage range for those accustomed to heavy bronze. They were true coins, in the tradition transmitted by Greece: clearly marked with recognizable types, circular in shape, and (for good measure) bearing marks of value. Their principal types were aptly

9, 10 chosen: Janus, god of beginnings and turning-points; Mercury, god of travel and

11, 12 commerce; Mars, the now active god of war; Venus, ancestor goddess of the Roman people. Here, then, was a coinage which, though it lacked the name of Rome in writing, proclaimed Rome in all its major types, and which catered for values from the unit—the As—down to 1/24th of the unit. It was to be the model for numerous other issues of *aes grave* (as it is technically known) from Rome's early Latin colonies—Cales, Luceria, Venusia, Hatria, Ariminum, and Firmum.[26]

Those first products of the *tresviri monetales* at Rome were designed in a strong, hard style which was in fact to be characteristic of a large part of Roman coinage down to the end of the Republic. No great desire existed, it is evident, to elaborate such details as the planes of relief in a profile head, or the waved masses of hair. The coins were clear and practical, but not in any way—to the modern eye at least—beautiful. However, a very different style marked the first silver struck in the name of the Romans—pieces of *c.* 7.25 g.[27] with *obv.* Bearded

23, 24 Mars-head, oak-branch behind, and *rev.* Bridled horse's head above a tablet inscribed ROMANO, corn-ear behind. Very similar to

these are bronze coins of *c.* 5.10 g. with the head of Minerva instead of Mars. Type- 25, 26 parallelism places these Greek-style silver didrachms early in the third century. The bearded Mars-head is a close copy of the head of Leucippus found on didrachms of Metapontum *c.* 300 B.C., and the bridled horse's head has very strong similarities to the coinage of Carthage, with which in fact Rome made an alliance in 306.[28] In all essentials the ROMANO Mars/Horse pieces are Greek coins: made of silver, equivalent to 2 drachmae, and bearing types characteristic of the central Mediterranean and rendered in fine Greek style, evidently by Greek artists. They were followed fairly quickly by a second series of silver didrachms with *obv.* Apollo head, ROMANO, 27, 28 and *rev.* Sun above cantering horse—again a Carthaginian echo.

The ROMANO didrachms with Mars and Apollo heads cannot easily be attributed to the new mint under the *tresviri monetales* at Rome, where even the importation of Greek artists from the south would probably have failed in the face of Rome's undeveloped technical standards. It is impossible to say where their production took place; but it is usually agreed now that they were struck in southern Italy by Roman military commanders calling both upon the services of Greek artists and craftsmen and also possibly upon supplies of silver partly derived from Carthage. After the outbreak of war with Pyrrhus in 280 B.C. the need for such a coinage would have been urgent: in order to buy services and materials in the silver-using south, Rome itself must pay in silver. One result of the contact with Greek monetary artists in the south seems to have been an improvement in aesthetic standards at Rome, as shown by a new series of *aes grave* featuring (like the second series of didrachms) the head of Apollo :

7, 18
19
20

As (*c.* 334 g.) [29]	Apollo head/Apollo head
Semis	Pegasus, s(emis)/Pegasus, s
Triens	Horse's head, 4 dots/Horse's head, 4 dots
Quadrans	Boar, 3 dots/Boar, 3 dots
Sextans	Dioscurus head, 2 dots/Dioscurus head, 2 dots
Uncia	Barley grain, 1 dot/Barley grain, 1 dot

The coins were not in any sense elegant : their large size and the very technique of casting prevented that. But the Apollo heads are not without grace in modelling and hair-treatment, while the Pegasus, horse's head and boar show some real fluency and life.

It was to 269 B.C., as already seen, that Pliny (either expressly or by implication) assigned the first denarii of the mint of Rome under the *tresviri monetales*—a view which has to be rejected on emphatic grounds.[30] What the Roman mint did produce in or about that year was its first silver coinage, consisting of didrachms (only marginally lighter than the southern Apollo/Horse coins) with *obv.* Young Hercules head, *rev.* Wolf and twins, ROMANO. The type of Hercules was copied from Syracusan bronze coins of 279 or after. The wolf and twins must look to the action of the brothers Cnaeus and Quintus Ogulnius in 296, when they added the twins to the Capitoline group; and the same Q. Ogulnius, consul in 269, could thus commemorate that earlier action on coins actually struck upon the Capitol.[31] No more positive a manner of declaring the origin of this coinage could be conceived. Its production was due, partly, to previous familiarity with a didrachm coinage struck on Roman

account in the south : these new silver coins of Rome could themselves be used anywhere in that south. Another cause, however, was the impending war with Carthage : the building up of military and naval forces and materials would call for large supplies of silver, and in fact the Hercules/Wolf and twins issue of didrachms was fairly closely followed by another, with *obv.* Roma head, *rev.* Victory, ROMANO— doubtless an assurance that Carthage would be defeated.[32] The didrachms of both these series were of fine Greek style : the *tresviri monetales* had clearly drafted in artists and workmen of real skill from the Greek south.

At about the same time as these didrachms two new series of *aes grave* appeared. One, with types Helmeted Roma-head/Helmeted Roma-head on the As, ran down to semuncia with types already seen before. The other began with triple As (tressis, marked III), double As (dupondius, marked II) and As, all with *obv.* Helmeted Roma-head, with a range of new obverse types down to sextans : all the reverses showed a six-spoked wheel. In both cases it is clear that the weight of the As was at this stage being substantially reduced : from a level of *c.* 334 g. in the Apollo/Apollo series (see above) it was slipping down, dropping to a point around or even below 270 g. This reduction

31, 32

has been variously interpreted. However, there is no need for over-subtle theory. Since the beginning of the third century Rome had been increasingly on a war-economy. The primary coinage metal of Rome was bronze, silver being produced originally for external purposes in the south: even now, Rome's silver coins lacked the denominational marks of value that were regular on the bronze. With an internal monetary system that was monometallic, in bronze, and with bronze in ever increasing demand for a developing programme of warfare, it was natural that its value should rise, with a consequent diminution in the weight-standard of *aes grave*. Bronze was, in fact, being slowly revalued upwards.[33]

This process was to continue in the period between the First and Second Punic Wars, when the output of the mint of Rome was in any case elaborated. Three issues of silver didrachms were made, again in fine Greek style :

33,34 1 *Obv.* Young Mars-head.
  Rev. Bridled horse's head; ROMA; symbol, sickle.
35,36 2 *Obv.* Young Mars-head; symbol, club.
  Rev. Prancing horse; ROMA; symbol, club.
37,38 3 *Obv.* Apollo-head.
  Rev. Prancing horse; ROMA.

Of these three didrachm issues (all struck at *c.* 6.55 g.), nos. 1 and 3 were accompanied by corresponding drachms; and a range of smallish struck bronzes, ranging from *c.* 6.25 to *c.* 1.65 g., was also produced, with the legend ROMA, for those areas which,

21,22 Republic. *Obv., two hens feeding, face to face ; between, two stars. Rev., two rostra, l. and r. ; between, two dolphins.* c. 260 B.C., Rome (cast bronze bar, 3500 gm., 164 by 93 mm., BM).

23,24 Republic. *Obv., head of Mars, helmeted ; oak-branch with acorn behind. Rev., bridled horse's head ; corn-ear behind ;* ROMANO *on tablet.* c. 280-260 B.C., south Italy (?) (silver didrachm, 7.56 gm., diam. 20 mm., BM).

25,26 Republic. *Obv., head of Minerva, helmeted ;* ROMANO. *Rev., bridled horse's head ;* ROMANO. c. 280-260 B.C., south Italy (?) (bronze half-litra, 5.91 gm., diam. 18 mm., BM).

27,28 Republic. *Obv., head of Apollo ;* ROMANO. *Rev., horse prancing ; star or sun above.* c. 275-260 B.C., south Italy (?) (silver didrachm, 6.84 gm., diam. 22 mm., BMCRR Romano-Campanian 21).

29,30 Republic. *Obv., head of young Hercules ; lion's skin and club at shoulder. Rev., wolf and twins ;* ROMANO. c. 269 B.C., Rome (silver didrachm, 7.03 gm., diam. 20 mm., BM).

31,32 Republic. *Obv., head of Roma wearing Phrygian helmet with gryphon's head crest. Rev., Victory attaching ribboned wreath to palm-branch ;* K, ROMANO. c. 265-260 B.C., Rome (silver didrachm, 6.76 gm., diam. 19 mm., BM).

22

21

23   **24**

25   **26**

27

28

29

30

31

32

33

34

35

36

37

38

39

40

41

42

33, 34 Republic. *Obv., head of Mars, slightly bearded ; helmet ornamented with gryphon. Rev., bridled horse's head ; sickle behind ;* ROMA. c. *260-240 B.C., Rome (silver didrachm, 6.71 gm., diam. 19.5 mm., BMCRR Romano-Campanian 57).*

35, 36 Republic. *Obv., head of Mars, slightly bearded, wearing helmet ; club behind. Rev., prancing horse ; club above ;* ROMA. c. *260-240 B.C., Rome (silver didrachm, 6.38 gm., diam. 19.5 mm., BMCRR Romano-Campanian 49).*

37, 38 Republic. *Obv., head of Apollo, long-haired. Rev., prancing horse ;* ROMA. c. *260-240 B.C., Rome (silver didrachm, 6.47 gm., diam. 19 mm., BMCRR Romano-Campanian 68).*

39, 40 Republic. *Obv., head of young Janus. Rev., head of Mercury wearing winged petasus ; sickle behind.* c. *260-240 B.C., Rome (cast As, 257.24 gm., diam. 37 mm., BM).*

41, 42 Republic. *Obv., head of Roma wearing Phrygian helmet ; club behind. Rev., head of Roma wearing Phrygian helmet ; club behind.* c. *250-240 B.C., Rome (cast As, 290 gm., diam. 34 mm., BM).*

requiring a didrachm coinage, preferred at the same time small struck bronzes to the heavy cast bronze values traditional at Rome itself.[34] The major visual change in these silver and bronze coins lies, of course, in the substitution of ROMA for ROMANO(*m*) (= *Romanorum*) : the genitive plural ethnic (analogous to the usage on Greek coins of south Italy) which had originally been employed for a Roman silver coinage intended for southern recipients and circulation now gave way to the clear and simple statement of place of origin, implying the actual state and government of Rome. It is of interest, too, that the types of Mars-head and Apollo-head, which were used for substantially earlier ROMANO didrachms (see above, p. 26), were now renewed after the intervention of the Hercules and Roma obverses. The same reversion to earlier types was seen also on the accompanying *aes grave* that was now produced.[35] Janus/ **39, 40** Mercury reappeared on the As of a series (down to uncia) which, with the As at c. 272 g., was much lighter than the original issue (p. 25) with the As at c. 320 g. : it was additionally distinguished by the sickle symbol on all its denominations. A new light Apollo/Apollo As (c. 283 g.) headed a range (incomplete) of denominational types already seen on the earlier and heavier series (with an As of c. 335 g.): the symbol was a vine-leaf. Finally, another Roma/ Roma As (c. 269 g.) headed a repeated range **41, 42** (down to uncia) all bearing the club symbol. These bronzes are the last to be found before the introduction of the famous Bearded Janus/Prow Asses of c. 267 g., **1, 3** with which (as will be seen) entirely new silver was associated, of diminished Greek

ETRURIA
Rome
Anagnia
Corfinium
Ostia
LATIUM
SAMNIUM
Capua
CAMPANIA
Beneventum
Naples
Metapontum
Tarentum
Brundisium
Epidamnus
Apollonia
EPIRUS
Corcyra
Actium
Croton
Zacynthus

0   220 Kms
0   140 Mls

CASPIAN SEA

BLACK SEA
THRACIA
Philippi
NIA
Pharsalus
Pergamum
ASIA
Sardis
Athens
Ephesus
Corinth
ACHAEA
Rhodes
Crete

PONTUS
ARMENIA

PARTHIA

SYRIA
Cyprus

Alexandria

AEGYPTUS   NABATAEA

idiom. Thus, the fact that the sickle and the club of the light Janus/Mercury and of the repeated Roma/Roma *aes grave* are found also on two out of the three didrachm issues just described must argue strongly (as does their change from ROMANO to ROMA) that these are the last of Rome's fully grecizing didrachm coinages.

The issues just described were produced *c.* 240 B.C., around 50 years after the establishment of the Rome mint under the *tresviri monetales*. During that half-century, which, following Rome's domination of central Italy, saw her involved first in the Pyrrhic war and then in the First Punic War, the weight of the Roman silver didrachm had declined from *c.* 7.25 to *c.* 6.55 g., i.e. about 10 per cent. That of the As had dropped more sharply, from *c.* 330 to *c.* 270 g., i.e. about 20 per cent. Not enough is known about possible fluctuations in metal-supply at that time to allow any firm theories about the increase of metal-prices through shortages at source. Nor can it be said with confidence of Rome in the mid-third century B.C. that monetary economics were so well understood as to prompt the deliberate production of each new issue at a weight not exceeding that of the partly worn average of its predecessors. The only plain fact, abundantly clear from a great mass of surviving coins, is that the value of silver appreciated, and that the value of bronze appreciated even more. It is not difficult to understand the reasons. Whatever the social advantages of coinage were understood to be at this period,[36] its principal objects were, without doubt, to enable the state to pay for the goods and services which it needed in order to maintain

43, 44 Republic. *Obv., head of Mars, bearded and helmeted ; behind,* VX *(= 60). Rev., eagle on thunderbolt ;* ROMA. *c. 211-209 B.C., Rome (gold 60-As piece, 3.42 gm., diam. 14 mm., BMCRR Rome 185).*

45 Republic. *Rev., two warriors, differently dressed and armed, and one bearded, touching with their swords a pig held by youth kneeling between them ;* ROMA. *c. 218-216 B.C., Rome (gold, 6.87 gm., diam. 18 mm., BMCRR Romano-Campanian 77).*

46

47

48

49

government, essential supplies and public works, and security. These, in a period of internal development and external warfare, were heavy liabilities; and it would seem that silver and bronze values were slowly but quite steadily raised—by various means of which the coinage alone now provides the constant evidence—so that the state might properly discharge those liabilities. It is necessary, perhaps, to remember no more than that Rome, during the First Punic War, had had to build fleet after fleet, the earliest to fight and win the victory at Mylae in 260, the last to fight and win off Aegusa in 242. The strain of war had been immense; and, even if a defeated Carthage, as well as surrendering Sicily, paid Rome an indemnity of 3200 talents, this great sum could not have offset the cost of 24 years of fighting.

After the First Punic War Rome dominated most of the Italian peninsula. The northern frontier still remained to be consolidated against Gaulish peoples; and the tribes and colonies of the Greek south were still independent, with continuing autonomous coinage.[37] But Rome's territorial scope was already impressive, and half a century of expansion had brought growing familiarity with monetary questions. It was at this moment that the Roman monetary system was fundamentally changed, in the first of two stages of which the Hannibalic war in Italy was to bring the second in due course.

This first stage consisted partly of the abandonment of Greek-style silver didrachms in favour of silver of the same weight, but of essentially Roman style, as follows:

46 Republic. *Obv., head of Mars, bearded and helmeted; behind,* XX (= 20). c. *211-209 B.C., Rome (gold 20-As piece, 1.12 gm., diam. 10 mm., BMCRR Rome 190).*

47, 48 Republic. *Obv., head of young Janus, laureate. Rev., Jupiter with thunderbolt and sceptre in quadriga driven by Victory;* ROMA. c. *235-213 B.C., Rome (quadrigatus, 6.77 gm., diam. 22 mm., BMCRR Romano-Campanian 83).*

49 Republic. *Rev., the Dioscuri, with stars above their heads, charging on horseback with couched spears; corn-ear below;* ROMA. c. *209-5 B.C., Sicily (denarius, 3.88 gm., diam. 17.5 mm., BMCRR Rome 281).*

47 *Obv.* Young Janus head, laureate.
48 *Rev.* Jupiter with sceptre and thunderbolt in quadriga driven by Victory : ROMA.[38]

Struck in very considerable quantity, these 'quadrigati' were accompanied by less common half-pieces, perhaps appearing earlier rather than later.[39] The choice of the young laureate Janus head has been explained, with good probability, as reflecting one of the rare occasions in Roman history when, in 235 B.C., the doors of the temple of Janus at Rome were triumphantly closed, marking the total absence of warfare.[40] Production of quadrigati continued for about two decades : the style in general, and the obverse type in particular, are exactly the same as those of gold coins (*c.* 6.80 g.) and their halves :

Obv. Young Janus head, laureate.
45• *Rev.* Two soldiers, differently dressed, performing oath over pig held by third figure : ROMA.[41]

The corruption in the text of Pliny's summary of early Roman coinage [42] makes it dangerous to rely upon any information which he may seem to give, but it is possible that he was recording the first Roman production of gold 51 years after the first Roman silver (269 B.C.), i.e. in 218 B.C. If so, this gold recalls the hoped-for unity between Rome and its Italian allies in the face of Hannibal's invasion of Italy in that year. And the very production of a gold coinage, after nearly 20 years of the issue of quadrigati, must point to an emergency drawing upon Roman financial reserves.[43]

The second element in the re-organization of the Roman monetary system after the First Punic War affected the bronze—and not less fundamentally. Hitherto there had been considerable type-variation in the Roman bronze; but now, probably very near in time to the introduction of the quadrigatus *c.* 235 B.C., a standard reverse type of a ship's prow was introduced for all denominations. The earliest series of this new bronze was all cast, and the 'Libral' 1*, 3 As (at *c.* 270–255 g.) was only slightly lighter than previous issues. Obverse types were as follows : As – bearded Janus; semis – Jupiter; triens – Minerva; quadrans – Hercules; sextans – Mercury; and uncia – Bellona. The marks of value (I, S, ..., etc.) appeared with the prow on the reverses.[44] The significance of the prow is uncertain, but it is evident that the Second Punic War saw Rome develop into a maritime power, in virtue of which not only Sicily, but Sardinia soon afterwards, had been added to the Roman possessions.

The series of quadrigati continued, as already mentioned, for about two decades, and with nothing except terminal change of detail, when the legend ROMA, originally incuse, came to appear in relief on a raised tablet or within a linear frame : these last also showed a corn-ear symbol of the reverse. In the bronze, however, there was a sharp reduction in weight, at a date which (since the 'Libral' series was evidently issued in large quantity) may have occurred in the later 220s. The weight of the As fell suddenly to *c.* 132 g., that is, to about half of the 'Libral' As; and with all the coins in the range proportionately smaller and lighter it was possible, while still casting all denominations from As to quadrans (with types unchanged), to strike the sextans and uncia (again with heads of Mercury and Bellona) and to add a struck semuncia and quartuncia, also respectively with Mercury and Bellona. On the reverses of all these struck denominations the legend ROMA was added.[45] The 'semi-libral' series did not last very long, being replaced by one still lighter, in which the As weighed *c*. 88 g. As well as possessing large multiples of 10, 3 and 2 Asses, this 'reduced semi-libral' series showed a range of mainly cast fractions from semis to quadrans, with struck sextans, uncia and semuncia. The types were unchanged from those of the 'semi-libral' series,[46] and a corn-ear appeared on certain of the smaller coins.

Such was the stage reached in the development of Roman coinage about the time when Hannibal, advancing from a well-moneyed base in Spain, let loose the Second Punic War upon Italy and Rome in 218 B.C. Seventy years had passed since the establishment of the mint at Rome under the *tresviri monetales*. For a few years that mint had confined its activities to producing heavy *aes grave*, with some bars as well. It then turned to the issuing of silver Greek-style didrachms with ROMANO and ROMA: during this period the weight of the As showed eventual decline, and there was an increase in the variety of small struck bronzes with types analogous to those of the didrachms. Probably about 235 B.C. the Greek-style didrachms gave way to the Roman-style quadrigati: these, ultimately accompanied by some gold for emergency purposes, appeared with the new 'prow' bronzes, the weight-standard of which, at first stable, began to fall quickly as the Second Punic War loomed near. The *tresviri monetales* had in fact performed the historical sequence in their official title: *aere argento auro flando feriundo*.

Silver, as will have been noted, maintained its weight well by contrast with bronze. But it must be remembered that it was the bronze upon which the Roman monetary system was based. For this reason, indeed, bronze coins at Rome had from the very beginning shown marks of value, from the largest to the smallest denomination. Silver showed no such value marks; nor, with extremely rare exceptions, did the 'oath-scene' gold. The precious-metal coins evidently circulated as bullion, and not as specie: they found their value in the money-markets according to the confidence extended to them. Bronze, however, was a coinage with fixed face-values; and it is not difficult to imagine what distress would have been caused to those who lent in a heavier series, and recovered their debts in a lighter, unless (a) the value of bronze actually rose, and (b) a sufficient volume of silver began to permeate the economy.

It is here accepted that all, or at any rate the overwhelming majority, of the coins described above were issued from the mint of Rome. Their chronology admittedly raises many problems.[47] But on the question of mintage, although specific evidence is slight, there should be no doubt. The late Harold Mattingly held to a theory of quadruple mintage ('Ostia', 'Beneventum', Rome, and 'Tarentum') for much of the didrachm and heavier *aes grave* coinage.[48] Apart from the fact that this fragmentation depends substantially, and dangerously, upon the subjective analysis of style, such a system would seem to fly in the face of those very reasons which must have prompted most strongly the official establishment of the Rome mint, namely, full security and full administrative control. These are factors which are seen to operate, clearly and consistently, in all the later coinage of Rome.

II. THE INTRODUCTION AND SUPREMACY OF THE DENARIUS, *c.* 211-100 B.C.

In the late 220s the clouds of fresh warfare had gathered, or were just beginning to darken widely different parts of the Roman horizon. Northern Italy was disturbed by a dangerous incursion of Gauls : their defeat by a very large Roman force was followed by the establishment of Roman colonies on the river Po. The Adriatic sea was harried by Illyrian pirates who imperilled the security of southern Italy : their subjection by a Roman fleet led to the extension of Roman protection over Apollonia and Epidamnus (useful entrepôts, incidentally, for the acquisition of north Balkan silver), as well as Corcyra. But the major threat came from Carthage, and was to develop, surprisingly, from Spain, where Punic activity had reached a level that led Rome, in 226, to attempt to set the river Ebro as a limit to its advance. The effort was in vain : Carthage in 219 besieged Saguntum, with which Rome had concluded an alliance, and when Saguntum fell in that same year Rome declared war on Carthage.[49]

It had probably been the Roman intention, in the event of a Second Punic War, to strike directly at the city of Carthage by naval attack. Punic strategy made all such plans too late. Hannibal, the young Carthaginian general in Spain, led his large army of infantry, cavalry, and elephants in a lightning march up through Spain and Gaul, over the Alps, and into northern Italy. For Rome, defeat followed defeat : Trebia in 218, and Lake Trasimene in 217, on each occasion with great loss. Hannibal did not attack the city of Rome itself. Instead, he set himself to strip Rome of all its surrounding friends and supporters. Capua and other allies were persuaded to revolt : the kingdom of Macedon joined Hannibal's cause; and even Sicily seemed likely to fall away. Hannibal had in fact made a cardinal error in deciding not to attack the city of Rome, but *c.* 212, when Roman fortunes were at their very lowest, it is doubtful if that was realized at Rome. New armies and fleets had constantly to be raised, and new weapons manufactured. The finances of the Roman state and its government were strained to limits, unknown previously, which were probably not paralleled during the later course of the Republic.

According to many earlier studies, these desperate financial straits left little mark, if any, upon the silver coinage of Rome. Those who, following Pliny, assigned the earliest denarii to *c.* 269 B.C. were in general prepared to agree with him that the denarius, originally valued at 10 bronze Asses, was re-valued during the Hannibalic war to 16 Asses. Some, still assigning the first denarii to 269, placed the revaluation much later than the Hannibalic war. There is, moreover, the problem of the bronze. Pliny recorded that the As was reduced to the weight of one ounce ('uncial') during that war : Festus, writing later but more fully, recorded that it was at that time reduced to the weight of two ounces ('sextantal'). An immense and complicated literature has grown up around the date of the first denarius, and around the extent of reduction in the bronze standard at the close of the third century.[50]

Many different kinds of argument have come to converge in recent studies. The weights of coins, silver as well as bronze, have been carefully tabulated. The borrowing of the types of one coinage by another has been chronologically analysed. Ancient written sources have been scrupulously criticised. To these methods others have been added—notably, archaeological evidence and comparative hoard-analysis. 'Of two hoards with some issues in common, that which is later will contain issues which do not occur in the other hoard and which are less worn'.[51] Thus, if Festus' association of the sextantal bronze standard with the Hannibalic war is accepted, 'there are four hoards which associate the latest coinage of the didrachm system [i.e. quadrigati] or the earliest coinage of the denarius system [i.e. sextantal bronze] with coins of Hieronymus or the Syracusan democracy [i.e. from 216 B.C.], both groups showing comparable degrees of wear'.[52] Finally, and with apparent conclusiveness, when a temple at Morgantina in Sicily was destroyed by a fire almost certainly datable to 211 B.C., its roof-debris fell in on a small hoard, contained in a jug, which included (with 'victoriati': see below) one denarius of the generally admitted earliest type, together with three corresponding quinarii (silver half-pieces) and one sestertius (silver quarter-piece).[53] In other words, the Morgantina finds suggest very strongly that the denarius and its fractions (together with the victoriatus) had appeared by 211 B.C. Finds elsewhere, however, suggest that these denominations had not appeared in the closely preceding years. The inescapable conclusion must be that the denarius was introduced immediately before 211 B.C.—perhaps 213 or 212 : a controversy which at various times has placed it as early as 269 B.C., or as late as 187, or even 169,[54] must be said to have been settled finally.

The revised Roman monetary system of *c.* 213/212 B.C. clearly reflected the prevailing financial stress. Bronze, which had until now enjoyed a loose bimetallic relationship with silver, now became in effect a subsidiary coinage : the 'reduced semi-libral' As of *c.* 88 g. (see above, p. 41) now sank to *c.* 55 g., the weight of an early heavy sextans, and was not destined to hold steady even there, falling soon to half that weight. The monetary emphasis passed to silver, part of which now for the first time bore a mark of value (X) expressed in terms of bronze Asses: the denarius (at *c.* 4.5 g.) was a 10-As piece, and

50, 5

was accompanied by its half, the quinarius (marked v), and its quarter, the sestertius (marked IIS). On the denarius and its fractions, struck in fine style and with good, well modelled relief, the types were :

50, 51   *Obv.* Helmeted head of Roma; x (= 10) or v or IIS behind.
     Rev. The Dioscuri, with stars above, riding with couched lances; ROMA.[55]

Very soon after the introduction of the x-marked denarius, and certainly by 209 B.C. (when Rome's gold-reserves of 4000 pounds were called upon),[56] gold coins were struck, and seemingly in larger quantity than the earlier Janus/Oath-scene pieces (see above, p. 40) of *c.* 218 B.C. This new gold, like a few of the earlier gold pieces, was value-marked, and the types were as follows :

43*   *Obv.* Head of Mars; below, VX (= 60),
46   XXXX (= 40), or XX (= 20).
44*   *Rev.* Eagle on thunderbolt; ROMA.

These three denominations were struck at *c.* 3.4, 2.3 and 1.1 g. respectively. Disagreement exists about the meaning of the value-marks, some interpreting them as sestertii (i.e. units of 2 1/2 Asses), and some as Asses. The latter view is preferable, partly because the new and immediately preceding denarius coinage was marked in terms of As values (a double system would surely have been misleading), and partly because valuation in Asses would have resulted in metal-ratios that conformed in general with those of the times—gold : silver *c.* 1 : 9; silver : bronze, *c.* 1 : 120; gold : bronze, *c.* 1 : 1000.[57]

Urgent pressures in the Hannibalic war had thus changed Rome's monetary system fundamentally. Bronze, already value-marked previously, suffered a sharp decline in weight, due most probably to its importance as a war-material. Silver, on a new standard and with new types, was value-marked in terms of bronze : supplies of silver would have come partly from the melting down of the earlier didrachms and quadrigati, and partly perhaps from newly available Illyrian sources. Finally, gold-reserves had to be coined, and here again value-marks were employed. The types of the gold and silver—Mars and Roma; eagle on thunderbolt and the Dioscuri; always with ROMA—were emphatically war types. It was the coinage of a Rome fully stretched in war. However, it was not the whole of Rome's coinage at this critical time. The Morgantina hoard[58] shows that it was at the same period that Rome produced silver coins (at first *c.* 3.4 g., though declining in subsequent years) which were known by the Romans as 'victoriati'[59] from their types :

Obv. Laureate head of Jupiter.   52
Rev. Victory crowning trophy of arms;   53
     ROMA.

These coins, issued in substantial quantity, bore no mark of value. That is to say, they were intended for recipients for whom the new Roman system of silver expressing bronze values had no relevance : recipients outside the Roman state, the Roman army, and the Roman navy. Their purpose was to provide a coinage, guaranteed by Rome, for payment to non-Romans, for whom silver within the weight-range of a Greek drachma would be wholly suitable.

Of this new Roman coinage—gold, denarii, victoriati, and lightened and lightening bronze—a large amount must have been produced at Rome itself by the *tresviri monetales*. But the necessities of war compelled the operation of mints elsewhere, some of which can be identified or reasonably conjectured. Livy, in describing the emergency-call upon the gold-reserves in 209 B.C., recorded that it was divided among the two consuls and two proconsuls (i.e. the four generals actually in the various fields of war) with a share also for the command in the citadel at Tarentum.[60] The implication is that coinage was to be undertaken locally. A reflection of such a system of dispersed war-mints is to be seen in the small symbols or letters which the coins of the new system, after beginning without them,[61] came to bear. In some cases the same symbol may mark the whole range of coinage. Thus a corn-ear—certainly to be associated with Sicily—appears on Mars/Eagle gold, denarii (and fractions), bronze, and victoriati, and this must be recognized as the coinage of Marcellus in Sicily, from which he drove a Punic army. Hoards found near Tarentum show a spearhead as the predominant symbol of the victoriati which they contain; and this symbol, appearing also on Mars/Eagle gold, denarii, and bronze, must be seen as marking coins produced at Tarentum, where the actual citadel successfully resisted the Carthaginians. Other symbols found on the Mars/Eagle gold (associated with a larger or smaller range of silver and bronze) are an

50, 51 Republic. *Obv., head of Roma wearing winged helmet ; X behind. Rev., the Dioscuri, with stars above their heads, charging on horseback with couched spears ;* ROMA. *c. 213-210 B.C., Rome (denarius, 4.81 gm., diam. 18 mm., BMCRR Rome 8).*

52, 53 Republic. *Obv., head of Jupiter, laureate. Rev., Victory crowning trophy of arms ;* ROMA. *c. 213-200 B.C., Rome (victoriatus, or drachma, 3.70 gm., diam. 19 mm., BMCRR Italy 242).*

54, 55 Republic. *Obv., head of Roma, helmeted ; X behind. Rev., Luna, with crescent on head, driving biga ; fly below horses ;* ROMA. *c. 200-190 B.C., Rome (denarius, 3.64 gm., diam. 20 mm., BMCRR Italy 376).*

56 Republic. *Rev., the Dioscuri, with stars above their heads, charging on horseback with couched spears ; dog below the horses ;* ROMA. *c. 200 B.C., Rome (denarius, 3.63 gm., diam. 20 mm., BMCRR Rome 486).*

57 Republic. *Rev., as on No. 56, but with* ME *(in ligature) below the horses. c. 195 B.C., Rome (denarius, 3.69 gm., diam. 19 mm., BMCRR Rome 532).*

58, 59 Republic. *Obv., head of Roma, helmeted ; X behind. Rev., Luna, with crescent on head, driving biga ;* TOD *below horses, with wren on the* T *;* ROMA. *c. 190-180 B.C., Rome (denarius, 3.73 gm., diam. 19 mm., BMCRR Rome 591).*

60, 61 Republic. *Obv., head of Roma, helmeted ; X behind. Rev., Victory driving biga, whip in hand ; below horses,* C TAL *(in ligature) ;* ROMA. *c. 165-150 B.C., Rome (denarius with serrated edge, 3.75 gm., diam. 20 mm., BMCRR Rome 771).*

62 Republic. *Rev., the Dioscuri, with stars above their heads, charging on horseback with couched spears ; below horses,* L CVP *(in ligature) ;* ROMA. *c. 160-150 B.C., Rome (denarius, 4.02 gm., diam. 19 mm., BMCRR Rome 850).*

63 Republic. *Rev., as on No. 62, but with dog below horses ;* ROMA. *[*C ANTESTI *in ligature on obv.] c. 160-150 B.C., Rome (denarius, 4.15 gm., diam. 19 mm., BMCRR Rome 859).*

50

51

52

53

54

55

56

57

58

59

60

61

62

63

64

65

66

67

64 Republic. *Rev., Mars, helmeted and with shield, with his arm round the goddess Nerio in quadriga, her hands bound behind her ;* CN GEL, ROMA. *c. 150 B.C., Rome (denarius, 3.79 gm., diam. 18.5 mm., BMCRR Rome 919).*

65 Republic. *Rev., Hercules, with club and lion's skin, driving biga of Centaurs, each with branch over shoulder ;* M AVRELI, ROMA. [COTA *on obv.*] *c. 150-140 B.C., Rome (denarius, 3.72 gm., diam. 18.5 mm., BMCRR Rome 917).*

66, 67 Republic. *Obv. head of Roma, helmeted ;* L COSCO(nius) M(arci) F(ilius) X. *Rev., Bituitus, naked, with spear, Gaulish shield and carnyx, in biga ;* L LIC CN DOM. *c. 118 B.C., Rome (serrated denarius, 3.76 gm., diam. 20.5 mm., BMCRR Rome 1189).*

68, 69 Republic. *Obv., head of Roma, helmeted ; behind, jug ; in front,* X. *Rev., Faustulus, with staff, standing by wolf and twins ; tree with birds behind ;* SEX PO FOSTLVS, ROMA. *c. 150-140 B.C., Rome (denarius, 3.89 gm., diam. 20 mm., BMCRR Rome 927).*

70 Republic. *Rev., male figure holding sceptre and corn-ears on column with bell on each side of capital and corn-ear on lion's head on each side of base ; on r. and l., togate figures with lituus and dish, one with foot on modius ;* C AVG. [ROMA *on obv.*] *c. 140 B.C., Rome (denarius, 3.99 gm., diam. 19.5 mm., BMCRR Rome 954).*

71, 72 Republic. *Obv., head of Roma, helmeted ; behind, anchor ;* X *below chin. Rev., Venus Genetrix, crowned by Cupid, driving biga ;* SEX IVLI *(with ligature)* CAISAR, ROMA. *c. 140-130 B.C., Rome (denarius, 3.92 gm., diam. 18 mm., BMCRR Rome 1140).*

73, 74 Republic. *Obv., head of Roma, with Phrygian helmet, star on neckpiece ;* X, ROMA. *Rev., Jupiter with thunderbolt driving biga of elephants and crowned by flying Victory ;* C METELLVS. *c. 130-125 B.C., Rome (denarius, 3.97 gm., diam. 18 mm., BMCRR Rome 1180).*

anchor, a pentagram, and a staff : the total of five symbols for gold are thus the marks of coinage struck from the five divisions of the reserve-gold. With this gold the generals in question coined also a supporting range of silver (denarii and/or victoriati), with or without bronze. Elsewhere similar measures were taken for the coinage of silver (or silver and bronze) alone. One group, bearing the letters C or AA or AR, is closely associated with Sardinia. Others bear monograms or even names which in some cases can clearly be attributed to known places, such as Croton and Corcyra, and even Rome itself. In a great many more cases the significance of the symbol, or the attribution of a letter or monogram, is still the subject of argument.[62]

The Mars/Eagle gold was presumably produced in and soon after 209 B.C., when the great gold-reserve was called upon. The production of victoriati continued, perhaps, for a decade or so after the Second Punic War ended (with Hannibal once expelled from Italy) in 202, when Rome's final terms for Carthaginian surrender included an enormous war-indemnity of 10,000 talents, a sum which would at least restore some part of the treasure which had had to be used in these long and dangerous years. At a date near the end of the war the appearance of the denarius was changed, perhaps as if to show that the period of war-coinage was at an end. Livy, writing the annals of Rome with documentary precision two centuries later, records 'bigati' in a number of passages dealing with the years 200-190 B.C.[63] This specific term can refer only to the denarii which were produced with the following new type :

54 *Obv.* Helmeted head of Roma; x behind (type as previously).

55 *Rev.* Luna driving two-horse chariot (*biga*); fly below; ROMA.[64]

Later on, when Rome had extended sovereignty over Macedonia and the eastern Aegean by defeating Perseus in 167, the figure of Luna was changed to one of Victory. For the moment, however, the 'bigatus' type was a new one. It did not altogether displace the original reverse of the Dioscuri; nor, when Victory took the place of Luna, did Victoria do so either. It is evident that from a date somewhere around 200 B.C. some variety in the reverse type of the denarius was permitted.

It is at this point that attention must be paid to the developing role of the *tresviri monetales* at Rome.[65] These young men, in their twenties, were junior magistrates, working in threes, who interpreted, through their day-to-day control of the mint, the financial policies laid down at higher level. The details of mint-organization and the systems of production would have been sharpened and hardened by the necessarily great output of coinage during the Hannibalic war; and the level of responsibility for coinage that was of good metal and weight, and well struck, would have been proportionately emphasized. It has already been seen how, during that war, issues of coinage struck outside Rome were given distinguishing marks (see above, p. 48). The same principle was adopted, at the same time, for coins struck in Rome itself. While the very earliest denarii, of *c.* 211–208, at first bore no symbol at all, later—whether they were of the Dioscuri or the bigatus

type—they unfailingly showed either a small symbol or a monogram. The symbol might be drawn from a wide but simple range: crescent, rudder, dog, star, and **56** anchor are characteristic examples. When a particular batch of coinage included bronze as well as silver, the chosen symbol was to be seen on the coins of both metals. Quite early there was a tendency to substitute for the symbol a monogram indicating a personal name: such monograms as AR, VAR, ME—to quote only easily inter- **57** preted examples—plainly indicate moneyers whose total names included as principal elements 'Aurelius', 'Varus', 'Metellus'. And it was not long before monograms were expanded into a fuller (if still often abbreviated) form of personal name, such as L. CVP(iennius), CN CALP(urnius), L. SAVF **62** (eius)—a stage which was to lead to the appearance of full names in the later second century. All these—symbols, monograms, and shorter or longer names—were simply magistrates' marks, applied by the *monetales* as an administrative distinction of their official output. Many a Greek city had come to employ similar administrative markings: most conspicuously, perhaps, Athens at the end of the third century B.C. They were purely a reflection of strict state control.[66]

The *tresviri monetales* were appointed annually, three at a time, to hold office for a year. Signatures of these *monetales* exist on the Roman coinage down to the end of the Republic, and even into the principate of Augustus (27 B.C.–A.D. 14). However, there are not enough names for allocation, three to a year, throughout the period in question: even at the rate of one a year (and leaving aside special coinages produced by other authority : see below, p. 69), the number is insufficient. Two conclusions are inescapable. First, it is very probable that coinage was not produced every year. Production was governed not by system but by need : sometimes existing currency stocks would suffice, sometimes they would require augmentation—and occasionally to a massive extent dictated by special military or social causes. Nevertheless, even in a year of non-coinage the *monetales* would not be idle. Short of coinage operations, there was metal to melt and refine and weigh and store and record: there was plant to renew; and there was technical staff to train. Secondly, it seems almost certain that, with some few exceptions, only the principal *monetalis* of any given year signed the coinage of that year: alternatively, the principal *monetalis* might sign the silver rather than the bronze, or show in some other such way his primacy among his colleagues.[67]

Given the high probability of these assumptions, it still remains that the whole huge mass of marked or signed Republican coinage from just before 200 B.C. has to be arranged in sequence. Between *c.* 200 and *c.* 100 B.C. there are few, if any, certainly fixed points. Although Republican denarii then came to bear a fascinatingly wide variety of types, these were mainly commemorative and retrospective, without any immediately topical value. One group of coinage, bearing among others the names L LIC(inius Crassus) CN DOM(itius Ahenobarbus), and certainly connected with the founding of the colony of Narbo by these commissioners in southern Gaul, probably fell *c.* 118 B.C. The revaluation of the denarius from a rate of 10 to a rate of 16 Asses, signified by a change from x to XVI (rarely) or ✕ (normally), has often been placed at about this same time, though it is possibly earlier.[68] No absolute chronology for this century of coinage can be achieved : all that is possible—and it is of great value—is the relative internal chronology of the coin-series, based on the massive comparative evidence of coin-hoards.[69] The basic principles in this method have already been made clear (see above, p. 46).

However, even with the relative chronology of the coinage of the first century B.C. thus made much more sure, there still remains a great problem. Excepting certain series (for example, that of Narbo just mentioned) which quite clearly lie outside the main stream of Republican coinage, was the Roman coinage from *c.* 200 onwards a coinage primarily—and indeed almost exclusively—produced at the mint of Rome itself ? This question cannot be answered with clear affirmative evidence : no author in antiquity stated specifically that the coinage of Republican Rome was issued, in the main, from the mint of Rome itself. Such, however, was the assumption until the middle of the nineteenth century, when Count de Salis set out to classify, chronologically and geographically, the Roman coins in the British Museum, including those of the Republic. In regard to the latter he distinguished two concurrent series, of Roman and (unspecified) Italian mintage. This distinction was adopted by subsequent English scholars, who proceeded to elaborate it.[70]

No clear evidence for any such distinction is to be found. Writing of the 'Italian' series Grueber noted :[71] 'these coinages

are precisely similar in their chief characteristics to those of the urban mint [i.e.
Rome], but in very many instances style
and fabric are almost the only guides which
enable us to separate them from the main
series'. Enough is known of stylistic and
technical differences within a series to allow
these to be recognized as the products of
men of differing abilities working at the
same time, often alongside each other:
stylistic analysis, once greatly respected, is
now regarded as dangerous ground.[72] With
this subjective criterion removed, no further
arguments for dualism in the Republican
coinage can be found. And there are
powerful arguments, indeed, against it.
Die-links prove that issues separated on de
Salis' classification were in fact from the
same mint. And the 'separatist' school has
never explained satisfactorily by what right
the *tresviri monetales* of Rome could have
issued and signed coins produced at mints
away from Rome.[73] Consequently, it is
here accepted that, apart from certain issues
demonstrably produced at mints other than
Rome, the main bulk of the long and
important Republican series was struck at
Rome, where alone the security of coinage-
metals and coinage-stocks, the control of
volume and purity, and the conduct of the
young *monetales* themselves could be properly assured by the government of the
Roman Senate.

A brief sketch has now been given of the
development of simple control-marks *c.* 200
B.C. into monograms and other more explicit forms of moneyers' names; and the
sequential classification of the moneyers,
together with the organization of their
work and output, have been discussed,

75 ▶
76 ▶

77

75, 76 Republic. *Obv., head of Roma, helmeted and
with pendant necklace ;* L MANLI PRO Q. *Rev.,
Sulla, togate and holding laurel, driving slow
quadriga and crowned by flying Victory ;* L
SVLLA IM(p). *c. 82-81 B.C., Rome (aureus,
10.83 gm., diam. 20 mm., BMCRR East 6).*

77 Republic. *Rev., equestrian statue of Sulla
togate and raising hand ;* L SVLL FE[LI DIC].
*c. 81 B.C., Rome (aureus, 10.87 gm., diam.
19 mm., BMCRR East 16). (For obv. see
No. 78.)*

78

79

80

with the finally expressed conclusion that the Republican coinage from that date was essentially a unitary series, produced at the mint of Rome. The demand for coinage during the next five or six decades was heavy. Rome was engaged in a long series of major hostilities: in Spain, almost continuously; in north Italy, in order to secure a still precarious frontier; in Macedon (twice) and Greece, culminating with the sack of Corinth in 146 B.C.; and against Carthage once more, in order to destroy Punic power for ever. The cost of warfare in itself was great: so, too, the cost of land-settlement, in Italy or elsewhere, for the many thousands of ex-service men who had fought those wars. It is a reflection of Rome's sound financial policies—and also of the increased supplies of coinage-metals which successive conquests brought—that during those decades the monetary system was virtually unaffected. The denarius, struck originally at *c.* 4.5 g. (see above, p. 46), settled finally *c.* 4.0 g. The bronze, even in the period of the Hannibalic war, had shown quick decline from the 'sextantal' As weight of *c.* 55 g. and was soon to be stabilized at the 'uncial' standard of about half that weight, with the minor denominations in proportion. Gold, in the absence of desperate emergency, was not coined.

In this period *c.* 200–150 B.C. the reverses of the denarii showed (as has been seen above, p. 54) variation between the original type of the Dioscuri, the type of Luna driving a *biga*, and the type of Victory driving a *biga*. Variation in technical and aesthetic standards was also apparent, both for the reverse types and also for the still

78 Republic. *Obv., bust of Roma draped, her helmet adorned with feathers* ; A MANLI [A F Q]. c. *81 B.C., Rome (aureus, 10.87 gm., diam. 20 mm., BMCRR East 16). (For rev. see No. 77.)*

79, 80 Republic. *Obv., head of Venus, diademed; in front, Cupid holding palm-branch* ; L SVLLA. *Rev., jug and lituus between two trophies;* IMPER ITERVM. c. *82-81 B.C., Rome (aureus, 10.73 gm., diam. 19.5 mm., BMCRR East 1).*

unchanging obverse (helmeted head of Roma, with x behind). To begin with, something of the well-rounded, soft modelling of the earliest denarii of the Hannibalic period was preserved: the influence of the Greek or grecized die-cutters of that time was not yet lost, and can still be traced **58, 59** in the denarii marked TOD (?Todillus) with **60, 61** wren (*rev.* Luna in *biga*) and C TAL(na) in monogram (*rev.* Victory in *biga*), though there was a clear tendency towards harder delineation and heavier emphasis, especially in the rendering of nose and mouth on the obverse and of the horses' legs on the reverse. This tendency was to be increased, and we must suppose that the now solid and permanent establishment of the mint at Rome was leading in turn to a characteristically Roman tradition of die-design and die-cutting. It was, by contrast, strict and strong. In the Roma-head an easy exaggeration is given to the details of eye, nose, mouth, helmet and hair; and the reverse types, and especially that of the Dioscuri, were treated in an increasingly harsh and mechanical idiom. This is well shown by **62** such issues as those of L. Cupiennius and **63** C. Antestius. Many (though by no means all) of the denarial issues were at this time accompanied by bronze, sometimes in complete series from As to uncia, sometimes more selectively: while all bronze denominations showed a ship's prow on the reverse, the obverses still varied, each denomination showing its traditional type.[74] In the 'sextantal' series (see above, p. 46) the comparatively large size of the As had necessitated production by casting instead of striking, but with the advent of the 'uncial' standard (p. 46) striking became

a possibility. The level of workmanship and care applied in the production of bronze had never been high ever since the time of the heavy, cast 'libral' pieces (p. 27). By now it was no better: the obverse heads could on occasion attract a die-engraver's interest and effort, and for those unskilled in portraiture the prow of the reverses could be built up into a strong design; but in general the very fact that the bronze types were repeated year after year without change resulted in their receiving little more than automatic treatment—sometimes of a very low level.

Although the types of the bronze were thus 'frozen', with a consequent decline in technical care, those of the denarii were deliberately varied with the passage of time. It is difficult to determine the exact date of the change. It coincided fairly nearly with the revaluation of the denarius from 10 Asses (x) to 16 Asses (XVI), for coins marked XVI, while they still show the traditional denarial types (for example, the Dioscuri, and Luna or Victory driving a *biga*), give way after a brief period to coins marked ✕ which show much greater freedom of type. Hoard-evidence, moreover, suggests that a change in denarial reverses had in fact preceded the XVI coins. The date of the revaluation from 10 to 16 Asses has been disputed, but it is likely that it took place not later than 140 B.C.[75] Variation in the types of the denarius may therefore have taken place in the period *c.* 150–140 B.C.

At first it was modest, taking the *biga* as a theme to be played with. The coins of Cn. Gellius showed Mars with the legendary **64** Nerio in a *quadriga*: those of C. Renius, Juno driving a *biga* of goats:[76] those of

C. Curiatius Trigeminus, Juno crowned by Victory in a *quadriga*; and those of M. Aure-
65 lius Cota, Hercules in a *biga* of Centaurs. Of the moneyers of the short XVI period (there were only six), one—M. Aufidius Rusticus —showed Jupiter in a *quadriga*. After the XVI period change was faster and more radical: moneyers broke away entirely from the reverse design of a *biga* or *quadriga*, in whatever form, and even varied the obverse. Thus Tiberius Veturius, within a very few years of the XVI period,[77] produced denarii with *obv*. Helmeted Mars-head, X, TI VET (in monogram), and *rev*. Oath-scene (re-produced from the emergency gold of 218; see above, p. 40), ROMA: his family had perhaps been involved in that earlier process of consolidating alliances with Rome in the face of Hannibal's invasion of Italy. And Sextus Pompeius Fostlus, at about the same time, while retaining (and appropriately) the Roma-head for the obverse of his denarii, showed on the reverse his tradi-
8, 69 tional ancestor Faustulus watching Romu-lus and Remus being suckled by a wolf, as legend said he found them, at the foot of the Palatine hill beneath a tree. A little later, C. Augurinus (still with an appro-priate Roma-head obverse) showed on his
70 reverses the monument—a statue on a column with bells—erected to commem-orate the action taken by his ancestor L. Minucius Augurinus in 439 B.C. to reduce the price of corn. Later again, Sextus Julius Caesar combined the Roma-head
1, 72 obverse with a reverse on which the *biga* is driven by Venus (with Cupid crowning her): it was from Iulus, grandson of Venus and Anchises, that the Julian family traced its descent.

All these types—and there were many others—referred in one way or another to the history of Rome, legendary or actual. But this history was seen in the context of the personalities of the great patrician families to which the *tresviri monetales*, aspirant senators, themselves belonged. It was, perhaps, chance that first led to the substitution of moneyers' names for a range of small symbols on the earliest denarii. Once names had appeared, the way was open, first, to a discreet modification of traditional types, and then to total change. The concept of Rome was still central; but Rome, in its now immensely developing strength, and with a growing range of important overseas possessions, was now synonymous with the great families who still (in spite of increasing popular agitation) monopolized the system of government. For a young *monetalis* to advertise on his coinage the family (*gens*) to which he belonged was to emphasize the strength of the political machine which would help him powerfully in his subsequent senatorial career. Moreover, by doing so he showed quite clearly that the principal *monetalis* of any annual college of three (see above, p. 55), though originally his coins bore designs laid down at some other and higher level, was able *c*. 150 B.C. to make a personal choice of what his coins should show. As the primary purpose of silver coinage, now as at other times, was to supply the means of state-payment (with army pay of chief importance), the widely disseminated rec-ord of the greater deeds and consequence of the greater families might well—it could be hoped—help to maintain their authority in government.[78] By contrast the bronze coinage, though it still continued to bear the principal moneyer's name, showed unchanged types. It was not of comparable importance in state payments : by no means every college of moneyers struck bronze at this time, and, when they did, the range of denominations was often very limited.[79]

The changing forms of Republican denarii after the middle of the second century B.C. were not accompanied by any change in artistic impulses at the mint of Rome. Dies were cut in an angular, strong, and hard style : often, indeed, harsh, with an almost brutal insistence on the linear elements in the Roma-portrait—wing-feathers, vizor, nose, and mouth—probably as a means of avoiding the subtle difficulties of modelling the features. Heads were large, with the wide-bowled helmet amply decorated; and to accommodate these the coins were struck upon noticeably wide, thin, and flat flans. Width of flan, even so, could not always contain the reverse design 68, 69 very easily. The scene on Fostlus's denarii —Faustulus, wolf and twins, tree, name, with ROMA below—might have been more comfortably composed in a style much less 70 coarse and heavy. That of Augurinus' denarii, simpler in composition and naive in presentation, was less coarse; but its 'spread' was too great for the available space. Republican designers were for some time to find difficulty in this limitation of space : as designs became more and more narrative and monumental, they were increasingly ill at ease in subjecting them to the confines of a small circle. Compared with the wholly Greek style of the Roman didrachms of the earlier and middle third century, and even with the hybrid but still

81 Republic. *Rev., galloping horseman in Greek armour with high-crested helmet, his spear couched ; behind, Macedonian helmet ;* Q PILIPVS, ROMA. c. *135-130* B.C., *Rome (denarius, 3.94 gm., diam. 19 mm., BMCRR Rome 1143).*

82 Republic. *Rev.,* M METELLVS Q F *around Macedonian shield with elephant's head in centre ; all in laurel-wreath.* c. *135-130* B.C., *Rome (denarius, 3.89 gm., diam. 18 mm., BMCRR Rome 1146).*

83, 84 Republic. *Obv., head of Roma, helmeted ; behind,* ✕ *above voting urn. Rev., Libertas driving galloping quadriga, holding cap of liberty and sceptre ;* C CASSI, ROMA. c. *130-125* B.C., *Rome (denarius, 3.90 gm., diam. 20 mm., BMCRR Rome 1032).*

85, 86 Republic. *Obv., head of Roma, wearing Phrygian helmet ;* M AVRELI, ROMA, ✕. *Rev., Bituitus, naked, with spear, Gaulish shield and carnyx, in biga ;* SCAVRI, L LIC CN DOM. c. *118* B.C., *Rome (serrated denarius, 3.93 gm., diam. 19.5 mm., BMCRR 1185).*

87 Republic. *Obv., head of Cybele, turreted and veiled ;* EX A PV. c. *100* B.C., *Rome (denarius, 3.63 gm., diam. 20 mm., BMCRR 1591).*

88 Republic. *Rev., Jupiter with sceptre and thunderbolt driving quadriga ;* D, L SENTI C F. c. *100* B.C., *Rome (denarius, 4.02 gm., diam. 20 mm., BMCRR 1646).*

89 Republic. *Obv., bust of young Hercules with lion's skin and club ; to l., shield ; to r., letter* I ; P E S C. c. *100-95* B.C., *Rome (denarius, 3.93 gm., diam. 17 mm., BMCRR Rome 1724).*

90, 91 Republic. *Obv., head of Saturn, bearded and laureate ; below, arrow ;* PISO CAEPIO Q. *Rev., two togate figures (Piso and Caepio) seated between ears of corn ;* AD FRV EMV EX S C. c. *100-95* B.C., *Rome (denarius, 3.99 gm., diam. 18 mm., BMCRR Rome 1125).*

92 Republic. *Rev., Victory placing helmet on trophy of arms which she is erecting ;* CN BLASIO CN F. c. *110* B.C., *Rome (As, 26.89 gm., diam. 32.5 mm., BMCRR Italy 632).*

81

82

83

84

85

86

87

88

89

90

91

92

93

94

95

96

97

98

99

100

101

102

103

104

105

106

93, 94 Republic (Social War Confederation). *Obv., head of Italia, laureate ;* ITALIA. *Rev., two groups of four warriors pointing with their swords towards pig held by kneeling youth between them in front of standard ;* IIII·. *c. 91-88 B.C., (?) Corfinium (denarius, 3.99 gm., diam. 20 mm., BMCRR Social War 3).*

95 Republic (Social War Confederation). *Rev., Victory crowning Italia, armed with spear and short sword, seated on pile of shields ;* C, ITALIA. *c. 91-88 B.C., (?) Corfinium (denarius, 3.93 gm., diam. 18 mm., BMCRR Social War 14).*

96, 97 Republic (Social War Confederation). *Obv., head of Italia, laureate ;* ꟼVƎHꓒ *(= Viteliu = Italia). Rev., warrior, helmeted and cloaked, and with spear and sword, treading on Roman standard ; recumbent bull beside him ;* ꟼ *(= A). c. 91-88 B.C., (?) Corfinium (denarius, 3.95 gm., diam. 18 mm., BMCRR Social War 19).*

98, 99 Republic (Social War Confederation). *Obv., head of young Bacchus wreathed with ivy ;* ꓷVꓕꓕꓭ8ꟽƎ ꓵꓕꟽV *(= Mutil[us] Embratur, i.e. Imperator). Rev., bull trampling and goring she-wolf ;* ꟾꟼꟼꟼꟼꟼ〉 *(= C Paapi[us]). c. 91-88 B.C., (?) Corfinium (denarius, 3.84 gm., diam. 20 mm., BMCRR Social War 41).*

100 Republic (Social War Confederation). *Rev., two soldiers, one with spear, clasping hands by prow of ship bearing ribboned sceptre and two spears and shields ;* A. *c. 91-88 B.C., (?) Corfinium (denarius, 4.22 gm., diam. 20 mm., BMCRR Social War 48).*

101, 102 Republic. *Obv., head of Apollo, laureate, with hair in ringlets ; behind, tanner's knife. Rev., naked horseman, galloping, and holding lighted torch ;* ✕, L PISO FRV N(epos) *above axe. c. 90-89 B.C., Rome (denarius, 3.85 gm., diam. 19 mm., BMCRR Rome 1860).*

103 Republic. *Rev., Victory advancing, holding wreath and palm-branch ;* L PISO FRVGI. *c. 90-89 B.C., Rome (quinarius, 1.96 gm., diam. 16 mm., BMCRR Rome 2138).*

104 Republic. *Rev., bridled horse galloping ;* E L P, FRVGI. *c. 90-89 B.C., Rome (silver sestertius, 0.95 gm., diam. 11 mm., BMCRR Rome 2177).*

105, 106 Republic. *Obv., mask of Silenus, bearded and wreathed with ivy ; below chin, two bells ;* PANSA. *Rev., mask of Pan, bearded and with goat's ears ; in front, sistrum ;* C VIBIVS C F. *c. 87 B.C., Rome (denarius, 3.95 gm., diam. 19 mm., BMCRR Rome 2310).*

elegant Greco-Roman style of the quadri-gati and earliest denarii, in all of which sensitive modelling and delicate line were combined with well proportioned and well accommodated design, the denarii from *c.* 150 B.C. show the abandonment of Greek artists and Greek concepts. They were the hard, strong product of a Roman school: Greek influence from south Italy had not yet been replaced by the Greek influence that was due to flow in, after an interval, from further afield.

In the new types which had been introduced soon after *c.* 150, moneyers had recalled the ancient history of Rome by reference to their own distinguished but long dead ancestors. Roman history was viewed, so to speak, through the wrong end of a telescope. But during the course of about a quarter of a century this discreetly remote view was changed, and changed surprisingly fast. The speed of the change was a symptom of the increasing stresses within the Roman political system. For many decades past the brunt of Roman expansion and Roman development had been borne, most heavily, by its ordinary citizens, without whom, as soldiers, the long series of wars could never have been undertaken. It was this ordinary citizenry which now increasingly began to claim a share in political power, political decision, and economic benefit; and it was against this popular movement, led most notably by the brothers Gracchus as tribunes of the people (Tiberius in 133, and Gaius in 124), that the old patrician families had to throw their weight. Thus the moneyers, in support of the patrician cause (which also tended to be their own), lost no time in moving towards more topical coin types. C. Metellus, showing Jupiter crowned by Victory in a *biga* of elephants, was content to look back for more than a century to his ancestor's victory over Punic forces (and Punic elephants) at Panormus in Sicily in 251 B.C.; and C. Serveilius came no nearer his own time than the representation of M. Serveilius, augur in 211 B.C., said to have been wounded and victorious in twenty-three single combats, and seen now on denarii engaged in one of them, his shield marked M. N. Fabius Pictor's coins showed his forebear of the same name, elected to the priestly flaminate in 190. Q. Pilipus chose a scene of Q. Marcius Philippus fighting on horseback in warfare (identified by a Macedonian helmet) against Perseus of Macedon in 169. The reverse of M. Metellus, with laurel wreath and Macedonian shield with elephant's head (the family badge), referred to the family's prowess in Macedon in 148. Finally, the denarii of C. Cassius (with *obv.* Voting-urn behind Roma-head, and *rev.* Libertas in *biga,* holding cap of liberty) seem to be looking back to that L. Cassius Longinus who, as tribune of the people in 137, proposed and carried a law ensuring vote by ballot in criminal cases tried by the people of Rome. The patricians had developed coin-types advertising the great patrician champions of the past. Now the same technique was being applied by representatives of the 'popular' party, and the dualism of party-politics had reached the coinage itself.

During the period after *c.* 120 B.C. various changes took place in both the fabric and also the control-methods of the great stream of Republican denarii. In regard to fabric, there was a tendency to make the flans smaller and thicker than before, leading to the necessity (not always well observed) of compressing the types more compactly. There also grew up—though at very irregular intervals—a habit of notching the edges of denarii by a chisel. A much earlier though isolated example of this practice occurred with the coins of C. TAL(na) in the first half of the second century. It was repeated on a quite large group of denarii, struck by five different *monetales,* which (with Roma-head obverse) bore a reverse looking clearly to the foundation of the colony of Narbo— the modern Narbonne—in southern Gaul about 118 B.C. after victory over the Gaulish chieftain Bituitus. This reverse, showing Bituitus with Gaulish arms in a *biga,* carried the names of the two founding commissioners, L. LIC(inius) and CN DOM (itius). Later, serration was to be seen again from time to time : in the last decade of the second century B.C., in the late 70s, and in and after the late 60s. Tacitus, writing in the later first century A.D., recorded that *serrati,* together with *bigati* (i.e. denarii from *c.* 200 B.C.), were popular with barbarian peoples beyond the imperial frontiers, presumably through respect for the silver, as serration might enable a man to see that a coin was not plated. From this, and from the coins commemorating the foundation of Narbo (some of which would have circulated in and around the colony), it has been concluded that serrated denarii were specifically produced for circulation outside Italy. But this must remain doubtful. Possibly moneyers resorted to serration in order to demonstrate the in-

tegrity of their denarii at a time when plated denarii (i.e. silver plating over a bronze core) were becoming so common as to disturb public confidence. However, the existence of plated *serrati* shows that such effort was in vain. All that is certain is that the effort was indeed great : the flans were chisel-notched, it seems, before they were struck, at 20 or more points around their circumference; and the manual labour involved in thus processing scores of thousands of flans must have been formidable.[80]

New methods of mint-control were probably caused by the continuing great volume of the late second-century denarial coinage, in conjunction with the sharpening suspicion and rivalry between the aristocratic and the popular factions in Rome. New colonies arose as a result of land-settlements in the Gracchan reforms. There was war in Mauretania against Jugurtha, war in northern Italy against hordes of Cimbri and Teutones, war against desperately rebellious slaves in Sicily. Perhaps it was felt that some improved methods of control must be introduced so as to check the great quantities of coin required—quantities which sometimes called for special requisitions of metals, as demonstrated by the formulae which many issues came to bear : D P P (*de publica pecunia*), D S S (*de senatus sententia*), EX A PV (*ex argento publico*), ARG PVB (*argentum publicum*), P E S C (*publice ex senatus consulto*), EX S C (*ex senatus consulto*).[81] The precise methods of control are still very obscure. It can be said, however, that they certainly included the marking of dies. This was done at first on a very simple system, which appeared originally on the denarii of N. Fabius Pictor (see above, p. 68), perhaps *c.* 130 B.C.

This *monetalis,* after a short production of coinage bearing no control-marks, then struck coins each bearing a letter on both obverse and reverse. However, there was no systematic relationship between obverse letters and reverse letters : they were used merely to identify the dies from which the coins were struck, and not to show how any given pair of marked dies was used in combination. In other words, individual dies were marked in simple letter-sequence as they were made : they could be used in any combination, e.g. A with X, or, more wastefully (because reverse dies had the shorter life), in strict parallelism—A with A, B with B, etc. It is not easy, now, to see what exact purposes such control-marks would have served. All that is evident is that the development of marking dies with a sequence letter must have had a purpose in its own time, that is, towards the end of the second century B.C.[82]

The advent of control-marks, the specification of metal as coming from a particular source or authority, and the very process whereby the choice of denarial types had apparently passed into the hands of the *monetales,* suggest in combination that the strictly simple system of mint-organization devised at the beginning of the second century was, a hundred years later, more complex and thus in a way looser, with greater possibilities of variation. Denarii (and bronze as well) could by now be signed by a wider range of officials.[83] Thus, between *c.* 120 and 110 B.C. the names of M CALID(ius), Q MET(ellus) and CN FOVL (vius) appeared jointly on their silver issue; and Q CVRT(ius) and M SILA(nus), signing silver jointly, were accompanied on bronze

by CN DOMI(tius). Nor did the *monetales* alone now sign coins. The quaestors— Rome's taxation and finance magistrates— also appeared as signatories, presumably in connexion with special coinages supplementing those of the *monetales.* Sometimes, as in the case of AP(pius) CL(audius) and T. MAL(lius) as Q(uaestores) VR(bani), both quaestors signed together : the same was true of PISO and CAEPIO as Q(uaestores) when in 100 B.C. they had to produce a special and senatorially authorized coinage in order to implement a new law enabling the people to buy cheap corn—a duty reflected in their reverse type, showing the quaestors with corn-ears and the legend AD FRV(mentum) EMV(ndum) EX S C.[84] Sometimes a single quaestor signed, as in the case of T CLOVLI (us) Q, whose half-denarii or quinarii (now without mark of value V : see p. 47 above) were—like those of other quaestorial issues of the same period—produced to implement the Clodian Law of *c.* 104 B.C., which reintroduced the denomination after a long lapse of time.[85]

Amid the great and continuing stream of silver in the latter part of the second century B.C. there was a marked diminution of bronze. The As was struck only occasionally—still (theoretically at least) at its previous uncial weight (see above, p. 46) : its fractions were less uncommon, though they were not produced with any regularity. In general, the earlier types of the bronze coins were retained, with the conventional range of heads of deities on the obverses, and a ship's prow on the reverses. However, there was also a tendency towards change, and the prow, often elaborated with various adjuncts, could be abandoned

90, 91

for quite different designs : thus the Asses of Cn. Blasio showed Victory crowning a trophy. In contrast to the workmanship and technique of the silver coinage, the bronze was remarkably rough and lacked any pretensions to elegance. It was as if it was now felt to be of definitely inferior status; necessary, without doubt, in transactions involving small values, but yielding all importance to the coinage of silver. This silver coinage, meanwhile, had had its previously strict range of types liberated and expanded in a remarkable manner; and, even if its style was not yet of very polished attainment, it had now reached a point where, simply because of constant type-change, it could and doubtless did contribute—neatly and clearly—something new all the time to the flood of political commentary. Restlessly extemporizing upon the themes of the day, the Republican coinage, like the Republican constitution itself, was now approaching a period of climax.

92

III. REPUBLICAN COINAGE IN THE TIME OF THE IMPERATORES, *c.* 100-48 B.C.

Until the end of the second century B.C. the constitution of the Roman Republic, had not been fundamentally changed. Its pattern, which combined certain democratic elements in a system effectively controlled by a senatorial oligarchy, had indeed come under strain. The mass of the Roman people had contributed immense effort during a long period of warfare; and their consciousness of a debt to be repaid in the form of wider political rights and better conditions of life was sharpened by such champions as the Gracchi (see above, p. 67) and, most recently Saturninus in 103. However, constitutional balance was heavily loaded against the *populares*—the 'popular' party. Ironically enough, the role of the *populares* in the first century B.C., when the political system of Rome rapidly decayed and fell apart, was to continue in the supplying of manpower for the armies of the series of great war-lords who destroyed that system. From the traditional constitution the Roman people might expect only a little by way of reward. From membership of a victorious army—even one that was engaged in civil war—a good deal more could be looked for in the shape of spoil, gratuities and land-distribution.

In 100 B.C. Marius, the great general who had beaten back the northern threat from the Cimbri and Teutones, held his sixth consulship, against all constitutional propriety. For twenty years thereafter the history of Rome was the history of the struggle between Marius, militarily popular but politically unskilled, and Sulla, perhaps less skilled in war but much more able and ruthless in his reactionary politics. The military context within which these two great leaders operated was varied and often dangerous. Most urgent, because nearest, was the danger in 90-89 B.C. from the neighbouring allied communities who, forming a confederacy, began the 'Social War' to extort from Rome a mass grant of Roman citizenship. In the end their claims were substantially met, but not before very large Roman forces had been engaged, some under Sulla. The insurgents themselves produced a denarial coinage in quantity, all in the name of 'Italia' in either Latin or Oscan (VꟼƎTIꟼ, 'Viteliu', Italia) char- 96 acters. The types chosen were in part derived from earlier Roman issues, in part newly devised or adapted. Obverses normally showed a head of Italia, so inscribed. 93 Among the reverses the dominant themes

73

were the oath of confederacy (expressed by
94 the apt revival of the oath-scene type used
for Roman gold during the Hannibalic war :
95 see above, p. 40), Italia being crowned by
96, 97 Victory, an Italic soldier trampling on a
98, 99 Roman standard, and—with *obv.* Bacchus—
a bull (Italia) trampling on a she-wolf
(Roma). There was also a reverse, showing
100 the welcome given to a person disembarking
from a ship, which would seem to reflect
the known hopes of help from the powerful
King Mithradates of Pontus, now poised
for war against Rome in Asia; and this
rebel coinage even includes a now unique
gold coin with types copied from a Pontic
original. The total volume of this confederacy issue (some of which bears the names
98, 99 of generals in Oscan letters)[86] was great,
and in many cases dies were marked with
94, 95 sequence-letters or numbers, on the Roman
97, 100 pattern.

This large and vigorously independent
war-coinage was rendered in a curious
mixture of technique and style. The flans
could be larger or smaller, and struck either
neatly or untidily; and the design of the
dies, sometimes strong, well proportioned
and capably modelled, showing an obvious
debt to the best Roman work of the preceding generation, was at other times flat,
weak or coarse. Production may have taken
place at more than one centre, although it is
likely to have been concentrated mainly at
the Pelignian town of Corfinium, chosen as
the centre of the confederacy and renamed
Italia or *Viteliu.* It was large enough, in
any case, to reflect a great war-effort; and
this in turn exacted equally great effort
from Rome. Not only did the Social War
itself necessitate a greatly increased volume

107
108

107, 108 Republic. *Obv., head of Africa wearing
elephant's skin ; behind, jug ; in front, lituus ;*
MAGNVS *; all within laurel-wreath. Rev.,
Victory with wreath flying above Pompey, holding
laurel-wreath, in slow quadriga ; a youth rides
the nearest horse ;* PRO COS. c. *61 B.C.(?),
uncertain mint (aureus, 8.93 gm., diam. 19 mm.,
BMCRR East 20).*

109, 110 Republic. *Obv., head of Venus or Pietas
wearing oak-wreath, her hair in jewelled knot ;*
LII *(= 52). Rev., trophy of Gaulish arms
(oval shield, carnyx, horned helmet) ; to r., axe ;*
CAESAR. c. *49-48 B.C., Rome (aureus, 8.63
gm., diam. 21 mm., BMCRR Rome 3953).*

109
110

111

112

113

114

of denarial coinage for payment to the Roman armies involved, but the Lex Plautia Papiria of *c.* 91/90 B.C., which provided for the extension of Roman citizenship among the neighbouring (and still loyal) Italian allies, expressly terminated non-Roman coinages (bronze as well as silver) yet surviving in the Italian peninsula, re-introduced silver sestertii (i.e. quarter-denarii), and reduced the weight of the As at Rome by half to the 'semuncial' standard. In other words, Rome was now to provide coinage for the whole of Italy without exception. The law was commemorated on the silver sestertii struck at once by the moneyer Silanus (alongside his much more copious denarii) by the letters E L(ege) P(lautia Papiria); and the reduction of the bronze standard was similarly advertised by the letters L P D A P (Lege Papiria de aere publico ?) on a full series of bronze, from As to quadrans, at about the same time. It was, however, after the issues of Silanus that the combined impact of the Social War and the Lex Plautia Papiria was most dramatically seen, in the coinage signed by the moneyer L. Calpurnius Piso Frugi.[87]

This coinage, of immense size, was in fact the largest issued by any signing *monetalis* during the whole of the Roman Republic. It consisted mainly of denarii, but included some quinarii and also a few silver sestertii marked (like those of Silanus) E L P; there was also a range of 'semuncial' bronze (As, semis and quadrans). Throughout the whole of the silver, in all denominations, the obverse type consisted of a laureate head of Apollo, in somewhat archaic style with long, stiff ringlets. For the quinarii the reverses showed the now

111,112 Republic. *Obv., as No. 109, but no jewels in knot. Rev., trophy of Gaulish arms, at base of which bearded and seated captive, his hands tied behind him ;* CAESAR. c. *49-48 B.C., Rome (denarius, 3.37 gm., diam. 20 mm., BMCRR Rome 3959).*

113,114 Republic. *Obv., head of Venus, diademed. Rev., Aeneas, holding palladium (archaic statuette of Pallas), with Anchises, in long tunic and hood, on his shoulders ;* CAESAR. c. *47 B.C., uncertain mint (denarius, 3.84 gm., diam. 17.5 mm., BMCRR East 34).*

104

101,102
103
104

conventional type of Victory, and for the sestertii, a bridled and galloping horse. On the massive series of denarii this horse bears a naked rider, bearing a torch or a palm-branch or a whip. The moneyer's ancestor, of the same name, had instituted the *Ludi Apollinares* in 212 B.C., to invoke the protection of Apollo against the forces of Hannibal. Such a type was again apt now, in the face of the Marsic confederacy; and there may indeed have been some further significance in the Apollo type. For in the closely succeeding years there is often a clear emphasis upon the choice between a head of Apollo and a head of Veiovis (young Jupiter) with thunderbolt for the obverse of Roman denarii; and it is not impossible that the Apollo-head stood for the party of Marius, and the Veiovis head for that of Sulla.[88]

Vast though the denarial coinage of Piso was, with a bewildering (but not systematically correlated) number of die-sequence marks in the form of symbols, letters and numbers—these last alone running up to some 150 (**CV**),[89] it was probably not the whole output of his year of office *c.* 90/89 B.C. It has been argued that this year of special monetary urgency prompted, unusually though not by any means uniquely, simultaneous signed coinage by all three *monetales*, and that the fairly large issues of C. Vibius Pansa and Q. Titius—each, like Piso's, with associated 'semuncial' bronze—were complementary.[90] There is an interesting contrast of style to be seen between these Roman issues of *c.* 90/89 and the 'Italic' coins of the rebel confederacy. At the end of the second century B.C. the die-engravers of Rome had suddenly and mark-

edly developed a new freedom of treatment, partly (no doubt) because traditional types had been abandoned, and partly also because the Roman conquest of Greece had resulted in the increasing employment at Rome of skilled Greek artisans. Hence the fluid sophistication and easy modelling of the types of such earlier *monetales* as L. Philippus (apparently commemorating the treaty of friendship made by his ancestor with Philip V of Macedon, whose head is shown), Cn. Blasio (of the Cornelian family, and showing what is probably the family portrait of Scipio Africanus the Elder), and Ti. Quinctius and L. Caesius (with busts of Hercules and Veiovis). By *c.* 90/89, if allowance is made for the urgency and pressure of a war-time coinage, the stylistic touch is seen to be even more assured, to the point, indeed, at which all but the least experienced die-engravers could feelingly reproduce the 'antique': the engravers working for Pansa and Titius—who were perhaps less pressed for time—produced heads of Apollo, Silenus, Pan (a punning type) and Mutinus Titinus (?)[91] with admirable incisiveness and decorative feeling, even if they were also consciously recreating an archaic style.

After 88 B.C. the rivalry between the factions of Marius and Sulla led to civil war, with irreparable damage to the Roman constitution. The Marians could claim credit for a policy of extended Roman citizenship and, thereby, the pacification of Italy. Sulla, the optimate, could base his reactionary political policy upon his personal services in defeating the power of Mithradates in Asia and recovering Athens from revolt. Declared a public enemy by

78

the Marians in 87, Sulla had by 82 returned with his army to Italy, captured Rome, assumed full power as *dictator*, proscribed the leading Marian supporters, and introduced a new and oligarchic constitution. There was still to be war, from various causes, elsewhere—against Sertorius in Spain (80–72), Mithradates in the east (from 75), and the slave-revolt in south Italy led by Spartacus (73–71). Sulla, retiring from public life in 79, died in 78; but there were new men to take his place, of whom Pompey, Caesar, and Cicero were already emerging.

The coinage of the late 80s clearly reflects Sulla's ruthless determination to oust the Marians and establish his own absolute position.[92] Under the moneyers of the earlier 80s—some signing in their triple collegiate entirety, some as senior *monetales*, and some in a special capacity as praetor or aedile—the general character of the types employed was not spectacular though occasionally it was topical: for example, an apparent reference in the serpent and altar of some of Dossenus' coins to the plague at Rome in 87, and the allusion by the denarii of the aediles Fannius and Critonius to the fact of a special coin-issue to pay for a distribution of corn *c.* 86.[93] But with Sulla's domination from 82 the whole character was changed. He at once authorized production of coinage in the provinces by his provincial subordinates: thus C. Valerius Flaccus, propraetor in Gaul *c.* 83, struck there a fairly large issue of denarii with *obv.* Victory (expected against Sertorius' threat), *rev.* legionary eagle and standards, C VAL FLA IMPERAT(or) EX S C; and C. Annius, proconsul in Spain imme-

diately afterwards, coined equally numerous denarii through his quaestors L. Fabius and C. Tarquitius, with *obv.* Head of Anna Perenna, C.ANNI T.F.T.N. PROCOS EX S C, and *rev.* Victory in *quadriga* or *biga*, L.FABI L.F. HISP (or C. TARQVITI P. F.) Q(uaestor). Similarly, and at about the same time, Q(uintus) C(aecilius) M(etellus) P(ius) I(mperator) coined denarii with *obv.* Head of Pietas, *rev.* Elephant (badge of the Metelli) or lituus and jug, IMPER in wreath, perhaps in northern Italy.[94] More important, however, than these coinages by Sulla's subordinates were the issues in the name of Sulla himself.

These were the first true forerunners of the imperial coinage proper, for they were struck, either in Italy or in Rome,[95] in the name of Sulla as supreme commander, and with types personal to him. It is notable, too, that these Sullan issues included gold —a mark of emergency in the past, but now perhaps a sign of his political purchasing power. The earliest of these issues, in gold as well as silver, and of strictly fine traditional style, were struck for Sulla by his proquaestor L. Manlius with *obv.* Head of Roma, L MANLI PRO Q, and *rev.* Victory crowing Sulla in triumphal *quadriga*, L SVLLA IM(perator) or IMP. Next, also in gold and silver, and much more coarse in treatment, was an issue with *obv.* Head of Venus (Sulla's chosen protectress) confronting Cupid with palm-branch, and *rev.* Lituus and jug (augural symbols) between two military trophies, IMPER(ator) ITERVM.[96] Last, again of good style, and in gold only, now produced by his quaestor A. Manlius, came coins with *obv.* Head of Roma, A MANLI AF Q(uaestor), and *rev.* Equestrian statue of Sulla, L SVLL(A) FELI(X) DIC(tator).[97] Bronze, some of it signed L SVL IMPE, but mostly anonymous though with Sullan types, accompanied this astonishing gold and silver. The earlier coinage of the Republic, produced by junior officials on behalf of the state, had thus given way to a coinage produced by a military commander who claimed to embody the state in his own person. With the rise of the politically motivated *imperator*, who needed to conciliate and maintain his professional and almost personal standing army, the old pattern of state-coinage had been fundamentally upset.

During the first two decades after 100 B.C. there were, apparently, some monetary troubles of other kinds, though it is now very difficult to estimate their nature and extent. Pliny the Elder recorded that Livius Drusus, as tribune of the people, instituted a 12 1/2 per cent debasement of the silver coinage. This, though it could have been done by M. Livius Drusus of 122 B.C., was more likely the work of his namesake of 91 B.C., as a preliminary to the predictable monetary strains about to occur in connexion with the Social War. Unfortunately little work has yet been done upon the silver-analysis of Republican coinage, and it is not possible either to pin-point the date of debasement or even to determine if it was consistently of the order of 12 1/2 per cent.[98] It is improbable that the Senate, then or at any other time, authorized the issue of plated coins, for those, when they occur in die-marked series, seem to show anomalies which suggest that they are the result of private forgery.[99] Nevertheless there was some loss of public confidence in the currency, for whatever reason. Cicero

115 Republic. *Rev., Victory advancing holding wreath and palm-branch and raising r. hand above serpent twined round altar ; L RVBRI.* [DOSSEN *on obv.*]. c. *87-86 B.C., Rome (quinarius, 1.98 gm., diam. 16 mm., BMCRR Rome 2459).*

116, 117 Republic. *Obv., head of Ceres wearing corn-wreath ;* AED(iles) PL(ebei). *Rev., the aediles Fannius and Critonius, togate, seated ; in front, corn-ear ; behind,* P(ublico) A(rgento) ; M FAN L CRIT. c. *86 B.C., Rome (denarius, 4.06 gm., diam. 19 mm., BMCRR Rome 2463).*

118, 119 Republic. *Obv., bust of Victory, draped, her hair braided and gathered in knot ; in front, caduceus. Rev., aquila between two standards inscribed respectively* H(astati) *and* P(rincipes) ; EX S C, C VAL FLA IMPERAT. c. *83 B.C., Gaul (denarius, 3.69 gm., diam. 18 mm., BMCRR Gaul 1).*

120, 121 Republic. *Obv., head of Pietas, diademed ; in front, stork. Rev., elephant with bell hanging from neck ;* Q C M P I. c. *83-80 B.C., (?) north Italy (denarius, 3.84 gm., diam. 18 mm., BMCRR Spain 43).*

122 Republic. *Rev., jug and lituus ;* IMPER ; *all in laurel-wreath.* c. *83-80 B.C., (?) north Italy (denarius, 3.89 gm., diam. 19 mm., BMCRR Spain 49).*

123, 124 Republic. *Obv., bust of Mercury, draped, wearing winged petasus ; behind, caduceus and* A. *Rev., Ulysses, wearing pileus and holding staff, greeting his dog Argus ;* C MAMIL LIMETAN. c. *81-80 B.C., Rome (denarius, 3.73 gm., diam. 20 mm., BMCRR Rome 2716).*

125, 126 Republic. *Obv., head of Hercules, with short curly hair ;* Q(uaestor) S C. *Rev., Victory flying to crown the Genius of the Roman People, seated on curule chair, holding cornucopiae and sceptre, and resting foot on globe ;* P LENT P F L(ucii) N(epos). c. *74 B.C., Rome (denarius, 4.13 gm., diam. 18 mm., BMCRR Rome 3329).*

116   117   115

118   119

120   121   122

123

124

125

126

127

128

129

130

131

132

133

134

135

136

137

138

139

140

127 Republic. *Obv., bust of Ceres, draped, her hair gathered in a net and ornamented with poppy heads ; behind, jug.* c. 68 B.C., Rome (denarius, 4.08 gm., diam. 18 mm., BMCRR Rome 3544).

128 Republic. *Obv., young male head (Bonus Eventus) with long hair ; behind, arrow.* c. 68 B.C., Rome (denarius, 3.95 gm., diam. 17.5 mm., BMCRR Rome 3554).

129, 130 Republic. *Obv., head of Apollo with hair rolled up over laurel-wreath ; behind, corded scroll. Rev., Clio in long drapery resting l. elbow on pedestal and holding open scroll ;* Q POMPONI MVSA. c. 67 B.C., Rome (denarius, 4.27 gm., diam. 17 mm., BMCRR Rome 3610).

131, 132 Republic. *Obv., king Aretas kneeling with ribboned olive-branch by saddled camel ;* M SCAVR AED CVR EX S C. *Rev., Jupiter hurling thunderbolt in galloping quadriga ;* P HYPSAEVS AED CVR C HYPSAE COS PREIVER CAPT. 58 B.C., Rome (denarius, 4.02 gm., diam. 20 mm., BMCRR Rome 3876).

133 Republic. *Rev., king Bocchus kneeling with olive-branch before Sulla, togate and seated, behind whom kneels king Jugurtha, his hands tied behind him ;* FELIX. c. 57 B.C., Rome (denarius, 3.87 gm., diam. 19 mm., BMCRR Rome 3824).

134 Republic. *Rev., L. Junius Brutus the Ancient walking between two lictors and preceded by*

another attendant ; BRVTVS. c. 54 B.C., Rome (denarius, 4.12 gm., diam. 20 mm., BMCRR Rome 3861).

135, 136 Republic. *Obv., bearded head of L. Junius Brutus the Ancient ;* BRVTVS. *Rev., bearded head of C. Servilius Ahala ;* AHALA. c. 54 B.C., Rome (denarius, 4.07 gm., diam. 18 mm., BMCRR Rome 3864).

137 Republic. *Obv., head of the consul C. Coelius Caldus ; behind, tablet inscribed* L(ibero) D(amno); C COEL CALDVS COS. c. 50 B.C., Rome (denarius, 3.97 gm., diam. 19 mm., BMCRR Rome 3833).

138 Republic. *Rev., the Basilica Aemilia, with shields fixed to the columns ;* M LEPIDVS AEMILIA REF(ecta) S C. c. 64 B.C., Rome (denarius, 3.74 gm., diam. 18 mm., BMCRR Rome 3650).

139 Republic. *Rev., temple of Venus at Eryx in Sicily, on rocky peak, surrounded by wall with gateway and towers ;* ERVC(ina). c. 56 B.C., Rome (denarius, 3.99 gm., diam. 18 mm., BMCRR Rome 3830).

140 Republic. *Rev., the Villa Publica in two storeys, both colonnaded, and the lower also arched ; sloping roof on top ;* T DIDI(us) IMP (erator) VIL(lam) PVB(licam refecit). c. 56 B.C., Rome (denarius, 4.00 gm., diam. 18 mm., BMCRR Rome 3856).

recorded that M. Marius Gratidianus, praetor in the mid-80s, received great popular acclaim for devising tests for false coin and for withdrawing all such coin. Gratidianus shortly afterwards lost his life under Sulla, who introduced his own law (the *lex Cornelia de falsis*) to deal with forgery.[100] Then again, the phenomenon of 'serration' (see above, p. 69) was re-introduced in the late 80s for denarii struck at Rome : it looks as if Sulla had to take special care to indicate that the coinage of the period of his supremacy was indeed of the best quality. Finally, and perhaps most surprising of all, coinage of bronze at the mint of Rome was totally suspended from the time of Sulla onwards :[101] provincial bronze was to be struck 40 years later by Pompeian or Caesarian adherents, and Roman *aes* began again some 60 years later, *c.* 23 B.C. Just how the public of Rome or other Italian cities and towns managed without supplementation in the supply of bronze coins is unknown : presumably older issues, worn and often halved or cut, were employed at a token valuation.[102] In any case the whole burden of confidence was cast—and at first, perhaps, not too happily—upon the silver.

For about 25 years after the Sullan interlude the coinage of the mint of Rome continued (now without bronze or any gold) along normal lines. But these were certainly not traditional lines. Freedom in the choice of types reached a new peak. Die-engravers were increasingly imbued with Greek conceptual idiom and Greek technical skill. The art of 'divine' portraiture moved forward to a point at which 'ancestral' portraiture could be undertaken with great distinction. Type-allusion acquired a more and more nearly immediate topicality. The precise sequence of this series of denarii, fascinating in its range of types and of treatment, is (as was the case with earlier series) impossible to establish. Hoards, as before, provide the firmest evidence for relative chronology.[103] There are, however, a few fixed or at least closely approximate points for dating, due principally to the fact that a number of special issues from time to time continued to be produced by magistrates other than the *tresviri monetales*, e.g. by P. Galba as curule aedile *c.* 69 B.C., by M. Scaurus and P. Hypsaeus as curule aediles in 58, and by A. Plautius and Cn. Plancius as curule aediles *c.* 55–4 B.C. Owing to the sheer variety of types used over this period no sequential commentary can possibly be attempted : instead, a few that are perhaps outstanding for design or content will be selected for brief mention.

Among the 'serrati' of the Sullan domination those of C. Mamilius Limetanus and A. Postumius Albinus possess special charm and interest, showing, in the one case, a head of Mercury, ancestor of Ulysses, who is seen on the reverse returning home to be greeted by his dog Argus, and, in the other a mourning head of Hispania (defeated with Sertorius) with *rev.* a togate figure standing between *fasces* and *aquila*. These are rendered in a style which is well-proportioned and clear, with a neatness which is more than merely pretty and a skill which is less than real artistry. Cn. Lentulus, coining as praetor and as CVR(ator) X (denariis) F(landis), chose types that were due to have great significance in the future—*obv.* Head of G(enius) P(opuli) R(omani) with sceptre, *rev.* the globe (of world power) between sceptre and rudder (of government). Another special issuer, P. Lentulus, a quaestor, also showed the Genius of the Roman people, this time ceremonially seated and 126 crowned by Victory, with *obv.* a beautifully designed and rendered head of Hercules. The many types included in the special issues (EX S C) of the curule aedile M. Plaetorius Cestianus were all of visual interest, with some of real beauty, e.g. the *obv.* Head 127 of Ceres, the corn-goddess, or Bonus 128 Eventus, combined with *rev.* Caduceus. Q. Pomponius Musa, with his set of coins (all with *obv.* Apollo) with reverses pun- 130 ningly devoted to the Muses, was sometimes more ambitious than distinguished in his results. C. Piso Frugi deliberately copied the types of his father's vast Social War coinage (see above, p. 77), with closer attention to the archaic head of Apollo. The very remarkable (if also far from ele- 132 gant) denarii of M. Scaurus and P. Hypsaeus as curule aediles in 58 showed *obv.* King Aretas of Nabataea kneeling in subjection, beside his camel, after the campaign against him by Scaurus in 64, and *rev.* Jupiter in quadriga—an old type, but appropriate with the legend declaring that Hypsaeus' ancestor C. Hypsaeus, as consul, captured Privernum (in 329 B.C.). Faustus Sulla commemorated his famous father, and also his father-in-law Pompey, with a number of types: one issue, with *obv.* Head of Diana, 33 has *rev.* showing Sulla the dictator receiving the submission of Bocchus, King of Mauretania, and the surrender of Jugurtha, King of Numidia. M. Junius Brutus, later to be notorious as one of Julius Caesar's assassins, was already able to proclaim his polit-

ical faith—in an age of crumbling democracy—by denarii with *obv.* Head of Libertas, LIBERTAS, and *rev.* L. Junius Brutus 134 (who as consul in 509 B.C. expelled the Tarquin kings from Rome) walking in procession, BRVTVS : other denarii of the same moneyer paired a portrait of his great ancestor with one of his mother's famous forebears, that Servilius Ahala who in 135, 136 439 B.C. slew Spurius Maelius as a traitor to the state. That Roman ancestral portraiture (and thereby the portraiture of the living) was now fast approaching the first flowering of its great strength and subtlety is well enough shown by the denarii of C. Coelius Caldus, with their superb repre- 137 sentation of the moneyer's grandfather. In such a coin the artistic feeling was wholly Roman, in contrast to such purely grecizing designs as those, for example, of L. Torquatus with *obv.* Head of Sibylla in wreath, *rev.* the Sibyl's tripod in wreath—allusions to the priesthood held by his family. Roman feeling was uppermost, too, in the architectural designs that now began to be seen —the Basilica Aemilia on coins of M. Lepi- 138 dus, the temple of Venus Erycina on coins 139 of C. Considius Nonianus, and the Villa Publica on coins of P. Fonteius Capito. 140

The whole (or virtually the whole) of this denarial coinage down to *c.* 55 B.C., with its urgently exciting changes of type, was struck at the mint of Rome, where lay the treasury from which alone the necessarily great quantities of coinage-metal could be drawn; [104] and, as already mentioned, this series of denarii (very occasionally supplemented by fractional pieces) was unaccompanied by any supporting bronze. In weight the denarius itself held steady

87

between limits of c. 3.85 and 4.36 g. Two highly exceptional and very puzzling gold issues, each of severely limited quantity, have to be noted if not explained. One, signed CN LENTVL(us), and known from only two examples, has obv. Head of Jupiter, rev. Eagle on thunderbolt: style and fabric are perhaps not Roman, and weight, at 7.87 g., is at variance with that of the aurei of Sulla (c. 10.75-11.00 g.). The date and the place of origin are alike difficult to define: it may fall even later in the Republican period. The other issue, also known from only two specimens, is of equal difficulty, and weighs c. 8.93 g. It was personal to Pompey, as the types show, with obv. Head of Africa, augural symbols, MAGNVS, in laurel-wreath, and rev. Victory crowning Pompey in triumphal quadriga, with his son riding on one of the horses, PRO COS. Of the possible dates of issue, Pompey's third triumph in 61 B.C. probably provides the most appropriate time; but it is very doubtful if even at that time Pompey (who, though keen for glory as a military leader, was slow in political initiative) would or could have encouraged the production of such an issue at Rome.[105] It was certainly from Rome, however, that the denarii of the time were pouring out.

During the years 60–50 B.C. the long-established dominance of the mint of Rome was at last to be broken. It was at that time that the rivalry between Pompey and Caesar assumed frightening proportions, which the studied moderation of that great patriot Cicero was unable to check. Caesar, consul in 59, received thereafter the assignment of military command in Gaul for five years, afterwards extended to ten; and in that period he secured for Rome, through the conquest of Gaul, her most important and most valuable provincial accession so far. Pompey, consul in 55, thereafter chose the command of Spain, by nature the richer province, but decided to leave his Spanish command to subordinates in order to go east once more. In 52 Pompey became sole consul. By 49 Caesar was determined: he first led an army to Spain to defeat the Pompeians there, and then chased Pompey from Italy to Pharsalus in Greece, crushing his army there. Pompey fled to Egypt, only to be killed; and Caesar, after arranging affairs in Egypt, returned to Rome in 47 as the holder of military experience, authority, and an imperium matched by no other living man, in the face of which the Senate found itself powerless.

Until c. 49 the mint of Rome functioned fairly normally, though with numerous issues from time to time in the names of magistrates senior to the tresviri monetales. In 49 the coinage was issued jointly by Q. Sicinius as tresvir and C. Coponius as praetor: both were 'Pompeians' and left Rome to join Pompey's forces during that year. Their reverse type of Hercules' club draped with a lion's skin doubtless looked to the confidence felt in Pompey's cause. Succeeding these moneyers, perhaps closely, came Manius Acilius, a 'Caesarian', whose types emphasized Salus and Valetudo—the health and welfare which the state might receive from Caesar. By now Caesar and Pompey were in open and armed opposition, and it was the campaigns in Spain and Greece that resulted, at last, in the large-scale production of coinage elsewhere than at Rome. Caesar financed his operations with

88

a vast coinage, possibly produced in Gaul, that was to all intents and purposes of im- 141 perial character, with *obv.* Elephant (= Caesar and his army) trampling serpent 142 (of opposition), CAESAR, and *rev.* Priestly symbols : Caesar, *pontifex maximus* since 63, had the ear of the gods. His opponents coined for Pompey (as MAGN PRO COS, and sometimes unnamed) in Sicily, Spain, and perhaps elsewhere : such types as the triskelis (badge of Sicily), Jupiter the thunderer, a ship's prow, and a sceptre between eagle and dolphin spell out the Pompeian cause, and its now all too unsure provincial context.[106]

With Pompey dead, the mint of Rome could, in 48 B.C., be controlled by secure Caesarian adherents. Decimus Postumius Albinus (later to join the conspiracy against Caesar) chose for his obverses heads of Mars and Pietas and even of his own father, 143 and for his reverses Gaulish weapons (he had served with distinction in Gaul), the clasped hands of concord, and a wreath of corn possibly symbolizing Caesar's distributions at Rome. C. Vibius Pansa repeated his father's punning Pan-mask (see above, p. 78), and introduced a head of Libertas : his reverses emphasized the victorious cause of Rome (under Caesar's leadership) and the corn-supply. L. Hostilius Saserna produced heads of Pietas, a mourning Gallia, and—of dramatic interest—a wild-haired warrior, surely the great Gaulish leader Vercingetorix himself, defender of Alesia. 144,145 In addition to these regular issues the mint of Rome put out a large victory coinage in the sole name of Caesar, with which his victorious army might be rewarded, and the loyalty of the population of Rome encouraged.[107] This was partly of gold, with *obv.* Head of Venus (or Pietas ?), *rev.* Trophy 109*,110* of Gallic arms, CAESAR, and partly of silver, both denarii and (after a long interval) quinarii. On these the same *obv.* head was accompanied by reverses showing CAESAR 111,112 and a military trophy, at the foot of which, on the denarii, sits a captive. All the obverses of this coinage, gold and silver alike, bear ⊥ΙΙ — most naturally explained as the Roman numeral 52 : Caesar's 52nd birthday fell probably *c.* 49 B.C.[108] The quasi-imperial quality of the 'elephant' coinage which he had produced on campaign in 49 was thus confirmed and extended in what he produced—at Rome itself—in 48. Only one element—his portrait—was needed to convert it into a fully imperial series.

IV. THE END OF THE ROMAN REPUBLIC, 48-27 B.C.

The concept and theory of *imperium*, so characteristically Roman in its combination of legal, political and military elements, had so far survived : by no means intact, indeed, but not yet fatally damaged. It could still be argued that the Senate, on behalf of the Roman people, was the agent which constitutionally conferred the chief *imperium*, military as well as civil, upon an annual pair of consuls, each a check upon the other; and, with Roman provincial territories now of immense extent, it was the Senate again which assigned *imperium*, technically subordinate to that of the consuls at Rome, to those who administered and defended the provinces—proconsuls in the larger and more important provinces, and lesser men with lesser *imperium* elsewhere. The essence of *imperium* was that its grade, its duration, and its field of operation were all specifically defined. What had happened between Pompey and Caesar was that two ambitious and powerful provincial proconsuls had each used his constitutionally conferred *imperium* against the other in an attempt to control the political machinery at Rome itself. The earlier essays of Marius and Sulla had already shown clearly the pressures which could be brought to bear upon the political constitution of Rome by strong military leaders; and Sulla, as *dictator* (a sole and supreme office originally devised for extreme emergency), had even used his power to force a reform of that constitution.

Caesar was consul in 48. Technically he was not re-eligible, and consequently he accepted the more absolute and more powerful office of *dictator*, for the first time in 48, and for the second (DICT ITER) in 47. In 46 he was again consul (COS TER(T)), and in 45–4 he reverted again to the dictatorship as DIC TER and DIC(T) QVAR(T), finally receiving the dictatorship for life—and just before his death—in February 44 (DICT PERPETVO). Throughout this period, with the Senate unable to oppose him, he received from its hands supreme *imperium* in one form or another; and he was careful to record these grants of *imperium* upon the coinage issued for him. By contrast, those who still opposed him in the provinces, and principally in Africa and Spain, had a much lesser *imperium* formerly delegated by Pompey when alive (e.g. LEG(atus) PRO PR(aetore), PR(o) Q(uaestor)); and some could not point to any at all—Pompey's sons Cnaeus, killed in 45, and Sextus, together with Q. Metellus Pius Scipio, could style themselves no more than IMP(erator), *de facto* army-generals.

In 47 B.C. the mint of Rome continued to function under its *tresviri monetales*, one of whom, C. Antius Restio, chose a superb 146 portrait of his father for his denarii, and also issued silver quinarii and sestertii.[109] In addition to the normal coinage of the *monetales*, Caesar produced coinage on his own account, presumably for military purposes: aurei emphasizing his priestly status and his victories,[110] denarii perhaps struck in Sicily,[111] and an immense series of denarii with *obv.* Head of Venus, *rev.* 113,114 Aeneas saving Anchises and the palladium from the sack of Troy.[112] The next year, 46, saw an even larger and more varied denarial series (again with fractions) from the *monetales*; many of the types were simply pro-Caesarian, but T. Carisius produced some denarii of unusual technical 147,148 interest, with *obv.* Head of Juno Moneta, *rev.* Vulcan's cap above the anvil, hammer and tongs of a mint-worker. Once more Caesar coined on his own account, producing a very large series of aurei through the agency of A. Hirtius, the city-prefect 149,150 —clumsy coins, with *obv.* Head of Pietas, C CAESAR COS TER, perhaps produced in haste by workmen unaccustomed to working in gold, as well as a range of denarii emphasizing Venus, his divine ancestor, and his victories in Gaul. This was the year in which Caesar celebrated four triumphs, distributed money to his troops and to the Roman citizens, dedicated a temple to Venus Genetrix, and prepared his forces for a campaign against the Pompeian remnants in Spain. There a varied coinage of denarii

had been struck since 49 in order to pay the troops who, under Cnaeus and Sextus Pompey (both now adopting their dead father's name MAGNVS), were still loyal to the Pompeian cause.[113] The types were of great interest. The obverses usually showed a portrait of Pompey the Great: reverses 151 concentrated upon Spanish loyalty to the Pompeians, as in the scenes of Cnaeus 152 Pompey being welcomed ashore by Spain(?) or Baetica(?) from a ship, or being given a laurel branch and wreath by two personifi- 153 cations—Baetica(?) and Tarraco(?). In addition, Cnaeus Pompey struck bronze Asses in some quantity, with *obv.* Head of Janus and *rev.* the traditional and now specially appropriate ship's prow.

The same general pattern of coinage continued in 45. From the *monetales* at Rome came a fairly large coinage of denarii and silver fractions with very varied types: those of L. Papius Celsus and L. Valerius Acisculus were mainly devoted, in the traditional Roman manner, to mythological and ancestral history, but Palikanus' coins, with heads specified as being those of Libertas, Honos and Felicitas, and with varied references to the Rostra, voting-methods, and curule chair, appear to look to political processes of the time. More gold—aurei and half-aurei—were specially struck for Caesar in Rome by L. Plancus as city-prefect in succession to those of Hirtius. These, with their *obv.* Bust of Victory, were doubtless produced for military distribution after his crushing defeat of the Pompeians at Munda in Spain (March, 45), when Cnaeus Pompey was killed and Sextus fled. The latter had the ability still to strike rough denarii (now as PIVS as well as

MAGNVS) and Asses (with the features of Pompey the Great seen in Janus' head): *pietas* was the reflection of a vow to avenge his father. The bronze coinage struck in 46–5 by the Pompeians in Spain, though it lay outside the series of the central mint of Rome, was in fact the first bronze to be produced in quantity since the suspension of Roman bronze in Sulla's time (see above, p. 86). Caesar himself may have been well aware of the need for low-value currency: at any rate C. Clovius, a *praefectus* in Cisalpine Gaul, produced a considerable issue of pieces with *obv.* Bust of Victory, CAESAR DIC TER, and *rev.* Armed Minerva with trophy and Medusa-shield, C. CLOVI PRAEF. These handsome coins may well have been made at Mediolanum (Milan), the principal centre of Cisalpine Gaul, lying near an important source of the mineral *cadmea*, for they were not of bronze (i.e. copper and tin) but of bright yellow *orichalcum* or brass (i.e. copper and zinc with *cadmea*).[114] Their denominational value is uncertain: at *c.* 15.25 g. they were substantially lighter than the As of the Pompeians at *c.* 22.75 g., but *orichalcum* was a better looking and more valuable metal than bronze or copper, so that they may have passed as dupondii, i.e. double Asses.[115]

The coinage of 44 B.C. clearly reflects the intensity of the political drama which culminated, on March 15, in Caesar' assassination at the hands of those who, for mixed reasons, feared the consolidation of his autocratic and near-monarchical government. Caesar himself, as part of his increase in the number of junior magistrates,[116] raised the *monetales* from the long-established figure of three to four; and the formula

IIII VIR appears on coins of L. Aemilius Buca, though it was omitted by the other three—M. Mettius, C. Cossutius Maridianus, and P. Sepullius Macer. That these were in fact the colleagues of Buca is, however, proved by the type-content of their coins (mainly denarii, with a few silver quinarii and sestertii). The denarii all bear Caesar's portrait on the obverse, with reverses given up to various representations of Venus Genetrix, his divine ancestress: at last the representation of a living Roman had been undertaken on the coinage of Rome, for Caesar *was* Rome. He began the year as DICT(ator) QVART(um). By February 15, when he declined the offer (made by the consul M. Antonius on behalf of the people) of actual kingship,[117] he was DICT PERPETVO; and such was his position when he died on March 15: coins of Macer and Maridianus combine this title with a posthumously veiled head. In April the office of dictator was abolished, and Caesar appeared for a short time, still veiled, as PARENS PATRIAE—a title of which Dio Cassius[118] recorded that it appeared by senatorial order on the coinage. The number of distinct types and issues produced by these four *monetales* between January and April of 44 was very considerable, and it is of interest that die-sequence letters were used by Mettius for his part of what appears to have been a supplementary series (probably struck for military pay) still with Caesar's portrait but with title IMP or IMPER. This was the last occasion on which such letters were used.[119]

The urgency with which the Caesarian coinage of 44 was struck is evident from the treatment of Caesar's portrait. For the first time in the history of their office the *monetales* could instruct their die-engravers to work from the features of a living man, and must instruct them to work to that man's satisfaction. What working models may have been available one cannot say; but at least it is clear that Mettius, at work earlier than his three colleagues (he alone struck for Caesar as DICT QVART), possessed a fine portrait model for his engravers to follow. This early head was fairly large, and of fine proportion. The features, if slightly dry, were firm and strong: the neck was long, but not thin; the hair was firmly rendered upon a well-shaped, deep head in no way dwarfed by the laurel wreath around it. With the passing of the weeks the treatment sadly deteriorated, and what was initially a portrait of strength, and even nobility, became almost a carica-ture, with a small head overburdened by a large wreath, pinched features, and a long and skinny neck. Not even the posthumous portraits recovered any of the original poise and stylishness. Nevertheless, whether well or badly rendered, Caesar's portraits in 44 had revolutionized the coinage of Rome. After 250 years of 'republican' aspect it had now become to all intents and purposes imperial. And it well reflected those tendencies which the conspirators hoped that they were destroying on the Ides of March.

However, the post-March types of Macer (who continued with Maridianus to coin for a time) showed how great the real de-struction was. Caesar's death had created a dangerous vacuum. Macer might well produce denarii with *obv.* Temple, CLE-MENTIAE CAESARIS—a temple promised by

141, 142 Republic. *Obv., elephant trampling on dragon ;* CAESAR. *Rev., pontifical emblems (ladle, sprinkler, axe, and priest's cap).* c. 49 B.C., Gaul (?) (denarius, 4.08 gm., diam. 18 mm., BMCRR Gaul 27).

143 Republic. *Rev., two Gaulish trumpets, crossed ; above and below, an oval and a round shield ;* ALBINVS BRVTI F(ilius). c. 48 B.C., Rome (denarius, 3.90 gm., diam. 20 mm., BMCRR Rome 3962).

144, 145 Republic. *Obv., Vercingetorix (?), with flowing hair and beard, a chain around his neck ; behind, long, pointed shield. Rev., naked warrior with spear and shield in galloping biga driven by charioteer with whip ;* L HOSTILIVS SASERNA. 48 B.C., Rome (denarius, 3.91 gm., diam. 20 mm., BMCRR Rome 3995).

146 Republic. *Obv., head of the tribune Antius Restio ;* RESTIO. 47 B.C., Rome (denarius, 4.04 gm., diam. 19 mm., BMCRR Rome 4029).

147, 148 Republic. *Obv., head of Juno Moneta, draped ;* MONETA. *Rev., Vulcan's cap* (pileus) *laureate above coining tongs, anvil, and hammer ; all in laurel-wreath ;* T CARISIVS. 46 B.C., Rome (denarius, 4.15 gm., diam. 20 mm., BMCRR Rome 4056).

149, 150 Republic. *Obv., head of Pietas, veiled ;* C CAESAR COS TER(tium). *Rev., sacrificial im-plements (lituus, jug, axe) ;* A HIRTIVS PR(aefec-tus). 46 B.C., Rome (aureus, 8.09 gm., diam. 20 mm., BMCRR Rome 4051).

151, 152 Republic. *Obv., head of Pompey the Great ;* CN MAGN IMP(erator). *Rev., Hispania (or Baetica), turreted, standing with spear on pile of arms and grasping the hand of Cnaeus Pompey with ship's stern behind him ;* M MINAT(ius) SABIN(us) PR(o) Q(uaestor). 46 B.C., Spain (denarius, 3.71 gm., diam. 18.5 mm., BMCRR Spain 77).

153 Republic. *Rev., Baetica (?), turreted, with caduceus, presenting laurel-branch to Cnaeus Pompey leaning on spear and crowned by Tarraco (?), turreted and with trophy of arms, behind him ;* M MINAT SABIN PR Q. 46 B.C., Spain (denarius, 3.77 gm., diam. 19 mm., BMCRR Spain 83).

141

142

143

144

145

146

147

148

149

150

151

152

153

154

155

156

157

158

159

160

161

162

163

164

165

166

154, 155 Republic. *Obv., bust of Victory, draped;* CAESAR DIC(tator) TER(tium). *Rev., Minerva, helmeted, advancing with trophy, spears, and gorgon shield; serpent erect before her;* C CLOVI PRAEF. *45 B.C., north Italy (Mediolanum?) (dupondius (?) of orichalcum, 15.29 gm., diam. 27 mm., BMCRR Rome 4125).*

156, 157 Republic. *Obv., head of Julius Caesar, laureate; lituus behind;* CAESAR DICT QVART (um). *Rev., Juno Sospita in goat's skin head-dress, with spear and shield in galloping biga;* M METTIVS. *44 B.C., Rome (denarius, 4.10 gm., diam. 18 mm., BMCRR Rome 4135).*

158 Republic. *Obv., head of Julius Caesar, laureate;* CAESAR DICT PERPETVO. *44 B.C., Rome (denarius, 3.90 gm., diam. 20 mm., BMCRR Rome 4157).*

159 Republic. *Obv., head of Julius Caesar, laureate and veiled;* CAESAR DICT PERPETVO. *44 B.C., Rome (denarius, 3.85 gm., diam. 18 mm., BMCRR Rome 4173).*

160, 161 Republic. *Obv., temple with doors closed and globe in pediment;* CLEMENTIAE CAESARIS. *Rev., horseman in conical cap and with whip riding the nearer of two galloping horses; wreath and palm-branch behind;* P SEPVLLIVS MACER. *44 B.C., Rome (denarius, 3.86 gm., diam. 21 mm., BMCRR Rome 4176).*

162 Republic. *Obv., head of Antony, bearded and veiled; lituus in front; jug behind; circular punch-mark.* 44 B.C., Rome (denarius, 4.28 gm., diam. 19.5 mm., BMCRR Rome 4178).

163 Republic. *Obv., head of Octavian, slightly bearded;* CAESAR III VIR R P C. *42 B.C., Rome (denarius, 3.29 gm., diam. 18 mm., BMCRR Rome 4279).*

164 Republic. *Obv., head of Lepidus;* M LEPIDVS III VIR R P C. *42 B.C., Rome (aureus, 8.02 gm., diam. 20 mm., BMCRR Rome 4232).*

165 Republic. *Obv., head of Julius Caesar, laureate; lituus behind;* DIVI IVLI. *40 B.C., Rome (denarius, 3.97 gm., diam. 18 mm., BMCRR Rome 4308). (Moneyer: Q. Voconius Vitulus.)*

166 Republic. *Obv., head of Octavian, with light beard;* DIVI IVLI F. *40 B.C., Rome (denarius, 3.84 gm., diam. 18 mm., BMCRR Rome 4314). (Moneyer: Ti. Sempronius Graccus.)*

the Senate before he died, and now perhaps set in train as an act of reparation, so as to lower the political temperature. At the same time Antony, as consul, could seek to raise that temperature, inciting the citizens of Rome against the assassins, and reading Caesar's will in public, with the bequest of nearly 19 denarii to every Roman. Power passed insensibly to Antony; and Antony's portrait promptly appeared on Macer's later coinage, in mourning veil and with priestly symbols as *augur*. In 43, still with four *monetales*, the types reverted to a more conventional level, though L. Flaminius Chilo, probably the senior colleague,[120] could pair Venus with Victory and a head of Caesar with Pax. This was the year during which Antony, supported by Lepidus, Caesar's *magister equitum*, sought to strengthen his personal position against the military forces of the conspirator Decimus Brutus in northernmost Italy, against a revived senatorial morale inspired by the elderly Cicero, and latterly against Octavian, the grand-nephew and heir of Caesar, who, not yet 20, returned to Rome from his studies in Greece to claim his inheritance, conciliate Rome, and block Antony's ambitions. These complex manoeuvres led to the formation of the Triumvirate. Antony, Octavian and Lepidus became *triumviri rei publicae constituendae* for five years: Antony was to command the Gauls; Octavian, Sicily and Africa; and Lepidus the Spains. Greece and the East were dominated by the conspirators M. Brutus and C. Cassius.

The four *monetales* of 42—L. Livineius Regulus, P. Clodius, L. Mussidius Longus, and C. Vibius Varus [121]—all gave prominent publicity to the Triumvirate on their large and varied coinage in gold and silver. Each had some personally chosen types, Varus showing Roma and Nemesis, and Regulus even his father's portrait; but each also struck elaborately varied portrait issues for each of the three Triumvirs (M. ANTO-NIVS, C. CAESAR (= Octavian), and M. LE-PIDVS) as IIIVIR R P C. The inclusion of large quantities of gold in the coinage of 42 was of course due to the fact that each Triumvir was busily building up his military strength in the area assigned to him. Antony and Octavian combined their strength to defeat Brutus and Cassius at Philippi in Macedonia, and the areas of command were then changed, Antony choosing the East and Octavian securing Italy, with Lepidus relegated to Africa. The mint of Rome thus fell within Octavian's influence, and the coins of 41 (from C. Clodius, M. Arrius Secundus, C. Numonius Vaala, and L. Servius Rufus) made no reference to the Triumvirate. Nor did the gold and silver of Ti. Sempronius Graccus and Q. Voconius Vitulus,[122] the only two *monetales* that can be assigned to 40: by contrast, the emphasis was upon Divus Julius (head of Caesar, DIVI IVLI) and Octavian, who as DIVI IVLI F(ilius) was now set upon the long stern path of vengeful ambition and total constitutional reform.

Regular output by *monetales* at the mint of Rome apparently ceased at this point. Its production had been brought to a peak in Caesar's final years. After his death, and especially after the formation of the Triumvirate, centrifugal forces began to operate strongly, for the wide dominions of Rome abroad contained rival armies under rival commanders who could no longer look to the mint of Rome for monetary supplies. The earlier coinages of the Pompeians in Spain have already been noticed (see above, p. 94). Since then, non-Roman coinages had been multiplying elsewhere. Of these, one clear but short-lived section[123] was struck in Greece and further east to finance the military operations of the 'Liberators'—the anti-Caesarians who, led by Brutus and Cassius, had withdrawn eastward from Italy to escape the unpopularity which their assassination of Caesar had brought down on them, only to find final defeat at Philippi. Brutus, who on occasions appears as BRVTVS or M. BRVTVS but more often (after his adoption by Q. Servilius Caepio) as Q. CAEPIO BRVTVS, was based in Greece and Macedonia. His coinage—aurei and denarii, with some quinarii—was put out partly in his own name alone, and partly with the names of subordinates added: L. Sestius as proquaestor, C. Flavius Hermicillus as propraetor, Costa simply as legatus, and Casca (a fellow conspirator) and L. Plaetorius Cestianus without specified rank. Its theme was the war which Brutus was fighting to restore liberty to the Roman world. 'Libertas' was the watchword of his forces, and her head appeared on some coins: others showed Apollo, Brutus the Ancient (the first elected consul after the expulsion of the Tarquin kings: cf. above, p. 87), and M. Brutus himself, most notably on the famous and ruthless denarii with *rev.* EID MAR (*Eidibus Martiis*, 'on the Ides of March') below two daggers and the cap of liberty which Caesar's murder was designed to obtain.[124] The types of Apollo, lyre and tripod suggest that Apollonia was Brutus' principal mint. For Cassius, too, based in Asia Minor, the theme of Libertas was dominant in the context of warfare. He also coined through subordinates : his mints probably included Rhodes and Sardis.[125] The defeat and death of Brutus and Cassius at Philippi in 42 brought this brave and almost moralistic coinage to an end. Henceforth the opposition to the still joint power of Antony and Octavian was to come from Sextus Pompey. Based in Sicily after being proscribed by the Triumvirs, he consolidated a powerful and successful navy, and to finance this navy (which seriously menaced the corn-supply to Rome) he struck a series of denarii, with a little gold, bearing a variety of types referring to naval warfare, Sicily, and south Italy.[126] The obverses included heads of Pompey the Great, of Neptune, and of Sextus himself, who appeared as MAG(nus) PIVS IMP(erator) ITER(um) and—specifying the original command assigned to him by a compliant Senate in 43—PRAEF(ectus) CLAS(sis) ET ORAE MARIT(imae) EX S C, 'Commander of the Fleet and Coast by decree of the Senate'. It was not until the autumn of 36 that Octavian's forces, admirably led by Marcus Agrippa, could decisively defeat Sextus Pompey at the battle of Naulochus. Only then were the sea-approaches to Italy at last free from a very dangerous threat : Scylla and Charybdis and the harbour of Messana need now fear nothing but the elements of nature.

It will be remembered that, according to the initial arrangement for the Triumvirate in 43 (see above, p. 101), the Gaulish provinces were assigned to Antony and the Spanish to Lepidus, while Octavian was fobbed off with Sicily and Africa. After Philippi (42), Antony chose to command, in preference, the whole of the East, leaving to Octavian the whole of the west. Italy itself was regarded in some sense as neutral or at least special territory. Lepidus, though assigned to Africa, was at first suspected of treasonable dealings with Sextus Pompey, and did not take up his command until 40. Such is the chronological framework within which the coins of the Triumvirs have to be arranged down to the battle of Actium in 31, when Octavian at length emerged supreme and without a rival. These issues in the period 43–31 are of some complexity, for they reflect little uniformity of usage. At first the theory of the Triumvirate was reasonably well observed. For example, Antony, coining in Gaul *c.* 43–2,[127] began (on a non-portrait series of silver) by making joint reference to himself and Lepidus, representing the Gaulish and Spanish provinces, each simply as IMP or COS IMP, with types alluding to Antony as *augur* and to Lepidus as *pontifex maximus*. But Antony's constitutionalism could not match his ambition : almost at once he initiated a portrait coinage in gold and silver, for Antony/ Lepidus and Antony/Octavian, as Triumviri, and he followed directly in Caesar's footsteps (see above, p. 89) by specifying his own age—A(nno) XL—on quinarii mintmarked LVGVDVNI (Lyons) on the occasion of his presence at its foundation in 43.[128] He also struck gold and silver on which his own portrait, with M ANTO(N)IMP, was paired with Caesar's portrait (with CAESAR DIC) : *pietas* towards the Dictator's memory in Gaul could do him nothing but good.

At this period Octavian could produce no coinage. Still very young, and lacking

, 175
, 177
179
180, 181
182
183, 184

167,168 Republic. *Obv., head of Antony, bearded ;* M ANTONIVS III VIR R P C. *Rev., the hero Anteon (son of Hercules and ancestor of the Antonian family) seated on rocks with spear, short sword, and shield ;* L REGVLVS IIII VIR A(uro) P(ublico) F(eriundo). *42 B.C., Rome (aureus, 7.98 gm., diam. 21 mm., BMCRR Rome 4255).*

169,170 Republic. *Obv., head of Antony ;* M ANTONIVS M(arci) F(ilius) M N(epos) AVGVR IMP TER. *Rev., head of Octavia, her hair knotted and plaited ;* COS (consul) DESIG (natus) ITER(um) ET TER III VIR R P C. *38 B.C., uncertain mint (aureus, 8.06 gm., diam. 19 mm., BMCRR East 144).*

171 Republic. *Obv., conjoined heads of Antony (ivy-wreathed) and Octavia ;* M ANTONIVS IMP COS DESIG ITER ET TERT. *39 B.C., Ephesus (?) (silver tetradrachm, 11.01 gm., diam. 27.5 mm., BMCRR East 135).*

172,173 Republic. *Obv., head of Antony, ivy-wreathed ; small lituus below ;* M ANTONIVS IMP COS DESIG ITER ET TERT. *Rev., draped bust of Octavia, her hair knotted and plaited, on cista mystica between two serpents ;* III VIR R P C. *39 B.C., Pergamum (?) (silver tetradrachm, 12.25 gm., diam. 27 mm., BMCRR East 133).*

174,175 Republic. *Obv., head of Pompey the Great ; lituus in front ; jug behind ;* MAG(nus) PIVS IMP ITER. *Rev., Neptune, foot on prow, and holding aplustre, between the brothers of Catana, Anapias and Amphinomus, bearing their parents on their shoulders ;* PRAEF CLAS ET ORAE MARIT EX S C. *c. 42 B.C., Sicily (denarius, 3.91 gm., diam. 19 mm., BMCRR Sicily 7).*

176,177 Republic. *Obv., head of Neptune, diademed ; trident behind ;* MAG PIVS IMP ITER. *Rev., trident above helmeted naval trophy including prow, aplustre, and monstrous heads of Scylla and Charybdis ;* PRAEF CLAS ET ORAE MARIT EX S C. *c. 40 B.C., Sicily (denarius, 4.04 gm., diam. 20 mm., BMCRR Sicily 15).*

178,179 Republic. *Obv., the Pharos of Messana surmounted by Neptune with trident and rudder, foot on prow ; below, war-ship with aquila in prow and aplustre, trident, and pennant in stern ;* MAG PIVS IMP ITER. *Rev., Scylla wielding rudder, her body terminating in two fish-tails and the foreparts of dogs ;* PRAEF CLAS ET ORAE MARIT EX S C. *c. 40 B.C., Sicily (denarius, 3.87 gm., diam. 18.5 mm., BMCRR Sicily 18).*

171

172

173

174

175

176

177

178

179

180

181

182

183

184

185

186

187

188

189

190

191

192

193

194

195

180,181 Republic. *Obv., head of Antony ; lituus behind ;* M ANTONIVS III VIR R P C. *Rev., head of Lepidus ; ladle* (simpulum) *and sprinkler* (aspergillum) *behind (symbols of the* pontifex maximus*) ;* M LEPIDVS III VIR R P C. c. *42 B.C., Gaul (aureus, 8.13 gm., diam. 20.5 mm., BMCRR Gaul 46).*

182 Republic. *Rev., head of Octavian ;* C CAESAR III VIR R P C. c. *42 B.C., Gaul (aureus, 7.94 gm., diam. 20.5 mm., BMCRR Gaul 47).*

183,184 Republic. *Obv., head of Antony, slightly bearded ; lituus behind ;* M ANTON [IMP]. *Rev., head of Julius Caesar, laureate ; jug behind ;* CAESAR DIC. c. *43 B.C., Gaul (denarius, 3.88 gm., diam. 19 mm., BMCRR Gaul 53).*

185,186 Republic. *Obv., head of Labienus, slightly bearded ;* Q LABIENVS PARTHICVS IMP. *Rev., horse, bridled and saddled, with (?) bow-case attached.* c. *40-39 B.C., eastern mint (denarius, 3.78 gm., diam. 18 mm., BMCRR East 132).*

187 Republic. *Rev., Armenian tiara, with bow and arrow crossed behind ;* IMP TERTIO III VIR R P C. *36 B.C., eastern mint (denarius, 3.89 gm., diam. 20 mm., BMCRR East 172).*

188,189 Republic. *Obv., head of Antony ; Armenian tiara behind ;* ANTONI ARMENIA DEVICTA.

Rev., bust of Cleopatra, diademed and draped ; stem of prow in front ; CLEOPATRAE REGINAE REGVM FILIORVM REGVM. c. *32 B.C., eastern mint (denarius, 3.90 gm., diam. 19 mm., BMCRR East 182).*

190,191 Republic. *Obv., war-ship with rowers ; standard at prow ;* ANT AVG(ur) III VIR R P C. *Rev., aquila between two standards ;* CHORTIVM PRAETORIARVM. c. *31 B.C., eastern mint (aureus, 8.06 gm., diam. 20 mm., BMCRR East 183).*

192 Republic. *Rev., three standards, each ornamented with two wreaths and prow ;* CHORTIS SPECVLATORVM. c. *31 B.C., eastern mint (denarius, 3.56 gm., diam. 18 mm., BMCRR East 185).*

193 Republic. *Rev., aquila between two standards ;* LEG(io) XVI. c. *31 B.C., eastern mint (denarius, 3.41 gm., diam. 17.5 mm., BMCRR East 211).*

194,195 Republic. *Obv., head of Antony ;* M ANTONIVS AVG(ur) IMP IIII COS TERT III VIR R P C. *Rev., Victory holding ribboned laurel-wreath and palm-branch ;* D TVR ; *all in laurel-wreath. 31 B.C., eastern mint (denarius, 3.80 gm., diam. 18 mm., BMCRR East 227).*

both fortune and political backing, he was engaged temporarily in repairing these deficiencies: his only strength was that he was Caesar's heir and, from 42 (when Caesar was deified) *divi filius*. Apart from this his position as Triumvir would have been empty indeed. However, Antony's removal to the East after Philippi, and Octavian's succession to him in Gaul, radically changed his position; and from about 41 or very soon after he was evidently able to find the means of producing his own coinage, in gold as well as silver, in order to pay the forces under his command.[129] It is difficult to be precise about his mints, but it is likely that these would have lain north of the Po, probably in Cisalpine Gaul, and possibly further afield in Gallia Narbonensis. The types of his coins showed a wide range, including conspicuous reference to the honours paid to Caesar and to those which he himself had received after returning to Rome in 44;[130] and there were heads of Octavian (as C. CAESAR with IMP or III VIR R P C), Caesar (DIC(T) PER(P)), Lepidus (PONT MAX III VIR R P C), and Mars (combined with Octavian's names and titles). Of Antony there was for a time no mention; the trouble caused by his brother, the consul L. Antonius, by concentrating in Perusia a pro-Antonian force which Octavian had to starve into submission (40 B.C.) may well have been one reason for this.[131] However, a total break with Antony was deferred for a time. The pact of Brundisium (in 40) and the agreement at Misenum (in 39) did something to cement relations outwardly; and the Triumvirate was in fact renewed in 37 for another five years. Even so, it is noticeable that Octavian's coinage from 38 onwards dropped all reference to his great Triumviral rival. In 39 it had showed paired portraits of Octavian and Antony as CAESAR IMP and ANTONIVS IMP. Thereafter it was devoted to Octavian alone, with subsidiary references to the deified Caesar and to Marcus Agrippa, victor at Naulochus (see above, p. 103); and Octavian, although he did not at once abandon his Triumviral title, made increasing play with his status as DIVI F(ilius), began to use IMP(erator) as a semi-personal forename, and laid conspicuous emphasis on the fact that, as early as 39, he was designated consul (in advance) for the second and third times—COS ITER ET TERT DESIG.[132] For the ordinary citizen of Rome and Italy the two most important cards in any political pack were now the traditionally great *imperium* of a consul and the personal succession, as adopted son, to the inheritance of Caesar, the deified Dictator.

These issues by Octavian down to the middle 30s were primarily of military character: legions had to be raised, fleets constructed (Sextus Pompey had destroyed one fleet before its replacement defeated him at Naulochus), and harbours created. Antony was under a parallel necessity. After going to the East (see above, p. 102) he first exacted indemnities from those cities in the province of Asia which had helped Brutus and Cassius, and then went to Egypt and Cleopatra. Parthian inroads into Syria (encouraged by the renegade Q. Labienus, self-styled 'Parthicus' and 'imperator', who struck his own gold and silver) he dealt with through P. Ventidius, but the imminence of war against Octavian in 40 brought him to Italy with a large fleet, until the pact of Brundisium (whereby he married Octavia, sister of Octavian) dissipated the threat of hostilities. He retired to administer his affairs for three years from Athens before Egypt and Cleopatra claimed him once more; and he assigned to Cleopatra certain eastern territories, now under Roman control, which had once belonged to the Ptolemies of Egypt, finally giving the title of king to the two sons born to him by Cleopatra. For a far-flung administration, an extravagant manner of life, and above all the maintenance of fleets and armies, money must be provided.

For Antony, as for Octavian, the identification of his minting-centres is substantially a matter of conjecture. It has been argued [133] that, Italy being a sort of neutral ground common to all the Triumvirs, Antony (and equally Octavian and Lepidus) put out Triumviral coinage from Italy itself —though not from Rome—and that Antony's mint lay at Anagnia, a few miles east of Rome : from Anagnia, it has been held, virtually the whole of his great war-coinage down to 31 was issued. Although the literary evidence for this view is admittedly strong, it is nevertheless a view difficult to accept. Even if the neutral status of Italy is granted to the degree at which Octavian would not have dared to interfere with the gold and silver monetary production of an unfriendly and suspect rival who spent long periods in Asia, Egypt, and Greece, all far from Anagnia, it is impossible to accept that Antony would have found it better, safer, and easier, from the point of view of supply and distribution, to coin at Anagnia rather than in one or other of his various eastern sojourning places. Nor should it be forgotten that the production of coinage was a process that could be undertaken almost anywhere at short notice, given the metal, a furnace, and some engravers and metal-smiths. Even in the Hannibalic war (see above, p. 48) Rome had been able to decentralize arrangements for coining gold and silver almost on the spur of the moment, and with excellent technical results. On balance, the recognition of Anagnia as the site of Antony's main pre-Actium mint must be held to be unacceptable. It is probable that a plurality of mints worked for him, some here, some there. They were under the direction of a variety of subordinates, their fortunes more or less closely linked with Antony's—M. Barbatius and L. Gellius, each as Q(uaestor) P(ropraetore); M. Nerva as PROQ(uaestore pro) P(raetore); M. Silanus as Q(uaestor) PROCOS; L. Plancus as PROCOS; and Cn. Domitius Ahenobarbus, who had destroyed a navy of Octavian in 42, as IMP(erator). The fact that there was comparatively little stylistic difference between these issues is most naturally to be explained by the employment, mint by mint, travelling or static, of Italian rather than provincial or Greek operatives. It is likely that Antony's treasure of coinage-metals journeyed with him or with his most active and trusted subordinates. And with the treasure the mint-workmen would have gone as well.

For some little time Antony paid outward respect to the Triumvirate, or at least to Octavian, whose head was paired with his own (both as IIIVIR R P C) on gold and silver; and after the pact of Brundisium the concept of the new alliance was emphasized afresh, and not least by silver quinarii with *obv.* Head of Concordia, IIIVIR R P C, and *rev.* two clasped hands, M ANTON C CAESAR. The politically inspired marriage between Antony and Octavia was perhaps specially emphasized in the province of Asia, where, at the mints of (probably) Ephesus and Pergamum,[134] Octavia featured on two abundant series of 'cistophoric' silver tetradrachms—the normal silver currency of the province of Asia.[135] In one she shares the obverse with Antony, in the other she appears in smaller form on the reverse, Antony being in both cases wreathed with Dionysiac ivy. Octavia appeared also on certain aurei of the time, but from the mid-30s there was a change: the type-content of Antony's aurei and denarii was given up, first, to military and naval themes, the royal tiara of Armenia (defeated by Antony in 34) being prominent, and then—and with all the surprise of ultimately perfect logic—to Antony and Cleopatra jointly on denarii with *obv.* Head of Antony, tiara in field, ANTONI ARMENIA DEVICTA, and *rev.* Bust of Cleopatra, CLEOPATRAE REGINAE REGVM FILIORVM REGVM—'Queen of Kings and of her sons who are Kings'.[136] These coins were struck *c.* 32, and it might be supposed that they were designed as much to challenge and shock western opinion as to please Cleopatra, whose material assistance to Antony was not inconsiderable: conceivably their production (which was not very great) took place at Ephesus, where Cleopatra joined Antony in that year—the year in which, at Rome, Antony's will was opened, disclosing his intentions in detail.

During the years from 42 to 32 B.C., when massive numbers of men were gath-

171
172, 173
169*, 170*

187

188, 189

196, 197 Republic. *Obv., head of L. Junius Brutus the Ancient;* L BRVTVS PRIM(us) COS; *all within oak-wreath. Rev., head of M. Junius Brutus, slightly bearded;* M BRVTVS IMP, COSTA LEG(atus) ; *all within oak-wreath. 42 B.C., Greek mint (aureus, 8.04 gm., diam. 19 mm., BMCRR East 58).*

198, 199 Republic. *Obv., head of Libertas, laureate;* C CASSI IMP. *Rev., aplustre with its branches ending in flowers (roses?) ;* M SERVILIVS LEG. *42 B.C., Rhodes (?) (aureus, 8.08 gm., diam. 20 mm., BMCRR East 82).*

200

201

202

203

ering in the armies of the two great rivals, whose treasure must have seemed limitless, an interesting change had crept into the monetary system of the Roman world. So far as gold and silver were concerned there was little alteration: the weight of the aureus had tended to decline once it had taken a permanent place in the system, but was settled now;[137] and the denarius held steady at 1/84 of a pound (3 1/2 scruples, or *c.* 3.95 g.). The Triumvirate had seen some silver quinarii produced, and even a very few silver sestertii.[138] However, there was evidently a need, dictated by whatever reasons, for some amount of supporting *aes* to provide greater availability of small change: the Pompeians in Spain had already experimented with the re-introduction of *aes* in the mid-40s (see above, p. 94), as had Caesar himself, with the coins of *orichalcum* put out by Clovius (see above, p. 95). In the earlier 30s Antony —in association with L. Bibulus as praetor designate, L. Atratinus as consul designate, and M. Oppius Capito as propraetor and admiral of the fleet—produced what was clearly a large and elaborate *aes* of predominantly naval character. Most of these coins are now very rare, but those that survive show that they were struck in denominations of sestertius (HS and *Δ*, = 4 Asses), tripondius or triple As (*Γ*), dupondius or double As (B), As (A), semis (S), and sextans (. .). Of these, the major denominations mostly have *obv.* Conjoined heads of Antony and Octavia, sometimes with Octavian as well, with *rev.* Antony and Octavia in *quadriga* of hippocamps (sestertius), or three galleys (tripondius), or two galleys (dupondius), or one galley (As).

200, 201 Republic. *Obv., head of M. Junius Brutus, slightly bearded ;* L PLAET(orius) CEST(ianus), BRVT IMP. *Rev., cap of liberty between two daggers ;* EID(ibus) MAR(tiis). *42 B.C., Greek mint (denarius, 3.80 gm., diam. 17.5 mm., BMCRR East 68).*

202, 203 Republic. *Obv., head of Libertas, laureate ;* C CASSEI IMP. *Rev., crab with aplustre in its claws ; below, diadem and rose ;* M SERVILIVS LEG. *42 B.C., Rhodes (?) (denarius, 3.84 gm., diam. 20 mm., BMCRR East 84).*

This carefully planned coinage of bronze [139] is best attributable to a mint or mints in south Italian ports, within the context of the loan of a fleet which Antony made to Octavian in 37 against Sextus Pompey.[140] About the same time Octavian produced remarkable and now very rare *aes* (without denominational mark) with *obv.* Head of Agrippa, M. AGRIPPA ORAE- - -CLAS(sis) PRAE (fectus) C(os), *rev.* The triskelis of Sicily, CAESAR III VIR R P C; and these were followed by two large and handsome *aes* issues—again without value mark—for Octavian respectively with *obv.* Head of Octavian, DIVI F, *rev.* DIVOS IVLIVS in wreath, and *obv.* Head of Octavian, CAESAR DIVI F, and *rev.* Head of Caesar, DIVOS IVLIVS. It is quite uncertain where these coinages of Octavian were struck : the style, at least, is of the finest Italian tradition.[141] A surprising number of other *aes* issues, both for Antony and for Octavian, was coined elsewhere during the 30s. That of Antony's supporter and subordinate C. Sosius, produced on the island of Zacynthus (ZA), was prominent;[142] but the forces of each of the two great Triumvirs were everywhere restlessly on the move : armies and fleets must be paid, some small change was now clearly needed after the long intermission of *aes* production of Rome, and it was left to subordinates, place by place, to see that it was produced. In all it must have amounted to a considerable quantity.[143]

It was presumably during 32–1, and perhaps at Ephesus, perhaps at some intermediate point, that Antony struck his final vast war-coinage, in silver with some gold —of such a size, indeed, and with such a tendency to debase the quality of the silver, that these denarii, obeying and demonstrating Gresham's Law, remained in currency or were hoarded over the next two centuries and more.[144] A single *obv.* type was used, ANT AVG(ur) III VIR R P C around a war-galley. For the reverses, three military standards appeared throughout, but with variant legends specifying these as the standards of each individual element in Antony's great armada. There were two special detachments—the *cohortes praetoriae*, [190] the bodyguard of mixed cavalry and infantry, and the *cohortes speculatorum*, troops [192] employed in the carrying of messages : coins were struck for both of these. But the great mass of this war-coinage was in the names of Antony's legions, ranging with certainty from the First (PRI) to the Twenty-third [193] (XXIII), possibly with some numbered even higher.[145] Most of these are, even today, very common indeed, though certain numbers are rare (e.g. PRI and XVIIII), and the gold, known only for very few legions, is extremely rare. At the time of issue, however, this was a coinage of enormous size. Its types, of jejune character, and without any Antonian portrait (a refinement which would have delayed production), were nevertheless clear and specific. This was the military issue of a man who, with a great army and navy, was poised to fight for the mastery of the whole Roman world. His expectation of victory was unambiguously expressed by the denarii struck independently for Antony as COS TERT (consul for the third time, i.e. in 31 B.C.) by D. Turullius, an admiral, with *obv.* a very fine [194] portrait of Antony, and *rev.* a laurel-wreath enclosing Victory with wreath and palm, of elegant style, with monogram D VR.

Octavian, for his part, had also accumulated a huge military and naval force, the command of the latter being given to M. Agrippa, as experienced as he was loyal. Octavian's political base of power in 32-31 was fragile. The extended Triumvirate had crumbled and was obviously worthless. He held no consulship, and had none in prospect. His only asset—and it was of great value—was his personal position as *Caesar divi filius*, inheritor of all the pro-Roman and pro-western policies of the now consecrated Julius Caesar. It was as such that, in 32, he powerfully rallied opinion in Italy and the west to support him in opposing the orientalizing autocracy threatened by Antony and Cleopatra. And it was as *Caesar divi f.* specifically that he produced his own war-coinage. Insufficiently recognized in the past,[146] this was not indeed so large as Antony's; but it was explicit, and depended principally on three pairs of cleverly integrated designs,[147] as follows :

205 1a. *Obv.* Head of Octavian.
     Rev. Standing Venus, armed, CAESAR DIVI F
207 1b. *Obv.* Head of Venus.
     Rev. Octavian in military dress, CAESAR DIVI F
209 2a. *Obv.* Head of Octavian.
     Rev. Pax with olive-branch and cornucopiae, CAESAR DIVI F
211 2b. *Obv.* Head of Pax.
     Rev. Octavian in attitude of address, CAESAR DIVI F
213 3a. *Obv.* Head of Octavian.
     Rev. Victory alighting on globe, CAESAR DIVI F
215 3b. *Obv.* Head of Victory.

Rev. Octavian, foot on globe, with naval trophy (*aplustre*), CAESAR DIVI F

These types registered no victory, but they promised it, and Peace as well—under the leadership of Octavian, shown personally in a fine, stern, 'Roman' portrait, and they reminded men, both through the legend and also through the Venus motif, that he was Caesar's adopted son and Caesar's heir. Where he produced these coins is quite uncertain : it must surely have been in south Italy, as near as possible to his military and naval base. Their style, too easily assigned in the past to eastern mints, is purely western. Octavian's portraits show the hard, dry realism visible in Roman coin-portraiture over the last twenty years; the 'portraits' of the deities—Venus, Pax and Victoria—are typically devoid of all characterization; while the reverse types display all that jejune neatness and economy which had been the hallmark of the mint of Rome throughout the history of the denarius.

At a date soon after the battle of Actium in 31—a victory for Octavian more decisive than spectacular—he changed his nomenclature from *Caesar divi f.* to *Imp. Caesar*. This was perhaps in 29, the year of his famous triple triumph at Rome, which told the Roman world again that he had emerged sole victor and supreme military leader after years of disastrous civil war.[148] The change of title was reflected in his coinage. Antony's defeat in the naval fight at Actium had been celebrated on denarii with *obv.* Victory on prow (borrowed and adapted 216 from the earlier Greek coinage of Demetrius Poliorcetes),[149] and *rev.* Octavian in

217   triumphal quadriga, CAESAR DIVI F. Exactly the same types appeared with IMP CAESAR,
and this was the title which was used on
Octavian's subsequent coinage (mostly silver but also with an increased proportion
of gold, due to the vast spoils of war) struck
in Italy down to 27, when he became
Augustus. Most of the coinage from 29 to
27 carried Octavian's portrait, the reverse
types being given up to the ideas of
218, 219   triumph, naval victory, the supremacy of
222, 223   personal power, and the recovery for Rome
of the eastern provinces which Antony had
220, 221   dominated, and the conquest of Egypt
which had led to Cleopatra's suicide. Perhaps the last in this series of post-Actium
issues struck in Italy was that of aurei
(struck in Rome itself?) with *obv.* CAESAR
224, 225   COS VII (from 1 Jan. 27) CIVIBVS SERVATEIS
around bare head, and *rev.* AVGVSTVS (from
16 Jan. 27), S C, eagle on wreath with laurel
branches. In this was mirrored the climax
of Octavian's patient and, in the end, mas-
sively successful military and political effort.

If these preceding issues were produced
in Italy, and some perhaps even at Rome
itself, there is no activity attributable to the
mint of Rome immediately after 27. The
Italian peninsula was well stocked with
gold and silver struck for war and for
victory—for victory, because Octavian
after Actium found himself in command of
some 60 legions, partly victorious, partly
defeated, more than half of which had to be
paid off and given grants of land or cash,
so that cash was plentiful. Isolated issues
took place elsewhere, as required, though
in no great quantity except for a coinage
of silver tetradrachms in the province of
Asia designed to supplement those of An-

204, 205 Sole rule of Augustus as Octavian.
*Obv., head of Octavian. Rev., Venus, with
helmet and sceptre, leaning on column against
which rests shield bearing star ;* CAESAR DIVI F.
*c. 31-29 B.C., (?) Italian mint (denarius,
3.56 gm., diam. 20 mm., BMCRE 599).*

206, 207 Sole rule of Augustus as Octavian.
*Obv., head of Venus. Rev., Octavian in military
dress advancing with spear ;* CAESAR DIVI F.
*c. 31-29 B.C., (?) Italian mint (denarius,
3.74 gm., diam. 19 mm., BMCRE 609).*

208, 209 Sole rule of Augustus as Octavian.
*Obv., head of Octavian. Rev., Pax holding
olive-branch and cornucopiae ;* CAESAR DIVI F.
*c. 31-29 B.C., (?) Italian mint (denarius,
4.02 gm., diam. 20.5 mm., BMCRE 605).*

210, 211 Sole rule of Augustus as Octavian.
*Obv., head of Pax ; olive-branch in front ;
cornucopiae behind. Rev., Octavian in military
dress, with spear, raising hand in gesture of
address ;* CAESAR DIVI F. *c. 31-29 B.C., (?)
Italian mint (denarius, 3.98 gm., diam. 20 mm.,
BMCRE 612).*

212, 213 Sole rule of Augustus as Octavian.
*Obv., head of Octavian. Rev., Victory on globe
holding wreath and palm ;* CAESAR DIVI F. *c.
31-29 B.C., (?) Italian mint (denarius,
3.84 gm., diam. 22.5 mm., BMCRE 603).*

214, 215 Sole rule of Augustus as Octavian.
*Obv., bust of Victory. Rev., Octavian as
Neptune (?), holding aplustre and sceptre, with
foot on globe ;* CAESAR DIVI F. *c. 31-29 B.C.,
(?) Italian mint (denarius, 3.67 gm., diam.
21 mm., BMCRE 615).*

204

205

206

207

208

209

210

211

212

213

214

215

216

217

218

219

220

221

222

223

224

225

226

227

tony (see above, p. 114). These were struck in 28, perhaps at Ephesus,[150] and like the *cos. vii* aurei just mentioned they drew the final veil over the past years of unhappy conflict. The laureate head of Octavian on the obverse was surrounded by CAESAR **226** DIVI F COS VI LIBERTATIS P R VINDEX ('champion of the constitutional liberties of the Roman people'), while the reverse, with a miniature Dionysiac *cista* in the field, **227** showed Pax, boldly labelled as such, standing upon a sword and holding the caduceus of free commerce, all within a victorious wreath of laurel. With the slow and painful emergence of Octavian as the sole, un-questioned, and unquestionable *imperator* [151] the Roman Republic was at an end.

216, 217 Sole rule of Augustus as Octavian. *Obv., Victory on ship's prow, holding wreath and palm. Rev., Octavian driving ornamented slow quadriga, holding branch ;* IMP CAESAR. *c. 29-27 B.C., (?) Italian mint (denarius, 3.98 gm., diam. 20 mm., BMCRE 617).*

218, 219 Sole rule of Augustus as Octavian. *Obv., head of Octavian. Rev., trophy of arms on prow with rudder and anchor ;* IMP CAESAR. *c. 29-27 B.C., (?) Italian mint (denarius, 3.97 gm., diam. 20 mm., BMCRE 625).*

220, 221 Sole rule of Augustus as Octavian. *Obv., head of Octavian ; lituus behind ;* CAESAR COS VI. *Rev., crocodile ;* AEGVPTO CAPTA. *28 B.C., (?) Italian mint (denarius, 3.89 gm., diam. 20 mm., BMCRE 650).*

222, 223 Sole rule of Augustus as Octavian. *Obv., head of Octavian ;* CAESAR IMP VII. *Rev., Victory with wreath and palm on cista mystica between two snakes ;* ASIA RECEPTA. *29-27 B.C., (?) Italian mint (quinarius, 1.91 gm., diam. 15 mm., BMCRE 647).*

224, 225 Augustus. *Obv., head of Augustus ;* CAESAR COS VII CIVIBVS SERVATEIS. *Rev., eagle on wreath between laurel-branches ;* AVGVS-TVS S C. *27 B.C., Italian mint (aureus, 7.81 gm., diam. 21 mm., BMCRE 656).*

226, 227 Sole rule of Augustus as Octavian. *Obv., head of Octavian ;* IMP CAESAR DIVI F COS VI LIBERTATIS P R VINDEX. *Rev., Pax with caduceus standing on sword ; cista mystica and snake behind ;* PAX ; *all in laurel-wreath. 28 B.C., Ephesus (tetradrachm, 11.76 gm., diam. 28 mm., BMCRE 691).*

V. THE REFORMED COINAGE OF AUGUSTUS
AND ITS DEVELOPMENT DOWN TO NERO, 27 B.C.-A.D. 68

Octavian had accepted his seventh consulship on 1 January 27 B.C. On 13 January he announced his surrender of all the special and imperatorial power which he had exercised. Three days later, with wide popular support, and at the urgent and undoubtedly pre-arranged request of the Roman Senate, he received proconsular power enabling him to administer the predominantly military or strategic provinces of the empire (the others being left to senatorial supervision), together with conspicuous public honours, including the appellation 'Augustus'—half name, half title, and with religious overtones. Consul, proconsul, commander of a huge army, he stood supreme, and without a rival: the whole wide empire, stretching along the Mediterranean from Spain to Egypt and Asia Minor, was at peace within itself; and, supported by fervent public emotion both in Italy and the provinces, he could mould the Senate of Rome to his will. Politically, and with Julius Caesar's fate in mind, he must suggest that, through internal tranquillity, he was restoring the Republic; and his revised political settlement of 23 B.C., which gave him *tribunicia potestas*—the power of people's tribune—and allowed him to drop the annual consulship, enhanced the appearance of constitutionalism which this ruthlessly strong yet wise and patient man sought to present. Whatever specified powers he held, he wished principally to act through a natural and undefined power—*auctoritas*—and to be quite simply the first man in the Roman state—*princeps*. And he was ready to become the focus of an almost divine cult.

He now administered a large part of the empire *de iure*, and the rest of it, through control of a mainly compliant Senate, *de facto*. The organization of these vast territories could now be viewed as a whole. So, too, could the finances of the empire; and Augustus, with the great treasures of conquered Egypt at his personal disposal, lost no time in putting them on a sound footing. Financial control included, of course, control of coinage. Contrary to what has often been stated, Augustus' control in matters of coinage was absolute throughout the empire. There was no question, in any case, about the authority for issues of gold and silver: these issues, of prime necessity for the payment of the armed and the civil services, were the sole responsibility of Augustus as proconsular

BRITANNIA

• Briconium

Londinium • • Camulodunum
• Rutupiae

• Bononia
• Ambianum
Rotomagus

GERMANIA

• Col. Agrippinensis
• Treveri

GALLIA

Lugdunum •

Mediolanum

GALLIA CISALPINA
Ticinum •

PANNO-
NIA
Aquileia •
• Siscia

Nemausus • • Arelate

ITALIA

Ravenna •

ILLYRICU

Sirmiu

Caesaraugusta •

HISPANIA

• Tarraco

Emerita •

• Col. Patricia

SARDINIA

Ostia • • Rome

M A U R E T A N I A

SICILIA

• Carthago

AFRICA

TRIPOLIS

II THE ROMAN EMPIRE

800 Kms

500 Mls

A C I A

nacium

CASPIAN SEA

B L A C K   S E A

ARMENIA

• Serdica

THRACIA

Constantinople

Heraclea

• Nicomedia

alonica

GALATIA

Cyzicus

• Caesarea

• Pergamum

CAPPA-

ASIA

DOCIA

• Ephesus

• Athens

PARTHIA

COMMAGENE

• Antioch

AEA

• Laodicea-ad-mare

SYRIA • Palmyra

Emesa

JUDAEA

• Alexandria

A E G Y P T U S

imperator; and it was Augustus who could, if he wished, delegate the right to coin gold and silver to regional and subordinate 'client kings' like Juba of Mauretania. Even the lesser and token coinages of copper, brass, or bronze were, however, directly or indirectly dependent upon his authorization : towns, regions, provinces, and (it now appears) Rome itself required Augustus' authority for base-metal issues. Nor was this surprising, for Augustus, in the name of the state, controlled also the major sources from which coinage-metals were mined. Although he and his successors were far from being able to impose a uniform coinage-system throughout the empire over provinces and cities alike, they could at least help to ensure, by close supervision, that the various urban and provincial issues, especially in the east, both harmonized with the Roman system and also (more important) acknowledged the supreme authority of the Roman emperor.[152]

Augustus showed cautious experiment and slow development in his political arrangements after 27 B.C. His monetary arrangements were similar. He had inherited from the Republic a coinage system which, for the western part of the empire, consisted of aurei and denarii of regular weight, with occasional and ultimately unadjusted *aes*, and for the east of cistophoric tetradrachms. He was to stabilize the aureus at *c.* 7.70-7.85 g. (probably representing a theoretical norm of 7 scruples = 7.96 g.), and the denarius at *c.* 3.75-3.80 g. (probably representing a theoretical norm of 3 1/2 scruples = 3.98 g.), with a gold : silver ratio of approximately 1 : 12 through the equivalence 1 aureus = 25 denarii. This

228 Augustus. *Rev., shield between spear-head and curved sword*; P CARISIVS LEG PRO PR. *c. 25-23 B.C., Emerita (denarius, 3.87 gm., diam. 21 mm., BMCRE 277).*

229 Augustus. *Rev., perspective view of walled town behind gateway inscribed* IMERITA; P CARISIVS LEG PRO PR. *c. 25-23 B.C., Emerita (denarius, 3.95 gm., diam. 17 mm., BMCRE 288).*

230 Augustus. *Rev.,* P CARISIVS LEG AVGVSTI. *c. 25-23 B.C., Emerita (As, 16.42 gm., diam. 30 mm., BMCRE 302).*

231, 232 Augustus. *Obv., heads of Augustus (laureate, to r.) and Agrippa with rostral crown back to back;* IMP DIVI F. *Rev., crocodile chained to palm-branch; wreath above;* COL NEM. *c. 10 B.C. onwards, Nemausus (aes, 13.47 gm., diam. 25 mm., BM).*

233 Augustus. *Rev., shield inscribed* CL V *between two laurel-branches;* CAESAR AVGVSTVS S P Q R. *After c. 25 B.C., 'uncertain Spanish mint 2 (Colonia Patricia?)' (aureus, 7.82 gm., diam. 21 mm., BMCRE 353).*

234 Augustus. *Rev., comet;* DIVVS IVLIVS. *After c. 25 B.C., 'uncertain Spanish mint 1 (Caesaraugusta?)' (denarius, 3.78 gm., diam. 20 mm., BMCRE 357).*

235 Augustus. *Rev., aquila and four miniature galloping horses in ornamented car of slow quadriga;* S P Q R. *After c. 25 B.C., 'Spanish mint 1' (denarius, 3.34 gm., diam. 19 mm., BMCRE 392).*

236 Augustus. *Rev., Victory with wreath flying above shield (originally with* CL V) *resting against column;* S P Q R. *After c. 25 B.C., 'Spanish mint 1' (denarius, 3.66 gm., diam. 22 mm., BMCRE 341).*

237 Augustus. *Rev., Victory crowning Augustus in elephant-biga on arch on viaduct;* QVOD VIAE MVN SVNT. *After c. 25 B.C., 'Spanish mint 2' (aureus, 7.83 gm., diam. 21 mm., BMCRE 432).*

238 Augustus. *Rev., helmeted Mars with aquila and standard;* SIGNIS RECEPTIS. *c. 20-17 B.C., 'Spanish mint 1' (denarius, 3.86 gm., diam. 20 mm., BMCRE 332).*

228

229

230

231

232

233

234

235

236

237

238

239   240

241   242

243   244

245

246

247

248

249

250

239, 240 Augustus. *Obv., wreath* (corona civica) *between laurel-branches ;* OB CIVIS SERVATOS. *Rev.,* C ASINIVS C F GALLVS III VIR A A A F F, S C. *c. 22 B.C., Rome (sestertius, 27.66 gm., diam. 36 mm., Oxford, Ashmolean Museum Cat. 502).*

241, 242 Augustus. *Obv.,* AVGVSTVS TRIBVNIC POTEST *in wreath. Rev.,* C ASINIVS GALLVS III VIR A A A F F, S C. *c. 22 B.C., Rome (dupondius, 11.90 gm., diam. 28 mm., Oxford, Ashmolean Museum Cat. 505).*

243, 244 Augustus. *Obv., head of Augustus ;* CAESAR AVGVSTVS TRIBVNIC POTEST. *Rev.,* C GALLIVS LVPERCVS III VIR A A A F F, S C. *c. 22 B.C., Rome (As, 10.50 gm., diam. 28 mm., Oxford, Ashmolean Museum Cat. 535).*

245, 246 Augustus. *Obv., hands crossed over caduceus ;* LAMIA SILIVS ANNIVS. *Rev.,* III VIR A A A F F, S C. *c. 9 B.C., Rome (quadrans, 3.33 gm., diam. 19 mm., Oxford, Ashmolean Museum Cat. 559).*

247 Augustus. *Rev., Parthian, wearing breeches and cloak, kneeling and extending standard with* X *on flag attached ;* CAESAR AVGVSTVS SIGN RECE. *c. 18 B.C., Rome (denarius, 4.00 gm., diam. 17 mm., BMCRE 40).*

248 Augustus. *Rev., ornamented altar inscribed* FOR RE ; CAESARI AVGVSTO EX S C. *c. 19 B.C., Rome (denarius, 3.82 gm., diam. 21 mm., BMCRE 4).*

249, 250 Augustus. *Obv.,* I O M S P Q R V S PR S IMP CAE QVOD PER EV R P IN AMP AT Q TRAN S E *in oak-wreath. Rev., cippus inscribed* IMP CAES AVGV COMM CONS ; L MESCINIVS RVFVS III VIR, S C. *16 B.C., Rome (denarius, 3.56 gm., diam. 19 mm., BMCRE 92).*

simple bimetallic system furnished what may be conveniently called the 'state coinages'—coinages of gold and silver for military and other state purposes. Beside these state coinages of gold and silver a variety of others grew up in copper, bronze, or brass : in some cases these were of an economic size and importance that justifies naming them as major regional coinages, since they served areas of more than merely provincial extent,[153] though they were developed unsystematically. The development of the gold and silver 'state coinages', however, suggests by its carefully overlapping stages that production was often connected in some degree with the personal presence or the high-level military strategy of Augustus himself. In general, the output of coinage under Augustus was immense. Modern methods of estimating ancient coinage output are still in their infancy,[154] but it is clear at least that the whole empire was abundantly supplied, official and ubiquitous gold and silver being everywhere supported by adequate and often common *aes*, regional, provincial, or urban. It is unnecessary to emphasize the resultant stimulus to industry, trade, and commerce.

The earliest western issues of Augustus were denarii and quinarii struck, as a dominantly military coinage *c.* 25–3 B.C., at Emerita (modern Merida), the military colony in Lusitania founded for time-expired soldiers paid off during and after the short but fierce war waged by the emperor in person to complete the conquest of Asturia-Cantabria in north-west Spain, so rich in gold.[155] P. Carisius was the governor of Lusitania : in his military capacity (*legatus Augusti pro praetore*) he signed the reverses of the denarii, all the obverses of which bore Augustus' portrait, and simultaneously, in his civilian capacity (*legatus Augusti*) 230 he issued quantities of copper Asses.[156] The types of the denarii are purely military : 228 Spanish weapons, trophies of arms, and —of chief documentary importance—a 229 view of the gateway of a fortified city inscribed EMERITA. In style and technique these Emeritan coins—silver and copper alike—betray speed in production; but they are valuable evidence, first, of Augustus' continuation of the 'imperatorial' coinages of the Republic, and secondly of Carisius' dual role, civilian as well as military, in the operation of Augustus' mint at Emerita—a mint which, once the war was won, was relegated to purely colonial status.[157] Moreover, the copper Asses of Emerita, struck at *c.* 10-12 g., are the precursors of Augustus' full monetary reforms at Rome in or after 23 B.C. (see below, p. 139).

Augustus' presence in Spain, and the final completion of a provincial conquest begun nearly two centuries earlier, may have prompted his interest in the currency needs of the western territories—Spain and southern Gaul—as a whole: they were well populated and well romanized. It is certain that, at a date not long after 27 B.C., the colony of Nemausus (modern Nîmes) converted its modest colonial *aes* coinage into a profuse series serving a wide regional purpose—something that could have been done only on imperial orders : for a decade or more these conspicuous coins, with the 231, 232 heads of Augustus and Agrippa on the obverse, and the Nemausan crocodile and palm-tree with COL(onia) NEM(ausus) on the reverse, spread widely in the west.[158] But

the source of two distinct and abundant series of aurei and **denarii**, with types appropriate for central or western consumption between the later 20s and *c.* 17 B.C., is quite uncertain. These have been assigned, conjecturally, to the mints of Colonia Caesaraugusta (Saragossa) and Colonia Patricia (Cordoba) in Spain—two great urban centres of which the profuse coinages (if they did in fact come from there) might, in respect of their splendidly strong idiom of portraiture, very well have influenced the portraiture, of the same idiom, seen on the many urban mints of Spain striking *aes* by Augustus' permission. But it is necessary to explain how, even as a result of theft, one of the dies used for striking aurei of the 'Patricia' class came to 233 be found impeccably at Nîmes; and this has not yet been done.[159] All that is clear is that somewhere in the west—not at Rome, of which the style had been and was to be quite different—two large issues of gold (with some halves) and silver succeeded the lesser silver series of Emerita. They were handsome coins, struck from well engraved dies on broad, flat flans; and they showed a fine sense of design, as well as an often superb skill in portraiture, with bold yet sensitive modelling. When the imperial portrait is accompanied by a legend, this is normally CAESAR AVGVSTVS, occasionally the dedicative and honorific CAESARI AVGVSTO. Reverse types recapitulate all the triumphant reconstruction for which Augustus could claim credit—the honours 233, paid him 27 B.C.; his adoptive descent from 235 the divine Julius; the triumphal quadriga; 236, Victory; the rebuilding of the great trunk-roads;[160] the recovery from Parthia of the 238 standards lost by Crassus in 53, with the surviving prisoners of war; and finally the Secular Games of 17 B.C.

In 24 Augustus returned from Spain to Rome to prepare for the revised political arrangements of 23 (see above, p. 129). At the same time, with an ample production of state coinage in gold and silver (and of regional but official *aes*) assured elsewhere, he decided to reopen the mint of Rome. He judged, evidently, that the real need in Italy and the central empire was for a truly ample *aes* coinage, of which no regular supply had been struck at Rome since Sulla's time (see above, p. 86), so that nothing was now centrally available except old Republican pieces, greatly worn, often halved, and treated as the merest tokens. To remedy the need he introduced a striking reform which set a tradition for imperial *aes* that survived for nearly three centuries. Four denominations were planned: in *orichalcum* (brass)—with which Julius Caesar had first experimented (see above, p. 95)—sestertii (*c.* 25 g., = 4 Asses) and dupondii (*c.* 12.5 g., = 2 Asses), and, in the less valuable and less attractive copper, Asses (*c.* 11 g.) and their quarters (quadrantes, *c.* 3 g.). It was with this *aes* system that the mint of Rome began work in or soon after 23, under the resurrected supervision of the *tresviri a.a.a.f.f.*,[161] whose names now again appeared on coins of standard type, as follows:

240 *Sestertius.* Civic crown, laurels, OB CIVIS SERVATOS/Moneyer's name round S C

242 *Dupondius.* Civic crown round AVGVSTVS TRIBVNIC POTEST/Moneyer's name round S C

As. Head of Augustus, CAESAR AVGVST(VS) (PONT MAX, after 12 B.C.) TRIBVNIC POT(EST)/Moneyer's name round S C [243, 244]

Quadrans. Types variable, but S C and moneyers' names constant. [245, 246]

Of great abundance and urgency, and sometimes therefore of rough technique, this *aes* flooded through Italy and the provinces in central and western Europe, circulating for long years to come, and giving the western empire an admirable small-change system at a time when industry and commerce, now stabilized, clearly demanded it. It was not, as sometimes thought, a 'senatorial' coinage: the conspicuous and constant S C primarily called universal attention to the honours, titles and powers which Augustus had received from the Senate. In contrast to aurei and denarii, the *aes* was essentially a civilian coinage; and it is notable that the As—the commonest of all the denominations—invariably showed Augustus' portrait.[162]

Portraiture of Augustus varied greatly from mint to mint, and also from time to time. Sketchy at Emerita, heroized at the (?) 'Spanish' mints, it was essentially 'civil' on the *aes* of Rome: elsewhere during his reign it presented widely different characteristics. It is reasonable to suppose that die-engravers at any given time were working from a particular model, either in a mint itself or in a nearby public place, from which a current version of the imperial features could be studied. Throughout all the great range of variation under Augustus— and variation greatly diminished afterwards

—there are some common threads to be seen : a lofty head; a straight nose; artlessly 'natural' hair; a small, firm mouth. But only the existence of a variety of models for reproduction could explain such variation in treatment on the coins; and it is likely that coin-designers and die-engravers, now as during the Republic also, made full use of authentic public monuments on which to base their work.[163]

Not long after the moneyer's *aes* was begun at Rome Augustus ordered the production—irregularly, rather sparingly, and perhaps in part for the prestige of the mint —of aurei and denarii. Their idiom was at first uncertain, seeming to revive the conventions of the old Republic, with heads of deities alternating with those of the emperor, and reverse types alluding often to the families and traditions of the *monetales* themselves. However, if one of the two types was personal to a *monetalis* the other was always personal to Augustus : a portrait, often rendered in a hard, realistic Roman style; or types referring to the honours of 27 B.C., or to the Parthian surrender of the standards, or to Augustus' safe return from overseas travel. The Secular Games of 17 B.C., knitting up all the triumph and emotion of recent years within the context of religion, produced a range of appropriate types; and in 16 B.C. the *tresviri*, on a dated coinage, reproduced in miniature a whole range of public monuments and public inscriptions set up in Augustus' honour,[164] of which the most remarkable, skilful, and beautiful was an *imago clipeata*—an honorific shield embossed with his nearly facing portrait. Thereafter, until this Roman gold and silver terminated

251, 252 Augustus. *Obv., three-quarters bust of Augustus embossed on shield within laurelwreath ;* S C OB R P CVM SALVT IMP CAESAR AVGVS CONS. *Rev., Mars with spear and short sword on pedestal inscribed* S P Q R V P S PR S ET RED AVG ; L MESCINIVS RVFVS III VIR. *16 B.C., Rome (denarius, 4.02 gm., diam. 20 mm., BM).*

253, 254 Augustus. *Obv., head of Augustus wearing oak-wreath ;* AVGVSTVS COS XI. *Rev., head of Agrippa wearing mural and rostral crown ;* M AGRIPPA COS TER, COSSVS LENTVLVS. *12 B.C., Rome (denarius, 3.71 gm., diam. 20 mm., BMCRE 121).*

255 Augustus. *Rev., Apollo citharoedus with plectrum and lyre ;* IMP X ACT. *c. 15-12 B.C., Lugdunum (aureus, 7.87 gm., diam. 21 mm., BMCRE 459).*

256 Augustus. *Rev., Augustus, seated on stool on platform, receiving olive-branches from two soldiers ;* IMP X. *c. 15-12 B.C., Lugdunum (denarius, 3.77 gm., diam. 19 mm., BMCRE 448).*

257, 258 Augustus. *Obv., head of Augustus, laureate ;* CAESAR PONT MAX. *Rev., decorated altar flanked by Victories on columns ;* ROM ET AVG. *From c. 10 B.C., Lugdunum (As, 11.10 gm., diam. 30 mm., Oxford, Ashmolean Museum Cat. 337).*

259 Augustus (for Tiberius). *Obv., head of Tiberius, laureate ;* TI CAESAR AVGVSTI F IMPERATOR V. *c. A.D. 10, Lugdunum (sestertius, 23.74 gm., diam. 39 mm., Oxford, Ashmolean Museum Cat. 374).*

260 Augustus (for Tiberius). *Obv., head of Tiberius ;* TI CAESAR AVGVST F IMPERAT V. *A.D. 10-11, Rome (As, 10.63 gm., diam. 29 mm., BMCRE 271).*

261 Augustus. *Obv., head of Augustus ;* IMP CAESAR DIVI F AVGVSTVS IMP ·XX. *A.D. 11-12, Rome (As, 10.64 gm., diam. 29 mm., BMCRE 276).*

262 Augustus. *Rev., Caius Caesar galloping, with spear and shield ; behind, aquila between two standards ;* C CAES AVGVS F. *c. 8 B.C., Lugdunum (denarius, 3.87 gm., diam. 19 mm., BMCRE 500).*

247
248
249, 250
251, 252

140

251

252

253

254

255

256

257

258

259

260

262

261

263

264

265

266

267

268

269

270

271

272

273

274

263, 264 Augustus. *Obv., head of Augustus, laureate ;* CAESAR AVGVSTVS DIVI F PATER PATRIAE. *Rev., Gaius and Lucius Caesar, togate, each with spear and shield ; lituus and jug above ;* C L CAESARES AVGVSTI F COS DESIG PRINC IVVENT. c. *2 B.C. onwards, Lugdunum (denarius, 3.82 gm., diam. 21 mm., Oxford, Ashmolean Museum Cat. 178).*

265, 266 Augustus. *Obv., head of Augustus ; in front, punch-mark ;* IMP CAESAR. *Rev., seated sphinx ;* AVGVSTVS. *Soon after 27 B.C., uncertain mint of the province of Asia (tetradrachm, 12.16 gm., diam. 27 mm., BMCRE 702).*

267 Augustus. *Rev., tied bunch of six corn-ears ;* AVGVSTVS. C. *24-20 B.C., Ephesus (tetradrachm, 11.94gm.,diam.26mm.,BMCRE 697).*

268 Augustus. *Rev., hexastyle temple, its entablature inscribed* ROM ET AVGVST *;* COM ASIAE. c. *19-18 B.C., Pergamum (tetradrachm, 11.92 gm., diam. 26 mm., BMCRE 705).*

269, 270 Tiberius. *Obv., head of Tiberius ;* TI CAESAR DIVI AVG F AVGVSTVS. *Rev., seated female, with sceptre and branch ;* PONTIF MAXIM. *A.D. 14-37, Lugdunum (denarius, 3.83 gm., diam. 19.5 mm., Oxford).*

271 Tiberius. *Rev., facing bust of Tiberius embossed within laurel-wreath on ornamented shield ;* CLEMENTIAE, S C. c. *A.D. 18-21, Rome (dupondius, 17.25 gm., diam. 32 mm., BMCRE 85).*

272 Tiberius (for Drusus). *Obv., head of Drusus ;* DRVSVS CAESAR TI AVG F DIVI AVG N. *A.D. 22-3, Rome (As, 10.75 gm., diam. 32 mm., BMCRE 99).*

273 Tiberius. *Rev., covered and ornamented car drawn by two mules ;* S P Q R IVLIAE AVGVST. *A.D. 22-3, Rome (sestertius, 26.78 gm., diam. 33 mm., BMCRE 76).*

274 Tiberius (for Drusus). *Obv., busts of twin boys on grape-hung cornucopiae crossed over caduceus. A.D. 22-3, Rome (sestertius, 27.18 gm., diam. 39 mm., Oxford).*

in 12 B.C.,[165] the conventions settled : the *monetales* still signed, but the obverse came regularly to bear Augustus' portrait—still hard, and often heavy, while the reverses celebrated his status or achievements, with some superb representations of the great Agrippa, whose marriage to Julia, Augustus' daughter, had produced Gaius and Lucius Caesar as potential imperial heirs.

253, 254

In 16 B.C. Augustus went to Gaul, where he remained for three years to co-ordinate the final conquest of the Alpine frontier. As in Spain a decade earlier, a large military coinage was required; and this was produced, beyond reasonable doubt, at Lugdunum (Lyons)—a notable *colonia* and focal point in Gaul, lying within sight of the mountains, and a known mint-centre in later years.[166] Both aurei and denarii were abundant. As befitted a war coinage they were at first dated by reference to Augustus' successive acclamations as *imperator*—IMP X to XIII (15, 12, 11 and 9 B.C.); and the reverse types, paired with Augustan portraits of quite new idiom (ranging from a clean, clear likeness, unwreathed, and with closely dressed hair, to a wreathed, softer and more mature representation), were the mirror of Augustus' military successes. Diana of Sicily and Apollo of Actium recalled the victories of 36 (Naulochus) and 31; the butting bull was the Latin Mars—the Roman army; and Augustus could be seen receiving the branches of triumph from his field-commanders Tiberius and Drusus. Once founded, the Lugdunum mint proliferated. In 10 B.C. the great Altar to Rome and Augustus was dedicated at Lyons, in Augustus' presence, and prompted the issue of a substantial *aes* coinage with *obv.*

255

256

257, 258 CAESAR PONT(ifex) MAX(imus),[167] wreathed portrait, and *rev.* ROM(ae) ET AVG(usto), altar flanked by Victories; and this was continued in later years, with a much 'older' portraiture and the title PATER PATRIAE. The two 'Altar' series comprised between them sestertii, dupondii, Asses, and sem-isses: coming as they did, and in great 259 quantity, from 10 B.C. onwards, they furnished a large part of western *aes* supply after the cessation of *aes* at Nemausus and Rome.[168]

It was at Lyons that Augustus finally concentrated his arrangements for production of gold and silver on an empire-wide scale: his reasons must have included the proximity of Lugdunum both to the rich mineral sources of Spain and also to the military installations along the Rhine. Aurei 262 and denarii commemorated Gaius Caesar's first military exercise in Gaul in 8 B.C., and the formal introduction of Gaius and Lu-263 264 cius as Augustus' adopted sons and heirs in 5 and 2 B.C. These latter coins were issued in vast numbers: the *rev.* type (the two young Caesars with ceremonial spears and shields, C L CAESARES AVGVSTI F(ilii) COS DESIG (consules designati) PRINC(ipes) IV-VENT(utis)) made Augustus' dynastic intentions plain to all the empire. The young men died in A.D. 2 and 4, and a reluctant Augustus was forced to recognize Tiberius as successor, though he did not advertise his choice on coinage until A.D. 13–14 on Lyons gold and silver. At the mint of Rome, specially reopened after more than a decade, it was advertised from A.D. 10 on 260 Asses struck in parallel for Tiberius and 261 Augustus. These coins are remarkable for a number of reasons. They show the first

full beauty of the art of fine lettering under the empire. Portraiture—idealized for both men—is delicate, sensitive and restrained. There are no moneyers' names. And the large S C on the reverses, no longer directly referable (as with the earlier Roman *aes* of the moneyers) to specific choice of type, now first appears as an automatic adjunct in *aes* coinage—a phenomenon due to last for two and a half centuries.[169]

All these coinages—from Spain, Gaul, and Rome—had combined to supply the empire at large with aurei and denarii, and the west with *aes* on the new Roman system (sestertius to quadrans). The Greek east had different denominational needs, and notably the rich province of Asia, where in 28 B.C. (see pp. 120, 125) Augustus had begun to supplant Antony's silver tetra-drachms with his own. Between *c.* 27 and 18 B.C. these were amplified by copious issues (enough to endure for long years to come) from mints that included Ephesus and Pergamum. Portraiture varied widely, according to the models available for re-production: except when pushed into an imitative rut it was, in all versions, intelligently conceived and strongly—sometimes nobly—executed, with what was clearly a hellenistic skill. Many of the reverses, too, were handsome, especially the sphinx—the 265, earlier form of Augustus' personal signet: of the others, the capricorn referred to his birth-sign; corn-ears to prosperity; an altar 267 to the Artemisium at Ephesus; a temple (with COM ASIAE) to the official cult-centre 268 of Rome and Augustus at Pergamum; and a triumphal arch (with S P R SIGNIS RECEP-TIS) and a military standard in a temple (with MART(i) VLTO(ri)) to the Parthian success of

20 B.C. References to Parthia appeared also on a small issue of aurei and denarii, manifestly of Pergamene workmanship, which must have been struck for Roman forces and officials at the same time. It is of interest that Ephesus and Pergamum—essentially imperial mints—followed the example of Roman moneyers' *aes* and employed, in each case, three simultaneous *officinae* or mint-subsections.[170]

Some other, and temporary and minor, issues of aurei and denarii were coined in the Aegean area, including some aurei of superb and fully Greek style, with *rev.* Heifer, of which the mint is open to conjecture, and aurei and denarii (of equally uncertain origin) with apparent references to the Secular Games of 17 B.C. Otherwise the principal eastern emphasis was on *aes*, in three major groups. One, with frequently fine portraits, and *rev.* Wreath enclosing c(ommune) A(siae), clearly came from Pergamum; another, less refined, and with *rev.* AVGVSTVS in wreath, has connections with the Ephesian tetradrachms; while the third, of very rough style, and *rev.* s c in wreath, must belong to Antioch.[171] These coinages were large and widely distributed, providing small change for a large eastern area. Antioch, as the metropolis of Syria, produced also a series of silver tetradrachms for regional use. Further south, the Greek mint of Alexandria continued the base and rather ugly coinage which Egypt—an imperial granary politically and economically separate from the rest of the empire—was compelled to use.[172]

Beginning in an almost opportunist manner—a mint here, a mint there, often dictated by his personal presence—and ending with a major concentration of gold and silver at Lyons, supported by various regional and urban bronze coinages, Augustus stocked the Roman world with currency. For Tiberius there was little to do save keep the pool of currency (and especially gold and silver) at a safe level. He did this in the simplest way, by continuing a mint for gold and silver at Lyons and by expanding the output of *aes* at Rome, in both cases carefully maintaining the weights and standards of Augustus' monetary system : subsidiary coinages elsewhere tended to be curtailed—doubtless reflecting the amplitude of Augustus' provision. Between Tiberius' gold and silver of Lyons and his *aes* of Rome there is a sharp and fascinating contrast. Lyons began with some special issues in honour of Augustus as *divus*—he was immediately consecrated after his death in A.D. 14—and of Tiberius as his soldier-successor. Thereafter, except for a specifically dated sequence of half-aurei between 15 and 37, the gold and silver bore a single reverse type only : seated female figure, 269, 270 PONTIF MAXIM.[173] The fact that Tiberius' obverse portrait shows him becoming older and older, until the skin is stretched over features that are gaunt, suggests a long-continuing series, perhaps until his death in 37 : as in all repetitive coinages, the technical standards tended to decline. At Rome, on the other hand, those first vigorous signs of artistic revival that were apparent in Augustus' final *aes* from A.D. 10 (see above, p. 146) developed into a full flowering of skill and beauty. And not only was there a revolution in aesthetic and technical standards at Rome : there was also a revolution in type-concept.

Under Augustus the presentation of the imperial 'image' and the imperial achievement had been effected with greatest pictorial variety and suggestiveness on the gold and silver: his *aes*, designed for mass-circulation, whether in west or east, had emphasized simple fundamentals—portrait, victories, powers, and quasi-religious status. Tiberius did not omit to put out similar 'basic' *aes*, though characteristically (since he succeeded Augustus only with reluctance) this *aes* consisted of a varied series in hon-

275* our of Divus Augustus Pater, the reverses including the seated lady (Livia?) of the

276* gold and silver, a temple, Victory, s c in

278 wreath, an altar with PROVIDENT(ia), a thunderbolt, and an eagle. Of these dupondii and Asses, the latter were mostly very common; and except for the 'eagle' and thunderbolt Asses (late in Tiberius' reign, when skill was declining) all these issues shared in the artistic renaissance, with portraits of delicacy and power, and lettering of astonishingly fine proportion. Alongside these 'basic' *aes* coins, however, the mint of Rome issued others (usually much less common, and perhaps therefore for Italian rather than general western circulation) which were extraordinarily explicit in their interpretation of Tiberius, his family, and his policy. Apart from their frequent beauty they raise the question of why such a coinage should appear for an emperor who disliked and disdained such outward expressions of his position.[174]

Among the first of these was a small, twin, die-linked series of dupondii struck for Tiberius as IMP VIII (i.e. from A.D. 18) and showing ceremonial portrait-shields

271 given to mark his 'Moderatio' and 'Cle-

275, 276 Tiberius (for Divus Augustus). *Obv., radiate head of Augustus;* DIVVS AVGVSTVS PATER. *Rev., circular temple, with lamb and calf on bases to r. and l.;* s c. *c. A.D. 22, Rome (dupondius, 15.18 gm., diam. 28 mm., BMCRE 141).*

277 Tiberius. *Obv., bust of Salus Augusta (? Livia);* SALVS AVGVSTA. *A.D. 22-3, Rome (dupondius, 14.48 gm., diam. 28 mm., BMCRE 82).*

278

279

280

mentia'—at a time when his reliance on informers was earning unpopularity at Rome. These reverses, if explicit, were too full and too complex; and it was not until A.D. 22–3 (Tiberius' *tr.pot.XXIIII*) that full freedom of both artistic and ideological expression was attained.[175] The former restraint of Augustus' *aes* designs was cast aside. Asses now bore portraits of the finest quality, their high relief combined with excellence of plastic modelling. So, too, with the dupondii, which bore personified heads of Pietas and Justitia, quietly monumental in feeling, as well as of Salus, with features of human rather than divine character (?Livia). The chief beauty and breadth of experiment were reserved for a range of splendid sestertii. Three varieties of these are linked by the use of a common lettered reverse die : DIVVS AVGVSTVS PATER, seated with radiate crown; CIVITATIBVS ASIAE RESTITVTIS, a similarly statuesque figure of Tiberius, after his relief-measures to victims of earthquake; and a scene drawn not from the repertoire of public monuments but rather from life and memory— S P Q R IVLIAE AVGVST(ae), the closed carriage used in thanksgiving procession after the recovery of Livia (IVLIA) from grave illness. A fourth, in the name of Tiberius' son Drusus, was perhaps one of the loveliest of all Roman coins : the obverse, without lettering, showed Drusus' newly born twins on crossed cornucopiae, in fluid and elegant balance, while the reverse consisted wholly of Drusus' name and titles with s c, in superbly proportioned lettering. Its designer uniquely combined the Roman qualities of *gravitas* and *gracilitas*.

278 Tiberius (for Divus Augustus). *Rev., panelled altar ;* PROVIDENT, s c. *c. A.D. 22-30, Rome (As, 11.17 gm., diam. 29 mm., BMCRE 149).*

279 Tiberius. *Obv., Tiberius, togate, on curule chair holding patera and sceptre ;* CIVITATIBVS ASIAE RESTITVTIS. *A.D. 22-3, Rome (sestertius, 27.41 gm., diam. 34.5 mm., BMCRE 70).*

280 Tiberius (?) (for M. Agrippa). *Obv., head of Agrippa, wearing rostral crown ;* M AGRIPPA L F COS III. *c. A.D. 30-40, Rome (As, 11.51 gm., diam. 27.5 mm., BMCRE 161).*

This Roman *aes* of 22–3, showing brilliant and radical changes under a strongly conservative emperor, was not of great volume : the main currency-burden continued to be borne by the 'Divus Auguster Pater' Asses (see above, p. 148), possibly helped by the earlier of the enormously common and very beautiful Asses portraying Agrippa, grandfather of Gaius (Caligula) who succeeded Tiberius. Now dead for nearly 280 50 years, Agrippa appears as the admiral— and the man of iron—who helped to establish Augustus.[176] Later in the reign the mint of Rome again resumed a wider coinage-range, including sestertii once more with conspicuously novel types : this large denomination, coined by now in fair quantity, had established its place as the major coinage medium for large pictorial and verbal pronouncement, thereby adding a new art-form to the Roman world. In general Tiberius' later *aes* (TR P XXXVI-XXXVIII, 34–7) showed a sharp decline from the artistic standards of 22–3, though at least one sestertius issue—possibly designed by the master of the Drusus 'twins' sestertius—stands out for its magnificence : an unlettered obverse showing the temple of Concordia in great monumental detail, and a reverse of fine and finely balanced lettering.

Occasional and short-term coinages were struck for Tiberius at Caesarea (Cappadocia), and in Commagene, Galatia and Syria. Syrian Antioch continued its silver tetradrachms; and Alexandria was active. Local city-coinages in *aes* continued, now as later, to supplement imperial *aes*, with those of Spain still prominent. As a whole, however, Tiberius' imperial coinage (in gold, silver, and *aes*) had tended strongly towards centralization. Gold and silver was confined to Lyons, and the *aes* of Rome was suddenly harnessed to imperial pronouncements.

This tendency was emphasized under Caligula, better called Gaius (37–41), for whom the modern vocabulary finds terms ranging from simple suspiciousness to neurosis or paranoia. A short, uneasy reign, ending in the first imperial assassination, saw the production of gold and silver apparently transferred from Lyons to Rome,[177] and the continued transformation of *aes* into an imperial medium of pronouncement. Parallel with both these developments, and indeed closely connected, was the emphasis laid upon Gaius' personal status and family : Tiberius' coinage had introduced a similar personal note, but with Gaius the personal emphasis was much sharper, and, while much was said of the *princeps* himself, virtually nothing was said of what the principate was doing in the empire at large.[178] The aurei and denarii, primarily the medium of payment for the armed and higher administrative services, showed a narrow range of types. Gaius' own portrait was combined alternatively with portraits of Divus Augustus and of his 287 mother and father, the late Agrippina and 288, Germanicus, specified as *Gaes*(aris) *Mat*(er) 282 and *P*(ater). In the last two years of his reign, when he turned against the concept of an 'imperial house', these types were abandoned in favour of a simple 'succession' type, S P Q R P P OB C(ives) s(ervatos) within oak-wreath. Portraiture on this gold (which included also some dated halves, as under Tiberius) and silver was harsh and pinched: Gaius' own features bear out Suetonius' description of thin neck, hollow eyes and temples, and broad, fierce brow. If the gold/silver mint did in fact now move from Lyons to Rome it evidently did not easily recover from the inelegant and badly modelled forms that had characterized Tiberius' long and unchanging Lugdunum series.

By contrast the *aes* struck at Rome for Gaius preserved much of the aesthetic beauty and technical excellence that had emerged so brilliantly under Tiberius. Portraiture, a little uncertain at the moment of accession, quickly attained massive sculptural distinction: lettering, if not so fine as Tiberius' finest, was still a conspicuous ornament; and the reverses displayed interesting variety, especially on the sestertii, which continued their development as a miniature art-form of real quality. Some among these *aes* coins followed or amplified tradition— the non-portrait quadrantes with *rev.* R C C (*remissa ducentesima*, remission of the half per cent. sales tax); Asses in Gaius' name 290 with *rev.* Seated Vesta, goddess of family, hearth, and home; Asses with commemorative portrait of Germanicus; dupondii showing Gaius' dead brothers Nero and Drusus on horseback; and sestertii with *obv.* Gaius' portrait, *rev.* S P Q R P P OB CIVES SERVATOS in oak-wreath, and *obv.* Pietas seated, *rev.* Sacrifice in front of the 291 temple of Divus Augustus—this last a scene of monumental splendour, deriving directly from Tiberian tradition. Others broke away from all previous tradition. The funeral car 293 of the dead Agrippina, modelled on the Tiberian type of A.D. 22–3 in honour of Livia (see above, p. 151), is paired with an

unprecedented *obv.* portrait of Agrippina 292 —the stern translation into coin-form of a marble original. On early sestertii Gaius accorded similarly unprecedented representation to his three sisters, before Drusilla 281* died and Julia and the younger Agrippina were banished. Equally novel were the sestertii with *rev.* ADLOCVT(io) COH(ortium), Gaius addressing the praetorian cohorts. These lacked the S C normal on *aes* and may have been struck, initially at least, by special imperial order for distribution to the praetorians.[179]

Although Gaius' *aes* was so varied in type, its volume was not very great, and it is probable that he neglected the needs of empire-wide *aes* circulation. The mint of Alexandria was closed during his reign. In Spain the urban mints, still numerous under Tiberius, stopped working,[180] together with other local *aes* mints in the west as well. No *aes* issues of substance—comparable with those of Augustus (see above, p. 138 ff.)—were coined in the east. Thus, while Gaius' coinage of aurei and denarii, supplemented in the east by silver didrachms and drachms from Caesarea Cappadociae, kept up the great pool of gold and silver, his *aes*—even with the relatively common 'Vesta' Asses—allowed the *aes* 290 pool to decline. The real importance of his brief coinage, historically speaking, was that, as well as its almost certain concentration at Rome, it continued both to liberate the choice of *aes* types and also to promote the artistic role of the sestertius in the tradition first seen under Tiberius. A series of inscriptions, mainly of Trajanic date, shows how the internal organization of the mint of Rome had by then developed, with its casters, trimmers, letterers, engravers, and hammer-men all under a quasi-military supervision.[181] The coinage of Gaius marks a substantial step forward towards that later and more complete system.

His uncle Claudius (41–54) succeeded to power by the whim of the praetorian guard, apparently with only his lineage to recommend him. Yet, though physically weak, and the frequent butt of sophisticated society, he had the underlying strength and perception of a learned man; and, while steeped in tradition, he could also look keenly forward.[182] This was fully evident in his coinage, which with good, practical sense emphasized the realities of his reign rather than (as under Gaius) the realities of the man. His gold and silver (now assumed to be of the mint of Rome: see above, p. 152) varied the themes cleverly during the first ten years.[183] Of the six types that appeared in his accession-year, two specifically acknowledged his debt to the praet-

284 orians: IMPER(ator) RECEPT(us), soldier on guard in battlemented camp, and PRAETOR

285 (ianus) RECEPT(us in fidem ?), emperor and soldier shaking hands. These continued to appear until 46/7. CONSTANTIAE AVGVSTI, with seated female figure in an attitude of restraint, re-appeared when the praetorian types were dropped. The 'accession type' par excellence—EX S C OB CIVES SERVATOS in oak-wreath—also re-appeared from 46/7. Triumphal arch with DE GERMANIS was used again once, in 46/7, when it was ac-

286 companied by an arch DE BRITANN(is): the latter appeared again in 49/50, now accompanied by a Victory type, still celebrating the conquest of Britain. And during most of these years the staple type was PACI

281 Gaius ('Caligula'). *Rev., Gaius' three sisters standing, each holding cornucopiae ; Agrippina as Securitas on l. rests arm on column ; Drusilla as Concordia in centre holds patera ; and Julia as Fortuna on r. holds rudder ;* AGRIPPINA DRVSILLA IVLIA, S C. *A.D. 37-8, Rome (sestertius, 29.10 gm., diam. 35 mm., BMCRE 37).*

282. 283 Gaius ('Caligula'). *Obv., head of Gaius ;* C CAESAR AVG GERM P M TR POT. *Rev., bust of Agrippina senior ;* AGRIPPINA MAT(er) C CAES(aris) AVG GERM. *A.D. 37-8, Rome (aureus, 7.69 gm., diam. 19 mm., BMCRE 14).*

284

285

286

AVGVSTAE, Pax-Nemesis—a complex and subtle piece of symbolism that would convey to the empire at large the basic ideas of Pax, Victoria, Salus and Moderatio.[184] Claudius claimed consciously to be statesman as well as soldier, and soldiers' protégé, and did not hesitate to express his imperial philosophy upon the coinage primarily used for the payment of the armed forces all over the Roman world.

A mixture of a different kind was devised for the *aes*, and (it may be thought) no less consciously : not the least of senatorial criticisms of Claudius was his increasing reliance upon the advice of a highly organized imperial civil service. The chronology of this *aes* has caused difficulty. It bears the formula TR(ibunicia) P(otestate) simply as a title, and not (as on the gold and silver) with annual numbering; and the major part of it, quantitatively, lacks the title P(ater) P(atriae)—conferred in January 42—which appears on the minor part. As P P did not become a regular element in the titulature of Claudius' gold and silver until 50–51, it has been argued convincingly that the very common *aes* without P P therefore covers not just 41–2, but 41–*c.* 50, the issues with P P falling *c.* 50–51.[185] The range of types was virtually the same in both series. Sestertii commemorated Claudius' accession (with the now normal wreath reverse), his father Nero Drusus, and—perhaps most important—the birth of his son Britannicus within a month of accession, now marked by a type of SPES AVGVSTA (the imperial hope) that was to endure as a dynastic type for two centuries. Dupondii, produced in some quantity, looked to Claudius' mother 294 Antonia (also honoured on gold) and to

284 Claudius. *Rev., the praetorian camp, on the upper level of which are fortifications with a pedimented building ; in front, soldier with spear, and aquila ;* IMPER RECEPT *on lower wall. A.D. 43-4, Rome (denarius, 3.70 gm., diam. 17.5 mm., BMCRE 21).*

285 Claudius. *Rev., Claudius, bare-headed and togate, clasping hand of praetorian soldier, long-haired, with shield and aquila ;* PRAETOR RECEPT. *A.D. 41-2, Rome (aureus, 7.77 gm., diam. 20 mm., BMCRE 8).*

286 Claudius. *Rev., equestrian statue between trophies on triumphal arch ; the rider raises hand in act of address ;* DE BRITANN *on architrave. A.D. 46-7, Rome (aureus, 7.70 gm., diam. 20 mm., BMCRE 32).*

Ceres, goddess of the corn-supply which the new harbour at Ostia was greatly to help. Asses were coined profusely: commonest of all were those with *rev.* fighting Minerva (the military protectiveness of a wise emperor), but there were also CONSTANTIAE AVGVSTI—this time a military concept—and LIBERTAS AVGVSTI. Liberty and resolute self-discipline must go together. Technically this *aes* showed some variation in excellence, perhaps through sheer pressure of work at the mint. Artistically, however, it marked an advance on Gaius' coinage, especially in portraiture, which not only showed a shrewdly faithful likeness but also contrived to suggest the imperial philosophy spelt out by the coin types themselves: personal resolution, imperial dignity, and grave humanity. Even on the associated gold and silver, the much smaller size of which still clearly hampered artistic development, many portraits began to achieve a similar effect with an almost gemlike precision and delicacy. Coin-portraiture had advanced, sometimes uncertainly and irregularly, ever since the dying days of the Republic: now it could begin to combine strong fidelity with a truly subjective and sensitive treatment.

In 48 Claudius' wife Messalina was executed: in 49 he married Agrippina, the immensely ambitious sister of Gaius (see above, p. 153); and in 50 he entitled her 'Augusta' and formally adopted her young son Nero. The gold and silver of 51–4 informed the Roman world accordingly, showing the portraits of the new empress and her son: some coins were given up to Nero alone, with *obv.* portrait and *rev.* priestly or public distinctions conferred

upon him, and a few very rare *aes* coins followed suit.[186] In the east, where Ephesus and Pergamum had both issued 'cistophoric' tetradrachms earlier in the reign (those of Ephesus showing the Artemisium and Diana's cult-statue), fresh issues celebrated the new marriage and the adoption. This eastern portraiture of Claudius was exaggeratedly heavy, almost to the point of grotesqueness: it was less so at Caesarea in Cappadocia, which did not however coin after its conspicuous compliment to Messalina and her children, including Britannicus, now superseded by Nero. At Alexandria Messalina received great prominence until her fall, and Agrippina an even greater prominence thereafter.[187]

Whatever the output of *aes* by Claudius it evidently could not satisfy the needs of the empire. The *aes* of Gaius was not profuse by any means; and Gaius had closed the local Spanish mints. There was no regular series of local *aes* from Gaul, as under Augustus.[188] Hence the flood of copies of Claudian *aes* (mainly Asses and dupondii) found widely in the western provinces. Not all of these, probably, are of Claudian date, for under Nero no *aes* at all was produced from 54 to 64: their production, no doubt tolerated by the Roman government, may lie between the broad limits of 41 and 64. Some are fine copies; some of strong local style; some wretched, in weight as in technique.[189] In other respects, too, the supervision of currency may have been slack under Claudius. While the weight of the denarius, at *c.* 3.75 g., remained close to the Augustan norm of 3.75–3.80 g., plated denarii (which had occurred sporadically since Augustus) became fairly common. Sometimes regarded as a sign of monetary inflation under Claudius, these were much more probably illicit productions by persons with improper access to dies : if so, they appeared in numbers that suggest inadequate security in the organization of the mint.[190]

Upon Claudius' sudden death, Nero (54–68) succeeded at the age of sixteen. Effective power, born of experience, must obviously lie elsewhere; and the coinage of his first eleven years shows with perfect clearness how in 54–5 his mother Agrippina sought to exercise that power before her exclusion by the formidable partnership of Seneca, the philosopher-politician, and Burrus, the praetorian prefect, who were in turn ousted by Nero in 61–4. During these years the mint of Rome struck no *aes* at all : the Claudian *aes* output, doubtless supplemented by continuous imitation, had to suffice. Gold and silver, however, were abundant—and abundantly necessary for military support. In 54 the obverses showed **303** the confronting portraits of Nero and Agrippina, with Agrippina's name as NERONIS CAES(aris) MATER : Nero's name and titles surrounded the civic crown 'accession' type on the reverses, with EX S C, denoting (as is clear from subsequent use of that formula) a revived senatorial claim to control precious-metal coinage.[191] Next year, in 55, Nero's portrait (now a little more **304** mature) was superimposed on Agrippina's, and his legend moved to the obverse, Agrippina's now going to the reverse showing the deified Augustus and Claudius in an elephant-quadriga. In 56 Agrippina appeared no longer : the coins of this and the four following years bore an austere, constitutional statement of Nero's position, with *obv.* Bare-headed portrait, NERO CAESAR **305** AVG IMP, and *rev.* PONTIF MAX TR P (with number) (COS IIII, 59–61) P P around wreath enclosing EX S C. From 60 to 64, however, as Nero's features grew heavy, with lips encompassed by flesh, jaw thickening, and a neck-roll of fat already conspicuous, new reverses were introduced—standing figures of Ceres, Virtus, and Roma, though still with EX S C; and these in turn displaced the wreath type. Burrus died in 62; and in the same year Nero divorced Octavia, Claudius' daughter by Messalina, in order to marry Poppaea, leading the way to Seneca's enforced suicide. At the age of twenty-five Nero could at length do as he wished.

He was by now increasingly absorbed in the enjoyment and promotion of music and the arts. But either he or his advisers could evidently see that monetary reform was needed; and in 64 that reform was carried out on a massive scale probably stimulated by the great fire which destroyed so much of Rome, involved huge expense in rebuilding, and thus necessarily demanded a greatly increased flow of money. Nero's reform, which was recorded by his contemporary, the elder Pliny, consisted primarily of the reduction in weight of both aureus and denarius. Augustus (see above, p. 132) had coined aurei at 1/42 of the Roman pound of gold, i.e. at *c.* 7.70-7.85 g., a figure which had slightly declined by Nero's earlier years, and denarii at 1/84 of a pound of silver, i.e. at *c.* 3.75-3.80 g., from which again a slight decline had taken place. From 64 the aureus was 1/45 of a pound (*c.* 7.30 g.) and the denarius 1/96 (*c.* 3.25 g.). There was no official demonetization of

287 Gaius ('Caligula') (for Divus Augustus). *Rev., radiate head of Augustus;* DIVVS AVG PATER PATRIAE. *A.D. 37-8, Rome (denarius, 3.71 gm., diam. 19 mm., BMCRE 17).*

288, 289 Gaius ('Caligula'). *Obv., head of Gaius;* C CAESAR AVG PON M TR POT III COS III. *Rev., bust of Agrippina senior;* AGRIPPINA MAT C CAES AVG GERM. *A.D. 40, Rome (denarius, 3.77 gm., diam. 19 mm., BMCRE 23).*

290 Gaius ('Caligula'). *Rev., Vesta, veiled, seated holding patera and sceptre;* VESTA, S C. *A.D. 39-40, Rome (As, 12.10 gm., diam. 30 mm., BMCRE 59).*

291 Gaius ('Caligula'). *Rev., Gaius, veiled and togate, sacrificing out of patera over garlanded altar in front of festooned temple of Divus Augustus adorned with statuary and surmounted by quadriga between Victories; Gaius is accompanied by two attendants, one with bull, one with patera;* DIVO AVG, S C. *A.D. 40-1, Rome (sestertius, 26.05 gm., diam. 37 mm., BMCRE 69).*

292, 293 Gaius ('Caligula') (for Agrippina senior). *Obv., bust of Agrippina;* AGRIPPINA M F MAT C CAESARIS AVGVSTI. *Rev., covered and ornamented car drawn by two mules;* S P Q R MEMORIAE AGRIPPINAE. *A.D. 37-41, Rome (sestertius, 26.33 gm., diam. 36 mm., BMCRE 84).*

294 Claudius (for Antonia). *Obv., bust of Antonia;* ANTONIA AVGVSTA. *c. A.D. 41-5, Rome (dupondius, 16.12 gm., diam. 30 mm., BMCRE 166).*

295 Claudius. *Rev., fighting Minerva, helmeted, with short spear and shield;* S C. *c. A.D. 41-5, Rome (As, 9.26 gm., diam. 30 mm., BMCRE 149).*

296 Claudius. *Rev., bust of the young Nero after adoption;* NERO CLAVD CAES DRVSVS GERM PRINC IVVENT. *A.D. 51-4, Rome (denarius, 3.69 gm., diam. 20 mm., BMCRE 80).*

297, 298 Claudius. *Obv., head of Claudius;* TI CLAVD CAESAR AVG. *Rev., temple of Diana at Ephesus, with sculptured pediment; within, cult-statue of Diana, with ribbons hanging from her wrists;* DIAN EPHE. *c. A.D. 41-2 (?), Ephesus (tetradrachm, 10.88 gm., diam. 26 mm., BMCRE 229).*

299, 300 Claudius (for Messallina). *Obv., bust of Messallina;* MESSALLINA AVGVSTI. *Rev., Octavia (on l.) clasping hands with Britannicus (centre); Antonia (on r.) holds cornucopiae;* OCTAVIA BRITANNICVS ANTONIA. *c. A.D. 46 (?), Caesarea in Cappadocia (didrachm, 6.69 gm., diam. 23 mm., BMCRE 242).*

301, 302 Claudius. *Obv., head of Claudius;* TI CLAVDIVS CAESAR AVG P M TR P IMP. *Rev., fighting Minerva, helmeted, with short spear and shield;* S C. *c. A.D. 41-50, copy from uncertain western mint (cf. No. 295) (As, 6.95 gm., diam. 28 mm., Oxford).*

287

288

289

290

291

292

293

294

295

296

297

298

299

300

301

302

303

304

305

306

307

311

312

313

303 Nero. *Obv., confronting busts of Nero and Agrippina junior ;* AGRIPP AVG DIVI CLAVD NERONIS CAES MATER. *A.D. 54, Rome (aureus, 7.60 gm., diam. 18 mm., BMCRE 1).*

304 Nero. *Obv., jugate busts of Nero, in front, and of Agrippina junior ;* NERO CLAVD DIVI F CAES AVG GERM IMP TR P COS. *A.D. 55, Rome (aureus, 7.61 gm., diam. 19 mm., BMCRE 7).*

305 Nero. *Obv., head of Nero, bare ;* NERO CAESAR AVG IMP. *A.D. 55-6, Rome (aureus, 7.70 gm., diam. 19 mm., BMCRE 9).*

306 Nero. *Rev., the domed, two-storey meat-market (macellum) built by Nero ; sceptred figure within ;* MAC AVG, S C, II. *A.D. 64-8, Rome (dupondius, 14.94 gm., diam. 30 mm., BMCRE 194).*

307 Nero. *Rev., Nero in flowing garment as Apollo the lyre-player ;* PONTIF MAX TR P IMP P P. *A.D. 64-8, Rome (As, 11.99 gm., diam. 30 mm., BMCRE 236).*

308 Nero. *Obv., head of Nero, radiate ;* NERO CLAVD CAESAR AVG GERM TR P IMP P P. *A.D. 64-8, Rome (dupondius, 15.25 gm., diam. 30 mm., BMCRE 215).*

309 Nero. *Rev., temple of Janus, its closed doors garlanded, and with latticed window in side wall ;* PACE P R TERRA MARIQ PARTA IANVM CLVSIT, S C. *A.D. 64-8, Lugdunum (sestertius, 27.59 gm., diam. 36 mm., BMCRE 321).*

310 Nero. *Rev., combined aerial and perspective view of the harbour of Ostia ; on l., crescent-shaped portico leading to figure at sacrifice and terminal building ; on r., crescent-shaped row of slips or docks ; at top, sceptred figure on sea-girt pedestal ; below, Neptune reclining with rudder and dolphin ; seven ships in harbour ;* AVGVSTI S POR OST C. *c. A.D. 64-8, Rome (sestertius, 29.84 gm., diam. 33 mm., BMCRE 132).*

311 Nero. *Rev., Nero, cuirassed and with spear, on prancing horse accompanied by mounted soldier with long standard ;* DECVRSIO, S C. *A.D. 64-8, Rome (sestertius, 28.28 gm., diam. 34 mm., BMCRE 143).*

312 Nero. *Rev., Annona with cornucopiae standing facing seated Ceres, holding corn-ears and torch ; between them, modius with corn-ears on garlanded altar ; ship's stern in background ;* ANNONA AVGVSTI CERES, S C. *A.D. 64-8, Rome (sestertius, 28.71 gm., diam. 36.5 mm., BMCRE 129).*

313 Nero. *Rev., Victory floating and holding shield inscribed* S P Q R *;* S C. *A.D. 64-8, Lugdunum (As, 9.95 gm., diam. 29 mm., BMCRE 388).*

earlier issues, which Gresham's Law would automatically remove from circulation: coin-hoards show the sharp distinction between the old and the new standards. In fineness of metal there was apparently little or no change: both gold and silver remained remarkably pure. Possibly the reduction in weight of the aureus and the denarius reflects some increasing tendency towards higher prices.[192]

But the reform of 64 went further. Orichalcum (brass), hitherto used for sestertii and dupondii only, was used also for Asses, semisses and quadrantes, though a return to copper for these three denominations was soon made. All the *aes* denominations, in whichever metal, were issued in great abundance: the *aes* deficiency of previous years was evidently made good, for copies of Nero's coins are uncommon. And—perhaps most important of all—the profuse *aes* of Rome was supplemented by a closely similar *aes* series which the evidence of distribution pins down to the west, and probably to Lugdunum. These Lyons issues (sestertius to semis), most easily recognized by a small globe at the point of the neck-truncation, also show a portraiture and lettering rougher, more ragged, and much less stylish than is to be seen on the series without globe, which continues and elaborates the elegant confidence which had been developing on the *aes* of Rome ever since Tiberius.[193]

It was on this double series of *aes* from 64 that a brilliant series of new types appeared, rendered for the most part with equal beauty and sense of artistic fitness. Nero's portrait, by now fully matured into grossness, was nevertheless formidable in its sternness and absolute strength: it was massive and ornate, poised upon a bull-like neck, its eye shadowed, its expression only occasionally falling short of the relentless. Of the reverses, the finest (according to closely previous tradition) were reserved for the sestertii. If, by a kind of analogy with classical Greek art, Augustan *aes* represents archaic achievement, and that from Tiberius to Claudius the emergence of early classical, with forms clearly understood and refined into a firm, clean, sculptural treatment, then the designers and engravers of Nero's *aes*—and especially of his sestertii—can be regarded as having reached full classical beauty, in which form, plastic skill, and ornament were splendidly combined. Of the figure-compositions, ROMA, DECVRSIO, and ANNONA AVGVSTI CERES are of elaborate beauty, alluding respectively to the re-building of the city, the praetorian guards, and the corn-supply. Others are based on public monuments: the temple of Janus, ceremonially closed in 66 as a mark of universal peace when Tiridates came to receive his Armenian crown from Nero's hands,[194] and the triumphal arch decreed in 58 to mark eastern victories. Others again borrow from the panoramic idiom of bas-relief or painting: ADLOCVT(io) COH(ortium), Nero addressing the praetorians (elaborated from Gaius' type, mentioned above, p. 153); the now completed Port of Ostia, ringed by wharves and thick with ships within the shelter of a light-house; and distribution of corn to the people at a *congiarium*.

These magnificent sestertii had achieved, at last, full freedom of design; and this extended, so far as space permitted, to the smaller *aes*, where Roma, Temple, and Arch reappeared, with the interesting addition of 306 MAC(ellum) AVG(usti)—Nero's newly built food-market—on dupondii, now generally 308* distinguished at Rome by a radiate crown instead of a laurel wreath on Nero's head.[195] Dupondii and Asses, however, had a wider part to play than sestertii : they were every man's every-day money, and, as under Nero's predecessors, they bore messages of 313 more general character, of which imperial Victory and a figure of Apollo playing the 307 lyre (surrounded by Nero's titles, and clearly suggesting the artist-emperor) were the commonest, again rendered with fluid, delicate, beauty. The smallest coins (semisses with portrait, quadrantes without) were devoted mainly to the themes of Nero's five-yearly games and the cult of Minerva.

The profuse and brilliant *aes* from 64 was accompanied by new-style gold and silver on the reduced standard. Here the artistic achievement was inferior : designers still could not come to terms with the difficulties of small dies that had to be produced quickly and regularly for the urgent primary need of military pay. But the types were interesting : as well as ROMA and Janus temple (much abbreviated) they included AVGVSTVS AVGVSTA (standing figures of Nero and Poppaea), CONCORDIA AVGVSTA, and two which commemorated the failure of the Pisonian conspiracy of 65—IVPPITER CVSTOS and SALVS. Here again, as with the *aes*, the total focus was a personal one upon the emperor himself, and there was absolute freedom in the choice of types, with little assistance from precedent.

It was Nero's personal absolutism—of which the coinage of 64–8 is a token—that alienated, not the provinces or the provincials, but the provincial governors; and rebellion in Gaul and Spain was quickly followed by his death in June 68. And with his death the formative years of the imperial coinage were completed. Augustus had coined as required : now here, now there, now in this metal, now in that, with an ultimate emphasis upon Lyons as the chief precious-metal mint, supplemented by Roman *aes*. Tiberius continued this pattern : Gaius centralized most coinage at Rome; and Claudius continued as Gaius had done. Nero, after his years of minority, devised a completely integrated coinage in all metals at Rome, with gold and silver reduced in weight, and supplemented this with ample western *aes*, probably from Lyons : in addition, Caesarea in Cappadocia and Alexandria continued their special activities. The imperial coinage, after 100 years of experiment and development, had now achieved a completeness, a regularity, a centrality, and an artistic and technical confidence which the Republican coinage had for so long been denied by political fluctuations and uncertainties.[196] For one and a half centuries to come successive emperors were to follow this essential model.

VI. DISSOLUTION AND THE NEW IMPERIAL DYNASTIES : THE FLAVIANS, TRAJANS, AND THE ANTONINES, A.D. 68-192

At Nero's death the empire momentarily collapsed. In theory, the Senate and People of Rome continued as the ultimate legal source of supreme power. In fact, supreme power rested with the powerful army-commanders in the provinces. One by one the rivals for power arose, their actions generally dignified by publicly expressed concern for the Roman state and for the Senate, People, and City of Rome. Between June 68 and December 69 repeated and dangerous shocks threatened the stability of the principate as established by Augustus, all of them reflected in the coinage of the time. Clodius Macer set himself up in Africa as the *soi-disant* representative of the Senate : he died late in 68. In Spain Galba, likewise styling himself a *legatus* of the Senate, was saluted as *imperator* by his troops and attracted powerful support from C. Julius Vindex, the Gallic-born governor of Lugdunese Gaul, until Vindex was defeated by Verginius Rufus, governor of Upper Germany. Galba, notwithstanding, fought his way to supremacy, and was emperor from June 68 to January 69, when he was murdered. His successor, Otho, held power briefly until April 69, followed (hardly less briefly) by Vitellius until De-cember 69. Vitellius was threatened on two fronts : Julius Civilis was in revolt in Lower Germany, and Vespasian, the powerful governor of Syria, was advancing westward upon Italy. Vespasian's defeat of Vitellius' forces was complete; and the weary Senate gratefully accepted a new and strong emperor. Throughout all these convulsions, so horribly reminiscent of the rivalries at the end of the Republic, Rome itself was the glittering prize. Rome contained the Senate, and it was for the Senate to confer supreme *imperium*.

Macer, coining in Africa,[197] struck in silver only : these denarii, of meagre style, are now rare. All bear the letters s c, claiming (quite falsely) that Macer was acting for the Senate. The obverses show heads of Roma, Africa (as LIBERATRIX), Carthage, and Victory, and sometimes also of Macer 320 himself : the reverses specify his numbered legions, or show a ship—an allusion to his 321 hope of capturing Sicily, to which two other types were given. Macer's threat, had he been able, was to move on Rome via Sicily, strangling Rome's corn-supply in the process. Little more than a pirate, he soon disappeared. Galba, by contrast, was an 327 experienced senator and soldier; and the spate of coins which he issued in Spain, supplemented by what Vindex struck in Gaul, leave no doubt either of the general unhappiness of the western empire at the time or of the resolve to restore imperial government at Rome to a proper level of dignity and responsibility.[198] Nor, when their types are carefully weighed against the content of previous types, can there be any doubt whatever that the coinage of Galba and Vindex in 68 was employed, urgently and directly, to advertise a cause —the armed rescue of the Roman state from the chaos into which Nero had led it.

322, 323 The coinage of Vindex showed obverses with heads or figures of Genius Populi Romani, Roma, Libertas, Mars Ultor (the avenger), Hercules Adsertor (the champion, a play on the name Vindex), Pax-Nemesis (see above, p. 154 f.), and Victory. That of Galba, struck for him initially as IMP (erator) only, bore his portrait. On each series, by types combined in almost desperate variety, the message was the same. From his base in Spain (HISPANIA), assisted by Vindex in Gaul (GALLIA; TRES GALLIAE; GALLIA HISPANIA; CONCORDIA HISPANIARVM ET GALLIARVM; CONCORDIA PROVINCIARVM), Galba would succeed to the vacant principate (SPQR with wreath), thereby

324, 325 restoring Rome (ROMA RENASCENS), the
326 people's liberty (LIBERTAS/RESTITVTA, with Brutus' 'Eid. Mar.' reverse : see above, p. 102), and the well-being of mankind (SALVS GENERIS HVMANI). Passions were strong, and the vision clear; and these issues, mainly of denarii but including some gold and (later) aes, told the soldiers of the western world exactly what the vision was.

By October 68 Galba was in Rome, as emperor; and for three months the mint of Rome produced a remarkably profuse coinage, supplemented by continuing provincial issues. The gold and silver still emphasized the 'loyalist' part played by the provinces of Spain and Gaul. The aes was perhaps more remarkable. It was immense in quantity—so much so that some issues have, erroneously, been regarded as posthumous. It included a brilliant series of 328, 32 sestertii, of varied type. And, although the 330 artistry of the gold and silver (as under Nero) was still generally—though not al- 327 ways—affected by limitations of size, that of the aes demonstrates afresh the splendid skill of designers and engravers as developed under Nero.[199] Portraiture was of a stern and noble fidelity : the hard-bitten features of a 73-year-old emperor were represented on a massive scale, perfectly poised above a long, pointed neck-truncation; and, though some reverses were a little banal in treatment, others excelled, especially the fluid, sculptural representations of Victory, the fine and strong HONOS 329 ET VIRTVS and HISPANIA CLVNIA SVL designs,[200] and the packed, frieze-like ADLO- 330 CVTIO type, a vivid reminder of the military basis of Galba's power.

Without the assistance of personal popularity that power quickly waned, and, with Galba's murder, passed to Otho for three troubled months. Otho struck no aes—the preceding issues of Nero and Galba furnished ample sufficiency of that[201]—but a full continuance of gold and silver, neces- 314*. sary for military pay. The types were of a pathetically correct range : Pax Orbis Terrarum, Aequitas, Ceres, Securitas, Victoria,

Vesta, and Jupiter. In these, Otho began to draw upon that almost standard selection of imperial concepts which was to appear, year by year, for long decades to come. Of greater interest is the treatment of his portrait: neat, well-finished, and 'civilis'—unwreathed and citizen-like. Even while Otho was settling to his new position, however, the watch-dog armies of the Rhine were plotting the succession of a former commander, Vitellius, in conspiracy with the praetorian guard at Rome. Anonymous denarii were struck to bribe the waverers,[202] with such types as FIDES EXERCITVVM, clasped hands/FIDES PRAETORIANORVM, clasped hands; and pro-Vitellian forces defeated Otho in northern Italy. Vitellius succeeded in April 69, to rule for nine months. Like Galba, he had support in Gaul and Spain, where the mints of Lugdunum and Tarraco struck gold and silver for him, the latter making considerable use of the repertoire of ideas devised earlier for Galba and Vindex (e.g. LIBERTAS RESTITVTA, ROMA RENASCENS, VESTA P(opuli) R(omani) QVIRITIVM), while Lugdunum laid almost exclusive emphasis upon the CONSENSVS and FIDES EXERCITVVM which carried him in power to Rome. He reached the capital in the early summer of 69, and between then and his death in December the mint of Rome coined amply for him in all metals. In general, the style of these issues was a continuation from those of Otho, though the clarity and neatness visible under Otho was not now matched: Vitellius' gold and silver gives the impression of greater haste and some consequent technical decline, with a portrait which, while often a perceptive study of a gross if genial glutton, is rather coarse in actual execution. It was in the *aes* again, and especially in the sestertii, that distinguished portraiture was achieved, of immense power and obvious fidelity, with the head still proportionately large within its circle of (now variably good) lettering. Some of Vitellius' *aes* reverses look back to previous reigns, as for example the ANNONA AVG to Nero's *Annona Augusti Ceres* (see above, p. 168), the CONCORD AVG and ROMA to Galba's identical types. Others brought their own newly conceived beauty, such as a striding Mars with trophy, and Victoria bending, with majestic delicacy, to inscribe OB CIVIS SERV(atos) upon a shield. Vitellius' major innovation, however, was the publicity which he gave both to his father Lucius, a censor under Claudius, and to his own two sons. On gold and silver *rev.* portraits were assigned to the father (as L VITELLIVS COS III CENSOR) and to the children (as LIBERI IMP GERM(anici) AVG); and gold, silver, and *aes* alike showed the father ceremonially seated as censor.

In 66 the province of Judaea had risen in revolt against Roman authority; and Nero had appointed T. Flavius Vespasianus, an experienced soldier of good Italian stock, to quell the rising. By 69 Jerusalem was tightly besieged, and in July Vespasian, hitherto loyal to Vitellius, yielded to the persuasion of those who urged him to march on Rome and claim the principate. The march was long, and it was six months before he found himself emperor in Rome, officially recognized by the Senate. Exactly 100 years had passed since Octavian defeated Antony at Actium and, by doing so, ended the destructive and costly rivalry of the Pompeian and Caesarian era. Now, within a period of eighteen months, Nero's death had been followed by Galba, Otho, and Vitellius, all dead after a series of army-confrontations. The cost to the state had been enormous : Vespasian's estimate of the current deficit at the time of his accession was the huge sum of ten thousand million denarii.[203] The cost to the spirit—the 'salus generis humani'—was incalculable. Vespasian's reorganization of the Roman state in his ten years of rule (he acceded at the age of sixty) was total, and it was designed to endure, for he made it plain from the outset that his successors should be his sons, first Titus and then Domitian. Augustus' dynasty had lasted, in loose form, for a century : Vespasian's much tighter, lasted for hardly more than a quarter of a century. Nevertheless, in that short time the machinery of empire was changed into a new and strong form; and the change was seen not least in the imperial coinage.

This now for the first time became systematic and regular, and was to remain so during nearly four centuries to come. Under the Republic coinage had been provided as required, sometimes in larger quantities, sometimes in smaller, the requirements of military pay being the chief determinant; and the provision of bronze, originally of central importance, had seriously diminished as silver, and latterly gold, gained a greater economic place. Augustus, while seeing from the first that a widespread *aes* coinage was necessary in a vast Graeco-Roman world where urbanization was steadily and peacefully growing, did not however advance to the point at which a

314

315

316

314 Otho. *Obv., head of Otho, bare ;* IMP M OTHO CAESAR AVG TR P. *A.D. 69, Rome (aureus, 7.30 gm., diam. 19 mm., BMCRE 1).*

315 Vitellius. *Obv., head of Vitellius, globe at point of neck ;* A VITELLIVS GER IMP AVG P MAX TR P. *A.D. 69, Lugdunum (aureus, 7.30 gm., diam. 17 mm., BMCRE 110). (For rev. see No. 318.)*

316 Vespasian. *Obv., head of Vespasian ;* IMP CAES VESPASIAN AVG P M TR P P P COS III. *A.D. 71, Rome (sestertius, 25.65 gm., diam. 32 mm., BMCRE 765). (For rev. see No. 319.)*

317

318

319

317 Otho. *Rev., Victory with wreath and palm;* VICTORIA OTHONIS. *A.D. 69, Rome (denarius, 3.41 gm., diam. 19 mm., BMCRE 24).*

318 Vitellius. *Rev., helmeted Mars with spear, aquila, and standard;* CONSENSVS EXERCITVVM. *A.D. 69, Lugdunum (aureus, 7.30 gm., diam. 18 mm., BMCRE 110). (For obv. see No. 315.)*

319 Vespasian. *Rev., prince, with spear and sword, foot on helmet, standing by palm-tree below which sits Jewish woman (Judaea) in mourning attitude on cuirass;* IVDAEA CAPTA, S C. *A.D. 71, Rome (sestertius, 25.65 gm., diam. 32.5 mm., BMCRE 765). (For obv. see No. 316.)*

regular annual output of gold and silver seems to have been predictable : his succession of mint-phases—Emerita, Spain or Gaul(?), Rome, Lugdunum—makes this clear. And although his successors down to Nero often produced quite long runs of coinage, there was no instance of absolutely continuous coinage in all metals. Hence the surprising gaps that occurred, sometimes in gold and silver, more often in *aes* : interruptions in gold and silver, for example, under Gaius and Claudius for a year or more at a time, and intermissions in *aes* of longer duration, as under Augustus for 15 years before A.D. 10, under Tiberius for a decade before 34, and under Nero from 54 to 64.

From 69 onwards regularity was the rule. Coinage, in general, was issued annually, as can be seen usually by the dated elements within an emperor's titles—a numbered consulship, a numbered tenure of *tribunicia potestas*, a numbered military acclamation, or the conferment of some independently dated title. Not all metals were necessarily struck in any given year, though it was not abnormal for all three to appear. Nor were all issues dated : side by side with dated issues there were frequently quite large blocks of undated coinage, in whatever metal, the chronology of which can be fairly closely fixed by a comparison of their types and portraiture with those of the dated issues. The general impression that arises, in contrast to the non-regularity of Julio-Claudian coinage down to 68, is that the imperial government thereafter took care to ensure that the empire-wide pool of available currency never fell below a certain level. In regard to gold and silver—the primary metals for military and official pay, and perhaps also for tax-payments—this was of high importance. But *aes* was also important in the daily life of the man in the street; and *aes*, moreover, had come by 68 to bear a wide range of imperially approved information. From the time of Claudius there had been a centralization of coin-production in Rome (see above, p. 154), interrupted only by the events of 68–9. Vespasian, in his first year or two, when he was marching upon Rome and thereafter re-deploying his forces, operated temporary mints in the east, in Illyricum, and in the west.[204] After that, his monetary production was virtually all in Rome. Imperial supervision of the mint was easy and direct at Rome. From the time of Augustus an imperial secretariat had been growing, staffed by imperial freedmen and slaves, already notorious by Claudius' time. Under Vespasian and his successors this private civil service operated more discreetly, though no less efficiently. Domitian's financial secretary, according to the poet Statius, co-ordinated and controlled all the basic elements of the imperial economy, including monetary provision—from the mines onwards to the quantity of coinage to be struck at Rome.[205]

There were, indeed, other mints also at work from 69 until the end of the second century of the Empire. Alexandria continued to strike profuse coinage on the special debased standard reserved for Egypt. Antioch and Caesarea retained their importance as major coining centres. In Asia Minor the issue of 'cistophoric' tetra-drachms, renewed on a big scale by Augustus (see above, p. 146) and supplemented by Claudius and the Flavians,[206] was under-taken afresh, and on an enormous scale, by Hadrian.[207] And although local *aes* coinages in the west (now well supplied by Rome) were virtually extinct, they continued to flourish in the cities of the Greek east, where, apart from the probable margin of profit on their production, their great variety of pictorial types called attention to the religious and architectural wonders of those ancient communities. But it was from Rome that the overwhelming bulk of imperial coinage was produced and disseminated, year after year. The predictability of this annual coinage of great size led, in turn, to a new use of coin-types. Down to the end of Nero's reign types had tended to emphasize what was immediately topical, within a framework of permanently suitable generalities. Thereafter, with the annual volume of coinage much increased, the generalities tended to outweigh the topicalities, and a range of impeccably respectable concepts came to occupy an annual pattern of issues which were not regularly enlivened by topicality. Some examples will fairly illustrate the trend. In 75 Vespasian's gold and silver, with *rev.* legend either simply COS VI or PON MAX TR P COS VI, showed unlabelled figure-types as follows: Mars, bull, capricorn, eagle, Pax, Securitas, Victory, and seated emperor. The *aes* of the same year showed PAX AVGVSTI, Pax; S C, Victory; S C, Minerva; FELICITAS PVBLICA, Felicitas; and AEQVITAS AVGVSTI, Aequitas.[208] In 100 Trajan's gold and silver, with *rev.* legend P M TR P COS III PP, showed unlabelled figure-types of Abundantia, Concordia, Fortuna, Germania, Hercules, Pax, Roma, Vesta, and Victory: the nearly parallel *aes*, mostly with *rev.* legend TR POT

COS III P P S C, showed Mars, Abundantia, Concordia, Pax, Securitas, Victory, triumphal arch, and emperor on horseback.[209] In 139 the gold and silver of Antoninus Pius, with *rev.* legend AVG PIVS P M TR P COS II spilling over from the obverse, showed Aequitas, Aeternitas, Fides, Fortuna, Pax, Pietas, Victory, clasped hands, priestly symbols, and military standards : *aes* of the same year, with variant legends (some specifically identifying the type), principally showed Annona, Felicitas, Fides, Fortuna, Libertas, Liberalitas, and Moneta, with some special sestertius types depicting Antoninus distributing largesse.[210]

366

It would be wrong to suppose that the choice of types from 69 to the end of the second century were always chosen so mechanically from a stock range. The exceptions to the rule were many, and often brilliantly conspicuous. For example, Vespasian coined in all metals for Titus from 71 and for Domitian from 72, giving them in each case the right of obverse portrait; and Titus as emperor was to do the same for Domitian.[211] Such advertisement of heirs or junior colleagues was again regular from Hadrian to Marcus Aurelius. The compliment of a portrait coinage was, moreover, extended to a wide range of imperial ladies, of whom Sabina, Hadrian's wife, and the elder and younger Faustina, wife and daughter of Antoninus, were most prominent. Commemorative coinages, too, were commonly used to honour the illustrious dead. Some of the most remarkable of these consisted of the 'restoration', with appropriately added legends, of well known coins of the earlier years of the Empire. Titus' short reign, for example, witnessed

384
367

370

the 'restoration' of a quite remarkable range of coins of those who were clearly regarded, officially, as the 'good' emperors—Augustus, Tiberius, Claudius and Galba, without Gaius or Nero;[212] and Trajan, at a time of currency-reform (see below, p. 208), restored a considerable number of old Republican types which by then faced the oblivion of being called in.[213] Quite apart from exceptional series such as these, which fell well outside the main stream of coinage, there were others more closely related to it : best known, perhaps, are those which Hadrian, the great imperial traveller, struck in gold, silver, and *aes* to honour individual provinces and army-corps.[214]

338, 339

363, 364

Over and above all such series as these there was, moreover, a host of sharply topical types embedded with varying frequency in the vast unfolding fabric of the imperial coinage of Rome : it is enough to note such justly famous *aes* coins as Vespasian's IVDAEA CAPTA series, Titus' 'Colosseum' sestertii, Nerva's issues commemorating the lifting of the postal tax in Italy (VEHICVLATIONE ITALIAE REMISSA) and the reform of the Jewish poll-tax (FISCI IVDAICI CALVMNIA SVBLATA), Trajan's with REX PARTHIS DATVS, and Hadrian's calling attention to his act of debt-cancellation (RELIQVA VETERA HS NOVIES-MILL ABOLITA). Moreover, in the smaller details of more conventional types there was many a sideglance at a victory, a largesse, an imperial journey, or the hope of an imperial heir. When all is said, however, it remains true that from 69 onwards the normal range of types contains much that is repetitive and conventional. These types, in fact, make up the monotone backcloth against which

316*, 319
337

348*
353

the exceptions could from time to time be excitingly displayed.

With the development of a regular coinage, produced on a virtually annual basis in all three categories, gold, silver, and *aes*, the study of coin-hoards becomes increasingly important in distinguishing between the staple issues, struck in great quantity, and what may be called the marginal and sometimes occasional issues. And the larger the hoard, the more clearly the distinction is seen. Two great hoards, both deposited in the third century A.D., though both also containing coins of much earlier date, have shown this convincingly. That found in 1936 at Dorchester (Dorset) comprised over 22,000 silver coins.[215] That found in 1929 at Réka-Devnia in Bulgaria was very much larger.[216] Statistical analysis of such huge deposits as these has demonstrated without doubt what the main structure of coinage was at any given time.[217] From this, in turn, it has been possible to deduce the number of separate but parallel working-sections (*officinae*) in the mint of Rome from time to time. Under Augustus there had been three *monetales* at Rome, and presumably three *officinae* (see above, p. 139). Under Nero there were possibly six; and in the second and third centuries the figure seems to have been five or six at different times.[218] Division of the mint into these working sections brought advantages of administration and security. It seems that a particular *officina* would be assigned the production of coins with a particular reverse type or range of reverse types. In this way any deficiency or fault in output or technique could easily be brought home to those who were responsible. Later on, from the period of

320, 321 Civil wars; Clodius Macer. *Obv., head of Clodius Macer ;* L CLODIVS MACER, S C. *Rev., galley to r., with high stern and standard at prow ;* PRO PRAE AFRICAE. *A.D. 68, Africa (? Carthage) (denarius, 3.06 gm., diam. 18 mm., BMCRE 2).*

322, 323 Civil wars; Gaul. *Obv., bust of the Genius of the Roman People, diademed, with sceptre over shoulder ;* GENIVS P R. *Rev., helmeted Mars with short spear and shield ; short sword at his side ;* MARS VLTOR. *A.D. 68, Gaul, uncertain mint (aureus, 7.29 gm., diam. 18 mm., BMCRE 21).*

324, 325 Galba. *Obv., head of Galba ; globe at point of neck ;* GALBA IMP. *Rev., Roma, helmeted, holding Victory and sceptre ;* ROMA RENASCENS. *A.D. 68-9, (?) Tarraco (denarius, 3.48 gm., diam. 18 mm., BMCRE 184).*

326 Civil wars; Spain. [*Legend* LIBERTAS *on obv.*] *Rev., two daggers flanking cap of liberty ;* RESTITVTA. *A.D. 68, Spain, uncertain mint (denarius, 3.65 gm., diam. 19 mm., BMCRE 7).*

327 Galba. *Obv., bust of Galba, cuirassed ;* SER GALBA CAESAR AVG. *A.D. 68, Rome (aureus, 7.31 gm., diam. 19.5 mm., Oxford).*

328 Galba. *Obv., draped bust of Galba ;* IMP SER GALBA CAE AVG TR P. *A.D. 68, Rome (sestertius, 26.01 gm., diam. 36 mm., BMCRE 106).*

329 Galba. *Rev., Honos, with cornucopiae and sceptre, facing Virtus, helmeted, with short sword and spear ;* HONOS ET VIRTVS, S C. *A.D. 68, Rome (sestertius, 25.50 gm., diam. 37 mm., BMCRE p. 375).*

330 Galba. *Rev., Galba on platform, accompanied by officer, addressing group of armed soldiers surrounding aquila and two standards ; a horse among them ;* ADLOCVTIO, S C. *A.D. 68, Rome (sestertius, 24.91 gm., diam. 37 mm., Oxford).*

320

321

322

323

324

325

326

327

328

329

330

331

332

333

334

335

336

337

338

339

340

341

342

343

344

331, 332 (Vitellius) Civil wars; Gaul. *Obv.,*
clasped hands ; FIDES EXERCITVVM. *Rev.,*
clasped hands ; FIDES PRAETORIANORVM.
A.D. 69, Upper Germany, uncertain mint
(denarius, 3.37 gm., diam. 16.5 mm., BMCRE
65).

333 Vitellius. *Rev., Mars, in full military dress,*
holding Victory and trophy ; MARS VICTOR, S C.
A.D. 69, Rome (sestertius, 25.50 gm., diam.
36 mm., BMCRE 52).

334 Vitellius. *Rev., confronting busts of the son*
(on l.) and daughter of Vitellius ; LIBERI IMP
GERM AVG. *A.D. 69, Rome (aureus, 7.32*
gm., diam. 20.5 mm., BMCRE 27).

335 Vespasian. *Rev., Pax with olive-branch and*
cornucopiae ; PAX AVGVSTI, S C. *A.D. 71*
(cos. III on obv.), Rome (sestertius, 27.62 gm.,
diam. 36 mm., BMCRE 558).

336 Vespasian. *Rev., Aequitas holding scales and*
palm-branch ; AEQVITAS AVGVSTI, S C. *A.D.*
71 (cos. III on obv.), Rome (As, 12.23 gm.,
diam. 29 mm., BMCRE 603).

337 Titus. *Rev., view of tiered front and the crowded*
interior of the Colosseum ; the two central rows
of outer tiers contain a variety of figures and
quadrigae ; the interior shows a topmost row of
boxes, below which is a continuous gallery above

the main public space ; meta *(turning post) to l. ;*
*building to r. A.D. 80-81 (*cos. VIII *on*
obv.), Rome (sestertius, 23.36 gm., diam. 34 mm.,
BMCRE 190).

338, 339 Titus. *Obv., head of Divus Augustus,*
radiate ; DIVVS AVGVSTVS PATER. *Rev., pan-*
elled altar ; PROVIDENT, S C, IMP T CAES AVG
REST(ituit). *A.D. 79-81, Rome (As, 11.39*
gm., diam. 28 mm., BMCRE 269).

340, 341 Domitian. *Obv., bust of Domitian, laur-*
eate, slightly bearded, and draped ; IMP CAES
DOMITIANVS AVG GERMANIC. *Rev., bust of*
Minerva, helmeted and draped ; P M TR POT
III IMP V COS X P P. *A.D. 84, Rome (aureus,*
7.69 gm., diam. 22 mm., BMCRE 45).

342, 343 Domitian. *Obv., head of Domitian, laur-*
eate ; IMP CAES DOMIT AVG GERM P M TR
POT V. *Rev., Germania seated on oblong shield,*
her head resting in attitude of sadness on her
hand ; broken spear below ; IMP VIII COS XI
CENS(oria) POT P P. *A.D. 85, Rome (silver*
5-denarius piece, 17.11 gm., diam. 34 mm.,
BMCRE 85).

344 Domitian. *Rev., Domitian, togate, holding*
palladium (archaic statuette of Pallas) ; TR P
COS VII DES(ignatus) VIII P P, S C. *A.D. 81,*
Rome (sestertius, 27.59 gm., diam. 36 mm.,
BMCRE 265).

481, 491 Gallienus onwards, coins were specifically marked with an *officina* number or letter, e.g. I, A (= 1), P(rima), etc.

The need for continuous large-scale production of imperial coinage at Rome from Flavian times, and the organization of the mint into separate but parallel *officinae*, may have led in turn to what has been called the cyclical system of actual production. Provision of coinage under the Empire was according to need, primarily; and it has been seen (see above, p. 180) how, under Domitian, the imperial finance secretary determined and acted upon that need. It must be assumed that the state normally had in hand some 'pool' of coinage, of which the level fluctuated, so that at any given time the level, in whatever metal, might have to be raised. The cyclical system of production, if correctly observed for the second and third centuries A.D., would mean only that when coinage in a given metal of denomination was required, its production was shared by all *officinae*, which, once that particular coinage was fulfilled, would then turn, again in unison, to the coinage of another metal or denomination, as required.[219] Granted the inability of the Roman government to estimate in advance, or upon the basis of averages, what coinage-needs would be from year to year, this was a simple and flexible system for the supplying of current needs with minimum delay. Its operation has been recognized as early as Trajan, and its origin may in fact lie earlier, under the Flavians. One of its major advantages was that it enabled special or specially appropriate types to be interposed at very short notice within the perennial range of 'stock' types.

Apart from those working *officinae* in the mint which actually struck the coins one must consider the section (or sections) in which the obverse and reverse dies were engraved (and lettered?) by the *sculptores*. The number of dies engraved for any one year's coinage was very great in itself, leading to an actual coin-output that was probably much larger than has been normally supposed.[220] Die-engraving, whether for the portrait obverse or for the more variable reverse, was to some extent repetitive work; and repetitive work often becomes bad work. It is therefore all the more remarkable that in the period of the Flavians, Trajan, and the Antonines, when production soared, the general standard was so high. It was also extraordinarily consistent. The comparison of coins, reign by reign, and especially of sestertii, where the portraits were large, and executed in superb detail, shows that as between one portrait-die and another the differences could be infinitesimally small— a lock of hair differently arranged; the forehead marginally higher or lower; the wreath-ties swinging in minutely varying pattern. It can be safely assumed that, in the period in question, an emperor's official profile likeness was available in the mint as a model for imitation by die-engravers. But imitation is always subject to the personal whims of the imitator, and it has therefore been conjectured, though never yet proved, that such a high degree of near-identity between portrait-dies is the result of 'hubbing', i.e. a process by which a master-punch in relief could have been used to punch a not necessarily complete design into a series of dies of which the finer details could afterwards have been hand-engraved, die by die individually.[221] Proof would come only from the finding of a certainly authentic 'hub', or series of hubs; and since it was, then as now, a matter of careful policy to destroy obsolete dies (hardly a handful of unquestionably genuine ones has survived),[222] the same would doubtless have been true of hubs.

Portraiture under the Julio-Claudians had varied greatly from emperor to emperor. For Augustus, in general, the 'heroic' idiom had been used, clear, often delicate, and with overtones of that beauty and grace which hellenism reserved for the half-divine. Under Tiberius, although there was a sudden and astonishing florescence in coin-design as a whole (see above, p. 148), portraiture inclined sharply towards the realistic. Under Gaius the sestertius was for the first time regularly invaded by the imperial portrait, large in scale and therefore detailed; and realism then became so stark as to be formidable, suggesting very clearly the spirit of that young, fierce emperor. Claudian portraiture brought a complete change, to a subtler, more sympathetically considered idiom which represented the emperor essentially as a man. There was yet another change with Nero, who was represented from 64 as combining the qualities of fierceness and robustness with all the artless abandon and romantic proliferation of long hair and curls. It was Galba who set the fashion for the Flavians: a large portrait, with features severely set, owing nothing to adornment, its treatment being wholly realistic in a manner which might seem brutal if it were not so obviously true to life.

It cannot be doubted that the portrait-engravers who worked for Galba continued under Vespasian, for the same characteristics were continued. The degree of successful achievement was, still, less on the aurei and denarii than on the *aes*: even with a comparatively large head the engravers generally found that the small size of the gold and silver coins limited their ability to work in fine detail, so that the heads, while usually bold, often tended towards a coarse or perfunctory treatment, which was not mitigated by any great fineness or elegance of lettering. Vespasian's *aes*, however, and not merely the sestertii, developed a full magnificence of portraiture. Again the heads were large, even massive, and normally in high relief, giving a strong impression of the purely profile view of sculpture in the round. And, because of the larger scale which this *aes* permitted, a wealth of detail could be achieved: close-cut hair, finely wrinkled brow, a minutely rendered profile eye, and all the jowls and neck-folds of an old man. The beauty of this work lay in its realism, strong in authority and yet delicate in execution; and it was in the addition of technical delicacy to strength of conception that Vespasian's coinage clearly excelled over that of Galba. It is enough to compare the work of the mint of Rome with that of Vespasian's provincial mints—Tarraco and Lugdunum —to see, moreover, how far the mint of Rome excelled over others of its own day.

With Titus (79–81) and Domitian (81–96) the same general characteristics were continued. In neither reign was portraiture on aurei and denarii really confident or distinguished, though Domitian's aurei, free from the long obverse legends which encumbered his denarii, came to bear conspicuously

345 Titus. *Obv., head of Titus, laureate and slightly bearded ;* IMP TITVS CAES VESPASIAN AVG P M. *A.D. 80, Rome (aureus, 7.31 gm., diam. 19 mm., BMCRE 65). (For rev. see No. 349.)*

346, 347 Domitian (for Domitia). *Obv., bust of Domitia, draped, her hair in long plait ;* DOMITIA AVGVSTA IMP(eratoris) DOMIT(iani uxor). *Rev., naked baby boy seated on zoned globe, with arms outstretched ; seven stars around ;* DIVVS CAESAR IMP DOMITIANI F(ilius). *A.D. 81-4, Rome (aureus, 7.73 gm., diam. 19 mm., BMCRE 62).*

348 Nerva. *Rev., two mules grazing in front of cart, its pole and harness tipped up ;* VEHICVLATIONE ITALIAE REMISSA, S C. *A.D. 97, Rome (sestertius, 24.35 gm., diam. 32 mm., BMCRE 119).*

349 Titus. *Rev., wreath above curule chair ;* TR P IX IMP XV COS VIII P P. *A.D. 80, Rome (aureus, 7.31 gm., diam. 19 mm., BMCRE 65). (For obv. see No. 345.)*

350, 351 Titus. *Obv., head of Titus, laureate ;* IMP T CAES VESP AVG P M TR P P P COS VIII. *Rev., mourning woman seated under palm-tree by which stands a Jew with hands bound ; helmet and uncertain object on r. ;* IVD CAP, S C. *A.D.*

80-1, Rome (sestertius, 25.85 gm., diam. 33 mm., BMCRE 164).

352 Nerva. *Obv., head of Nerva, laureate ;* IMP NERVA CAES AVG P M TR P COS II P P. *A.D. 96, Rome (aureus, 7.63 gm., diam. 19 mm., BMCRE 16).*

353 Nerva. *Rev., palm-tree ;* FISCI IVDAICI CALVMNIA SVBLATA, S C. *A.D. 97, Rome (sestertius, 26.07 gm., diam. 32 mm., BMCRE 105).*

354 Trajan. *Obv., head of Trajan, laureate ;* IMP CAES NERVA TRAIAN AVG GERM. *A.D. 100, Rome (denarius, 3.08 gm., diam. 19 mm., BMCRE 72).*

355 Trajan. *Rev., bound Dacian, wearing cap, long tunic, and breeches, seated on pile of shields with spears and curved swords ;* COS V P P S P Q R OPTIMO PRINC, DAC CAP. *c. A.D. 107-11, Rome (denarius, 3.27 gm., diam. 19 mm., BMCRE 385).*

356 Trajan. *Rev., an elevation of Trajan's Forum ; central doorway between recessed shrines with statues surmounted by shields ; on top, quadriga, soldiers, trophies of arms, and (?) Victories ;* FORVM TRAIAN(i). *c. A.D. 112-15, Rome (aureus, 7.32 gm., diam. 20 mm., BMCRE 509).*

349

350

351

352

353

354

355

356

357

358

359

360

361

362

363

364

365

366

367

368

369

370

371

372

357 Trajan. *Rev., view of the Circus Maximus with colonnaded front ; on l. one arch, on r. two, all surmounted by quadrigae ; in central space one large and some smaller obelisks ; beyond, colonnades with temple surmounted by radiate bust ;* S P Q R OPTIMO PRINCIPI, S C. *A.D. 104-11, Rome (sestertius, 28.51 gm., diam. 36 mm., BMCRE 853).*

358 Hadrian. *Obv., head of Hadrian, laureate ;* HADRIANVS AVGVSTVS. c. *A.D. 125-8, Rome (aureus, 7.15 gm., diam. 20 mm., BMCRE 430).*

359 Hadrian (for L. Aelius). *Obv., head of Aelius ;* L AELIVS CAESAR. *A.D. 137, Rome (denarius, 3.51 gm., diam. 19 mm., BMCRE 989).*

360, 361 Hadrian. *Obv., bust of Hadrian, draped ;* HADRIANVS AVG COS III P P. *Rev., archaic cult-statue of Diana, veiled and in high headdress, and with garlands hanging from her wrists ;* DIANA EPHESIA. c. *A.D. 134-8, Ephesus (silver tetradrachm, 10.24 gm., diam. 28 mm., BMCRE 1091).*

362 Hadrian. *Rev., Hadrian, togate, on the rostra in front of temple addressing group of citizens ;* COS III, S C. *A.D. 119-38, Rome (sestertius, 28.14 gm., diam. 36 mm., Oxford).*

363 Hadrian. *Rev., Hadrian in military dress on platform addressing officer (with sword) and three soldiers (with aquila, standard and shield, and standard respectively) ;* EXERC(itus) HISPAN(icus), S C. c. *A.D. 134-8, Rome (sestertius, 23.88 gm., diam. 35 mm., BMCRE 1680).*

364 Hadrian. *Rev., Nilus (personification of the Nile) reclining against rock, holding reed and cornucopiae, with which two children play ; to r., hippopotamus ; below in water, crocodile ;* NILVS, S C. c. *A.D. 134-8, Rome (sestertius, 24.62 gm., diam. 35 mm., BMCRE 1770).*

365, 366 Antoninus Pius. *Obv., head of Antoninus, laureate ;* ANTONINVS AVG PIVS P P TR P COS III. *Rev., Antoninus seated on platform, hand extended, by Liberalitas holding abacus and cornucopiae ; below, citizen holding out fold of toga ;* LIBERALITAS AVG III. *A.D. 140-4, Rome (aureus, 7.33 gm., diam. 20 mm., BMCRE 218).*

367 Antoninus Pius (for Faustina II). *Obv., bust of Faustina II, draped, her hair waved and coiled on the back of her head ;* FAVSTINA AVG (usta) ANTONINI AVG PII FIL(ia). c. *A.D. 152-6, Rome (aureus, 7.23 gm., diam. 20 mm., BMCRE 1083).*

368, 369 Antoninus Pius. *Obv., head of Antoninus, laureate ;* ANTONINVS AVG PIVS P P. *Rev., personification of Alexandria, lotus on head, holding crown ; to l. and r., corn-ears and crocodile ;* ALEXANDRIA, COS II, S C. *A.D. 139, Rome (sestertius, 25.68 gm., diam. 33 mm., BMCRE 1179).*

370 Antoninus Pius (for Diva Faustina). *Rev., ornamented and draped throne ; peacock below, with tail spread ;* IVNONI REGINAE, S C. *A.D. 139-41, Rome (sestertius, 23.33 gm., diam. 35 mm., BMCRE 1118).*

371 Marcus Aurelius (L. Verus). *Obv., head of Lucius Verus ;* L VERVS AVG ARMENIACVS. *A.D. 163-4, Rome (aureus, 7.24 gm., diam. 19 mm., BMCRE 294).*

372 Marcus Aurelius (for Commodus). *Rev., Commodus, in military dress, standing with branch and sceptre by trophy of arms ;* PRINC IVVENT. *A.D. 175, Rome (aureus, 7.19 gm., diam. 20 mm., BMCRE 638).*

good portraits between the evenly bracketing DOMITIANVS AVGVSTVS. Equally good portraiture was achieved on gold for his wife Domitia and his sister Julia. Once more it was the *aes* which encouraged portrait-engravers to their full powers. Titus' florid geniality perhaps presented a less interesting exercise than Vespasian's shrewd, hard-bitten concentration, and the details were rendered much less minutely, perhaps with more poise than character. But the essence of the man was well shown: the great, flat-backed head inclined slightly forward upon an immensely thick neck, masterful and yet humane. Domitian's *aes*, by contrast, tended to show a smaller head —smaller, no doubt, so that it might be seen to be held high and proud upon the great column of a neck adorned above the breast by the gorgoneion. If the attitude was proud, the expression was one of critical disdain, of a kind familiar to the medallists of Louis XIV seventeen centuries later.

After Domitian's murder the Senate, weary of the fruits of dynastic succession, assigned supreme power to Nerva (96–8), an elderly nobleman who should show, it was hoped, that supreme power rested best in the hands of him who was best, thus beginning the philosophical conception of the 'Optimus Princeps'. After a generation of work in high relief on full, bold, rounded heads the portrait-designers of Rome found themselves confronted, for a brief period, by lean, angular, and very strongly aquiline features. They found the change difficult, and it was even more difficult for mints abroad. The aurei and denarii only seldom achieved any consistency of representation, the relationship of hollowed eye to bony

nose causing great problems. Nor was the *aes* much more successful : although some few engravers produced a tour-de-force, marvellously suggesting a shrivelled old scion of the nobility, most were content with a portrait of grotesque proportion and expression, the effect heightened by the still normally bold relief. Realism, as a basic idiom, had not been abandoned; but it was realism gone awry. Perhaps it was because of the exhaustion of an idiom that had lost its flexibility that Trajan (98–117) introduced a totally new tradition—probably a totally new school—of portrait artists at the mint of Rome.

This was a change of a very curious kind, and one which can be said only to have been for the worse, certainly for the gold and silver, and probably also for the *aes*. Until the latter part of his reign, when portrait-engravers recovered some assurance (seen in a better balanced treatment, with finer detail), the aurei and denarii were remarkable for the harsh, flat treatment of portraits engraved in a hard, dry, unsympathetic manner, with hair often coarsely rendered, and 'character'—in the absence of furrows, lines or wrinkles in the face—expressed only by a wide, level eye and a small, firmly pursed mouth. The same idiom was repeated on the *aes*, through here the technique was more polished and the proportions of portrait-mass and encircling space much better understood. Even on the *aes*, however, more skilful and more assured though it certainly was, the impression given by this flat and generally rather ageless and characterless portraiture is disappointingly empty. With one or two quite brilliant exceptions, clearly the work of specially gifted engravers, the *aes* of Trajan suggests that the portrait-artists were following, not a model of intimate size, intimately conceived, but a model of 'colossal' character, devoid of the subtleties that convey personality. It was portraiture with individuality, certainly, but with little humanity.[223]

There was another great change under Hadrian (117–38), who, as has been well demonstrated,[224] fostered a revival of art-forms based on Greek aesthetics. The change did not come at once. For the first few years of his reign the dry, hard style of the Trajanic coinage continued, its effect perhaps even accentuated by giving Hadrian a deep-chested bust which in turn necessitated a conspicuously small head in the space available. Even so, however, the engravers found material for modest ornament (lacking with Trajan) in the thick hair, the beard, and the chest, draped or undraped. And when the idiom changed after *c.* 125 a succession of very fine and often superb portraits was elaborated, not only on the *aes*, but also on aurei and denarii : it was, in fact, under Hadrian that the mint of Rome first fully mastered the art of the fine small-scale portrait—an art in which the splendid *aes* designers from Galba onwards had apparently been deficient. Hadrian, like Trajan before him, embodied the conception of the Optimus Princeps; and his portraits exhibit seriousness without severity, thoughtfulness without tension, and a sort of detached nobility which reaches its heights when the emperor is shown bareheaded—civilian instead of soldier. The standard of conception thus became philosophical; and the standard of

engraving soared to a new level of delicate beauty and strength, in which 'character' could be successfully conveyed by as little as the minute rendering of the eye well placed in the massive profile. Portraits of Hadrian's wife Sabina, and of his successive heirs Aelius and Antoninus, were rendered with more variable skill.

The full beauty of the Hadrianic school survived into the reign of Antoninus Pius (138–61), at least during the earlier years, when, as well as very fine *aes* portraits, there were splendid representations on the precious-metal issues, and particularly on gold. Antoninus' nobly melancholy features, combining serenity with still continuing seriousness, admirably express the spirit of the time, when the great stream of *romanitas* flowing through the whole broad empire was directed and controlled by the wisdom of yet another Optimus Princeps. But the seeds of artistic decay were visible. Hadrian's engravers were masters of the art of relief. Those of Antoninus, for all their great skill, began to lose that mastery. Their treatment of hair, beard, and eye was still fine; but the hollow features of the ageing emperor, sometimes accentuated by furrows, led to a devitalization not compensated by emphasis on the profile line of forehead and nose. The same changed idiom persisted under Marcus Aurelius (161–80), Lucius Verus (161–9), and Commodus (180–93). In a period which saw an unhappy return to the dynastic principle, serenity and grace of portraiture were diminished; features became harder, with a staring, unsubtle eye; hair and beard were rendered more mechanically; and engraving, while accurate, was harsh. There were, of

382

384
359

365, 368,
380*

385*
371

373, 374 Trajan. *Obv., bust of Trajan, laureate, draped and cuirassed ; small globe below ;* IMP TRAIANO AVG GER DAC P M TR P COS VI P P. *Rev., Jupiter, with sceptre, holding thunderbolt over small togate figure of Trajan with branch ;* CONSERVATORI PATRIS PATRIAE. *A.D. 112-7, Rome (aureus, 7.22 gm., diam. 20 mm.,* BMCRE *493).*

375 Trajan. *Rev., covered bridge arching over river with moored boat ; statues above the nearer gateway and at the further end ;* S P Q R OPTIMO PRINCIPI, S C. *A.D. 104 onwards, Rome (sestertius, 26.11 gm., diam. 33 mm.,* BMCRE *849).*

376 Trajan (for his father). *Rev., bust of Trajan senior, draped ;* DIVVS PATER TRAIANVS. *A.D. 112-7, Rome (aureus, 7.15 gm., diam. 18.5 mm.,* BMCRE *506).*

377 Trajan (for Plotina). *Obv., bust of Plotina, draped, her hair dressed high and secured by stephane, with queue down her neck ;* PLOTINA AVG IMP TRAIANI (uxor). *c. A.D. 112-5, Rome (denarius, 3.14 gm., diam. 20 mm.,* BMCRE *528).*

378 Trajan (for Marciana). *Obv., bust of Marciana, draped, her hair dressed high and secured by stephane ;* DIVA AVGVSTA MARCIANA. *c. A.D. 113, Rome (aureus, 7.24 gm., diam. 19 mm.,* BMCRE *649).*

376

377

378

382

383

384

379 Hadrian. *Rev., Hadrian, in military dress, followed by three soldiers (with two standards and one aquila) and a centurion (with staff) ;* DISCIPLIN AVG, S C. *A.D. 119-38, Rome (sestertius, 25.66 gm., diam. 31 mm., BMCRE 1484).*

380, 381 Antoninus Pius. *Obv., head of Antoninus, laureate ;* ANTONINVS AVG PIVS P P TR P COS III. *Rev., Britannia, in tunic, cuirass and breeches, seated on rock holding standard and shield ;* BRITANNIA, S C. c. *A.D. 143-4, Rome (sestertius, 29.46 gm., diam. 26 mm., BMCRE 1637).*

382, 383 Hadrian. *Obv., bust of Hadrian, left shoulder draped ;* HADRIANVS AVG COS III P P. *Rev., confronting busts of Trajan, draped and cuirassed, and Plotina, draped, with stephane ; a star above each ;* DIVIS PARENTIBVS. c. *A.D. 134-8, Rome (aureus, 7.35 gm., diam. 19.5 mm., BMCRE 603).*

384 Hadrian (for Sabina). *Obv., bust of Sabina, draped, her hair piled and coiled with triple stephane ;* SABINA AVGVSTA HADRIANI AVG P P (uxor). c. *A.D. 128-34, Rome (aureus, 7.30 gm., diam. 20 mm., BMCRE 893).*

course, splendid exceptions : the artists who worked under Commodus, for example, could still produce brilliantly successful studies of that emperor as the living Hercules,[225] weary but resolute under the world's burdens, of admirable technique, relief, and proportion.

392,394,395

Such special portraits as these may be assumed to be the work of artists of special skill reserved for engraving dies for what are now termed medallions.[226] Gold multiples, of the weight of 4 aurei, had been produced for Augustus, doubtless as pieces of special presentation-value; and silver multiples, worth 5 and 4 denarii, perhaps also with a gold multiple, were made for Domitian. Similar precious-metal multiples were struck for Trajan and Hadrian. But it was with *aes* medallions that the most interesting developments took place. These could be of the size and weight of normal *aes* coins, but differentiated from them by the absence of the s c formula and by the use of portrait-forms and reverse types which fell sharply outside the general run of *aes* coins proper. Finally, Hadrian's reign saw the production of *aes* medallions of a size and weight which did not conform with *aes* monetary denominations; and these large pieces, often pre-eminent for their portraiture and for the elaborate beauty of their reverses, were henceforth to be frequent, being often accompanied in the late Roman period by magnificent gold and silver money-multiples.[227]

342, 343

It was noted above (pp. 180-181) that from Vespasian onward the annual production of coinage led to the regular appearance of a wide range of unremarkable basic types like Aequitas, Fides, Moneta, Victoria, etc.

These could be varied, through the 'cyclical' system of minting (p. 187 f.), by the introduction at any moment of types of specially topical interest, of which a few examples were given. It must not be thought, however, that the run of imperial reverse types from 69 to 193 was necessarily monotonous. The exceptions were frequent and compelling; and on the *aes* especially there was in general a fine mastery of aesthetic composition and of technique. Under the Flavians the princeps himself and his family were given increasingly interesting prominence. Vespasian's earliest denarii, for example, included a splendid issue with *obv.* Head of Sol, *rev.* Emperor in act of public address : it was from the eastern provinces that Rome's salvation had come. He prominently advertised the coming succession of his sons : dynastically, this was an age of plenty. Domitian, in particular, called great attention to his role in the state by such fine *aes* types as those which showed him holding the palladium,[228] or at sacrifice (including the ceremonies of the Ludi Saeculares of 88). Ladies of the imperial family were conspicuously honoured—Julia, associated with the bountiful Ceres, under her father Titus; Domitia, under her husband Domitian, seen on one touching issue of fine aurei with *rev.* commemorating the consecration of their dead baby, shown as an infant Jupiter straddling the earth and heavens. Titus, whose gold and silver was remarkable for a variety of static, symbolic types, introduced into his *aes* a wide range of 'restored' coins, exactly repeating the types of earlier emperors (though with inevitable difference in style) with an added legend specifying the restoration. Multi-

344

346*

349

338,

figure types of statuesque nobility and beauty were common. The famous 'Judaea Capta' type, somewhat cramped on Vespasian's gold, is magnificently rendered in the larger field of the *aes* of Vespasian and Titus. 351 Sestertii of Vespasian with *rev.* ROMA RESVRGES (emperor raising a kneeling Rome) and of Titus with *rev.* PIETAS AVGVST (Pietas joining the hands of Titus and Domitian) show a wonderful ability to adapt the large-scale material of monument or frieze to the small scale of a coin. Even with the general run of types of deities there was frequent beauty and interest. Unusual reverse portraits could be introduced, as for Pax Orbis 341 Terrarum by Vespasian, or for Minerva by Domitian, whose coinage as a whole testified loudly to her patronage of the emperor. And a sense of great dignity and religious reality could be given by engravers of skill to repeatedly used figure-types of deities, 336 such as Aequitas and Pax under Vespasian, Ceres under Titus, and Fides Publica and Fortuna under Domitian.[229] Finally, there were of course frequent reverse types, in these as in later reigns, calling attention to conspicuous military campaigns or con-343 quests : Domitian's emphasis on Germany was great.

352 Nerva's brief and uncomfortable reign brought reverse types which looked not so much to himself as to his policy. After Domitian's tyranny there was to be political freedom, looking back to that of Augustus, whose coins alone he restored; and freedom must include the sense of equity which he displayed in mitigating such burdens as the impost in Italy to pay 348· for imperial couriers (VEHICVLATIONE ITALIAE REMISSA) and the incidence of the tax-

system upon the Jews (FISCI IVDAICI 363 CALVMNIA SVBLATA). But Nerva's main anxiety lay in the army : the CONCORDIA EXERCITVVM which he invoked with clasped-hands types was an appeal for their loyalty towards an essentially civilian emperor, who desperately needed Fortuna. With Trajan the armies got the professional soldier that they required, and, taken as a whole, his reverse types reflected to a high (and new) degree his personal prominence, whether simply as constitutional 'Optimus Princeps' (S P Q R OPTIMO PRINCIPI in civic 355, 357 crown), or as the great general who crossed the Danube to conquer Dacia or acquired 375· new eastern conquests, or as the great builder who, with his treasury the richer for his Dacian conquest, could add to Rome's architectural splendours or remake the road from Beneventum to Brundisium as the Via Traiana. Trajan's architectural types, 356, 357, 375· with all their deficiencies in the art of perspective, are of great importance. Vespasian's rebuilding in Rome after the terrors of 68–9, as also Nero's after the fire of 64, had been notable. But Trajan, in continuing the process, took care to do what Pericles had done with Athens : he proclaimed it as a great city to be seen by all who could, and the coins advertised his wish and intention. He could boast that, as Pater Patriae, he was under the protection of Jupiter him- 373·, 374· self. The lesser deities and the 'personifications' were not neglected : the latter, indeed, appeared in seemingly endless profusion, their identities by now so well known that they needed no labelling, being often surrounded simply by the overflow of Trajan's many titles from the obverse,[230] or by the subsequently common formula S P Q R

OPTIMO PRINCIPI. These, on the denarii, rank as dull and uninformative types, rendered in a small and cramped style. The chief interest and vigour, apart from the aurei (invariably executed with greater skill), is to be seen in the types of the *aes*, where, even if composition and engraving fell below the best Flavian standards, there is a fine variety.

In glorifying himself Trajan did not omit to glorify his own family as well. He coined for his wife Plotina and (after her death and consecration) for his sister Marciana, both ladies appearing with head-dresses of stately elaboration. He coined, too, in honour of his father, likewise consecrated after death. To these exceptional issues were added others, notably a series commemorating the 'good' emperors from Julius Caesar onwards, i.e. omitting Gaius, Nero, Otho, Vitellius and Domitian. These commemorative coins were part of a currency reform in 107 when, as has been recorded, Trajan 'melted down all the worn-out coinage'.[231] In doing so he rescued from near-oblivion many Republican denarial types—for some Republican denarii still survived, as hoards show. The types 'restored' (and some were even invented) ranged from the old x-denarii (see above, p. 47) down to the very end of the Republic; and the programme of restoration suggests that the more learned and antiquarian heads in the imperial civil service kept a keen eye upon the repertoire of coin-designs, past as well as present.[232]

The vast coinage of Hadrian, already noted (see above, p. 199) as having brought imperial portraiture to a new pitch of beauty, brought other changes too. It is

385, 386 Marcus Aurelius. *Obv., head of Marcus Aurelius, laureate, draped and cuirassed;* M ANTONINVS AVG TR P XXVI. *Rev., Victory setting shield inscribed* VIC GER *on palm-tree;* IMP VI COS III. *A.D. 171, Rome (aureus, 7.29 gm., diam. 19 mm., BMCRE 564).*

387, 388 Commodus (for Crispina). *Obv., bust of Crispina, draped, her hair gathered above her neck;* CRISPINA AVGVSTA. *Rev., Venus seated with sceptre, holding wreath-bearing Victory; dove below;* VENVS FELIX. *c. A.D. 180-3, Rome (aureus, 7.36 gm., diam. 20 mm., BMCRE 49).*

389

390

391

evident that the most highly skilled die-engravers were reserved for work on aurei and sestertii : denarii and the smaller *aes*,[233] though well engraved and struck, were of consistently lower quality. And it is evident, too, that Hadrian, while not averse to topical types by any means, always preferred to clothe them in stately references to his own active part in the government of the empire. There was indeed a very large and continual range of stock types of stock deities, sometimes specifically labelled, more often left to declare their identity by means of their attributes. Taken as a whole, however, the coinage surveyed the broad, unfolding tapestry of events as a focus upon Hadrian himself, from whose personal qualities it was possible for the Golden Age to arise, seen in the type of a young Genius, holding phoenix on globe (symbol of eternity), stepping out of a frame (of the years ?) above the legend SAEC(ulum) AVR(eum).[234] It was Hadrian who visited provinces, sailing the seas with fair winds 364 and wishes; Hadrian who reorganized provinces; Hadrian who led and honoured 363 armies; Hadrian who spoke to assembled 362 citizens; Hadrian whose *disciplina* guided 379· and informed the empire and its forces. This identification of emperor with empire was delicately done. The emperor was great, and appeared so on the obverse. The 358 achievements, on the reverse, were great too; but here the emperor was no more than a man (even if *princeps*) among men—a man, moreover, whose portrait could often appear without wreath. And, for all this overwhelming emphasis on his own personality, he did not neglect to coin with equal artistic magnificence for his wife

389, 390 Marcus Aurelius (for Divus Antoninus). *Obv., bust of Divus Antoninus, left shoulder draped ;* DIVVS ANTONINVS. *Rev., four-tiered funeral pyre ; quadriga on top ;* CONSECRATIO. c. *A.D. 161, Rome (aureus, 7.32 gm., diam. 19 mm., BMCRE 56).*

391 Antoninus Pius (for Faustina II). *Obv., bust of Faustina II, draped, her hair in bun over neck ;* FAVSTINA AVG(usta) ANTONINI AVG(usti) PII FIL(ia). c. *A.D. 152-6, Rome (aureus, 7.23 gm., diam. 20 mm., BMCRE 1083).*

Sabina and for his two heirs, first Aelius and then Antoninus. His fairly large series of eastern denarii followed along the general lines set by Rome; and even his copious re-coinage of Asiatic 'cistophori' (see above, p. 180), while including a number of types of strong traditional significance, underlined the spirit of the age by their close adherence to the portraiture of Rome.

Hadrian's coinage set the tone for that of the Antonines, although there were to be new developments. For the next 50 years, however, it remained true that the gold (usually produced with superb skill) bore types of a special nature seldom seen on the silver (often rather roughly produced), and that the sestertii enjoyed the same sort of superiority over the smaller *aes*. Technique as a whole tended to decline, and not only in portraiture (see above, p. 199): engraving, apart from that of the aurei, became notice-ably coarser, especially from 161 onwards; lettering began to lose its sense of confident proportion and spacing; and the flans them-selves, and particularly those of the sestertii, tended to lose that circularity which had previously been so evident, suggesting that changes in their manufacture had taken place, and for the worse.

The reverse types of Antoninus Pius put a heavy emphasis on his wife Faustina, associated with Juno and Venus in her life-time, and consecrated after her early death; and also on his adopted son Marcus Aure-lius, married to his daughter, the younger Faustina, and thereby cementing the full degree of imperial *concordia*. For the rest, the profuse issues of Antoninus consisted, so far as silver and smaller *aes* were concerned, mainly of the standard deities and

personifications, either labelled explicitly or not. The tendency throughout was to equate the spirit of the reverse with that of the em-peror seen on the obverse: a corn-measure; a largesse; a robust and graceful figure of Alexandria, honorific crown in hand; a thunderbolt; a figure of Britannia securely on her rock; [235] priestly symbols—all these looked to the man who, as vice-gerent for Jupiter, ruled the world with that combination of wisdom and strength and piety which made up the 'Optimus Princeps', and to whom specific reference could occasionally be made, as for example when his first ten years in power were due for celebration.

Under Marcus Aurelius and his co-emperor Lucius Verus (who dutifully com-memorated the dead Antoninus and hon-oured the imperial ladies) there was an inevitable shift in emphasis. War in the east and in Germany now for the first time began to destroy the serene equilibrium which Trajan and Hadrian had established, and Antoninus maintained; and by contrast with the peaceful types of Antoninus the reverses now look to Armenia, Parthia, the Germani and the Sarmati. Commodus him-self, now being trained by his father Marcus Aurelius to succeed him, appears as *princeps iuventutis*—that Julio-Claudian promotion connoting military proficiency and leader-ship which had been absent since the end of the first century. With the unhappy reign of Commodus all serenity was spent. He might pay lip-service to the conventions of previous coinages (e.g. in honouring Cris-pina with a prayer to the gods of marriage), but the emphasis must be on the *princeps*, who, if the armies remained loyal and

384, 359 360, 361 370 367, 391 365, 3 368, 3 380*, 389, 3 371 385*, 372 387*

212

Fortune stayed with him, would soldier on in luxurious stupidity to bear the burdens of the world. He was the first emperor to be assassinated (in 192) since Domitian's death in 96.

In a period of a century and a quarter which began with Galba and ended with Commodus, it would be true to say that the imperial coinage, in the course of a stately progress and proliferation that embraced two of the topmost peaks of artistic and technical beauty, moved steadily from the joint concept of the emperor and Rome towards that of the emperor alone. That movement was to continue, and with increasing emphasis, during the next century, reflecting the political realities of the times. Another movement, too, reflecting economic realities with equal clarity, was in progress. Coinage in gold continued during this period to be abundant, and of excellent fineness. That of silver was also abundant, but its fineness had been sinking steadily throughout the second century, until at the end of that century it was no more than about three-quarters fine.[236] Parallel with this change there was a strong tendency to produce more sestertii and fewer of the minor *aes* denominations. Whether or not the causes are to be sought in inflation or in a changing price-structure or both, these were symptoms of an economic imbalance that was to become dangerously clear in the third century, when the bimetallic rule of gold and silver supported by *aes* yielded more and more to a confidence in gold alone.

VII. INFLATION, DECENTRALIZATION, AND REFORM: FROM THE SEVERI TO DIOCLETIAN, A.D. 193-305

The murder of Commodus in 192 left a vacuum hard to fill, for he was the last of an imperial line which extended back, without violence or interruption, as far as any man could remember, and there was no dynastic successor. As after Nero's death, therefore, although the formal choice of an emperor lay with the Senate, the actual choice lay with the army, which invited P. Helvius Pertinax, an elderly and upright senator, imbued with all proper constitutional ideas, to assume the burden. Pertinax lasted only for three months, having failed to satisfy the hopes of the praetorian guards for a rich donative; and the praetorians then literally auctioned the empire, which went to Didius Julianus upon his offer of 6250 denarii a man. Julianus lasted only for two months. Public reaction to events was hostile, and a call went out to Pescennius Niger, the respected governor of Syria, whose legions proclaimed him emperor. Meanwhile Septimius Severus, governor of the much nearer Upper Pannonia, acted for himself. Proclaimed by the legions of the Danube and Rhine frontiers, he first conciliated the influential Clodius Albinus, governor of Britain, naming him his Caesar. In June 193 Severus entered Rome as the successor of Pertinax, whom he deified. By 195 he had defeated and killed Niger in the east, which he sternly reorganized. In 196 he gave the style of Caesar to Caracalla, his son by Julia Domna, and adopted the name Antoninus for himself and his family. In 197 Clodius Albinus, having by now set himself up as a rival emperor, was defeated and killed at Lyons; and Severus was at length free to wage war against Parthia. Five years were thus necessary to settle the convulsion caused by Commodus' death; and it was only after 198, with Severus entitled 'Parthicus Maximus', Caracalla as joint Augustus, and Geta as Caesar, that the central problems of administration could be systematically undertaken, themselves to be overtaken in turn by the campaign in Britain, leading to Severus' death at York in 211.[237]

This was an expensive period of years. Each new emperor, or aspirant to empire, had to buy his way in, either by outright largesse or by the ability to secure normal payment for his troops. Moreover Severus, once established, made altogether six great distributions of largesse to the Roman public, at an estimated cost of 220 million denarii.[238] In addition there were public

215

games and charities, and a programme of public building. Not only, therefore, was there an immense total issue of coinage: silver supplies were also 'stretched' by a sharply increased debasement of the denarius, and the weight of the denarius (as also that of the sestertius) showed instability.[239] The general availability of coinage-metals cannot have been easy. Down to the time of Commodus the vast majority of Roman imperial coinage, in all metals, had been issued centrally at Rome itself. Rome, indeed, was now still the great central mint, striking in turn for Pertinax, for Didius Julianus, and for Severus (with Clodius Albinus—at first his Caesar—and with his wife Julia Domna and his sons Caracalla and Geta all honoured and advertised by coinage in their names). But other mints also had to be supplied. Albinus, once in revolt, coined in all metals at Lugdunum, explicitly named on one issue: Pescennius Niger struck gold and silver only, probably at Antioch. Severus himself, with his focus of military action drawn eastward by Pescennius and then Parthia, may have operated mints at Laodicea, Emesa, and Alexandria.[240]

The short coinage of Pertinax at Rome, in gold, silver and *aes*, was produced with a beauty which belies its brevity. Commodus, it will be remembered, had latterly enjoyed the services of die-engravers who had been able to break away from the rigid sterility that was evident under Marcus Aurelius and Lucius Verus (see p. 199). The new school of engravers—for such it must have been—now made some portraits of splendid quality, with an amplitude, an honesty, and a decorative sense which

(certainly intended to emphasize the old man's well known virtues) had not been inspired in engravers since Antoninus Pius' time. As previously, aurei and sestertii received most care, and in all metals the reverses are distinctly less elaborate than the obverse portraits. But the content of the reverses was striking enough. LIBERATIS CIVIBVS frankly records the end of Commodus' tyranny. The dedication to Mens Laudanda is to that great goddess who could retrieve disaster, in Hannibal's time, after Lake Trasimene. Laetitia Temporum speaks of newly found rejoicing; and Providential Deorum supplies the shining star of power now to be seized by Rome in the person of Pertinax, himself both protected by the gods (DIS CVSTODIBVS) and also the provider of public largesse. No such stirring messages appeared on the coins of Didius Julianus, which, again well engraved, though with more evident haste, concentrated on military concord and imperial good fortune (each urgently needed), as well as on Manlia Scantilla and Didia Clara, his wife and daughter, with portraits of distinction.

Severus, until his death in 211, issued an immense coinage in all metals from Rome; and, reverting to earlier practice, he gave wide advertisement to members of the imperial house—to Julia Domna, his wife; to Caracalla and (initially) Albinus as his Caesars; to Caracalla as co-Augustus, with his wife Plautilla; and to his younger son Geta first as Caesar and finally (from 209) also as co-Augustus. As noted above, he coined also at eastern mints. The range of types was very great: though it included very many from the now traditional stock of standard motifs, there were often novelties, deftly applied, and rendered (as now usual) with a fine degree of skill on the gold and the sestertii, and less well on the denarii and smaller *aes*.[241] Severus' earliest issues, in which his portraiture had not yet settled to the assured proportions and decorative instinct of his mid-reign period, emphasized the loyalty of his legions, the high prestige of his wife Domna, and the fact that the gods were on his side: a loyal glance of his own was given to his native province of Africa, and coins in the name of his Caesar Albinus paid compliment to the circumstance of his association. Albinus, in his brief revolt, coined silver at Lyons—military in content, and rough in style. After Albinus' death there, Severus, who had already given great publicity to Caracalla as his Caesar, openly designating him as his successor, created him Augustus (in 198), with the younger son Geta as the new Caesar; and he could now safely go east to fight and defeat Pescennius, whose silver coins, rough and even sometimes illiterate, went out of their way to underline the legitimacy of his imperial claims ('Iustitia Aug', 'Victoria Iusti Aug').

In the middle years of Severus' coinage the conceptual and technical skill of the mint of Rome reached a fine level—a level, incidentally, which since it was never at all matched in eastern mints shows that those mints had to rely on local (and inferior) artists and workmen. As earlier, the majority of types fell within the now standard range, but there was a continuing desire to publicize Julia Domna (seen as Rome's 'Vesta Mater'), Caracalla and his wife Plautilla, and Geta, whose position was further

enhanced when he too was promoted Augustus (in 209). In these closing years of Severus' life, however, artistic skills at the mint of Rome were declining, and the portraiture which had until then been firm and controlled, with a clear indication of individuality, began to show signs of a feebler and more slipshod approach: the sense of inspiration generated by Severus' succession to Commodus was perhaps fading. Nevertheless Severus' vast coinage, taken as a whole from 193 to 211, is certainly one of the finest and most interesting of the empire, and not least because of its presentation of the concept of the imperial house.

For about a year after Severus' death and consecration power was shared by Caracalla and Geta as joint Augusti: they returned from Britain to Rome to an uneasy equilibrium maintained by their mother Domna, 'mother of the Augusti, mother of the Senate, mother of the fatherland'. But in June 212 Caracalla had Geta murdered. The coinage of his sole reign (to 217) has many points of interest. Type-emphasis shifted to new religious concepts, of eastern origin, including Aesculapius, Isis, Serapis, Luna and Sol, though Julia Domna still typified the Roman virtues of Vesta: in addition, Caracalla duly celebrated his victories in war, and the glories of the Circus Maximus. Portraiture received fresh stimulus, and Caracalla's features, especially on the sestertii, were magnificently rendered: wreath, cuirass and paludamentum combined with tight curls and good relief and modelling to produce portraits of formidable strength. Portraiture on the gold was perhaps less good than under Severus; but on silver it underwent a sudden improvement owing to the introduction of a new and larger denomination. This, now called the 'antoninianus' (without any real authority),[242] was almost certainly intended to pass as a double denarius—it showed the radiate crown which had long since marked the dupondius as a double As, and, under Trajan Decius, later distinguished the double sestertius. As such it was substantially larger in diameter than the denarius, weighing about 5 g. against the *c.* 3.10 of the denarius. On these new and larger coins the emperor's portrait achieved a strength and realism previously lacking on the smaller denarii, and the same was true of Domna, whose antoniniani show her bust upon a crescent. The antoniniani were handsome coins. Their silver content was no better than that of denarii, i.e. they were almost half alloy, and they did not even weigh twice the weight of denarii; but at a time when there was great pressure on currency supplies their good looks may well have achieved a readier acceptibility.[243] They did in fact constitute the first great overt act of depreciation in the currency of the Roman empire; and they must have tempted wary financiers to consider the possibility of a run on gold aurei, now a little lighter than they had been, but still (if the gold-price was tending to rise) absolutely reliable.

Caracalla was murdered in 217, while in the east: the troops there chose Macrinus as his successor, later confirmed at Rome, with his son Diadumenian as his Caesar. Macrinus never came to Rome, and so the mint of Rome, lacking a true version of his features, produced portraits totally unlike those of Macrinus' eastern mint (presum-

392, 393 Commodus. *Obv., head of Commodus, laureate ;* M COMM ANT P FEL(ix) AVG BRIT(annicus). *Rev., seated Fortuna holding bridled horse and cornucopiae ;* FORTVNAE MANENTI, C(OS) V P P. *A.D. 186-9, Rome (denarius, 2.72 gm., diam. 17.5 mm., BMCRE 231).*

394, 395 Commodus. *Obv., head of Commodus, laureate ;* M COMMOD ANT P FELIX AVG BRIT P P. *Rev., Hercules, with cornucopiae, sacrificing over garlanded altar, against which his club leans ; lion's skin on tree nearby ;* HERC(uli) COMMODIANO P M TR P XVI, COS VI, S C. *A.D. 190-1, Rome (sestertius, 27.09 gm., diam. 32 mm., BMCRE 669).*

396 Septimius Severus. *Rev., personification of Africa with elephant-skin head-dress ; lion at her feet ;* AFRICA, S C. *A.D. 194-5, Rome (dupondius, 11.37 gm., diam. 26 mm., BMCRE 523).*

397 Septimius Severus (for Clodius Albinus). *Obv., head of Albinus, left shoulder draped ;* D CLOD SEPT ALBINVS CAES. *A.D. 194-5, Rome (aureus, 7.39 gm., diam. 20 mm., BMCRE 93).*

398, 399 Septimius Severus (for Julia Domna). *Obv., bust of Domna, draped, her hair waved ;* IVLIA DOMNA AVG. *Rev., Venus holding apple and palm-branch and leaning on column ;* VENERI VICTR(ici). *c. A.D. 193-6, Rome (aureus, 7.31 gm., diam. 20 mm., BMCRE 47).*

400, 401 Septimius Severus. *Obv., bust of Septimius, laureate, draped and cuirassed ;* L SEPT SEV PERT AVG IMP VIIII. *Rev., confronting busts of Septimius, laureate and draped, and Geta draped and cuirassed ;* IMPERII FELICITAS. *A.D. 197, Rome (aureus, 7.28 gm., diam. 20 mm., BMCRE 221).*

402 Clodius Albinus. *Obv., head of Albinus, laureate ;* IMP CAES D CLO SEP ALB AVG. *A.D. 195-7, Lugdunum (denarius, 3.17 gm., diam. 19.1 mm., BMCRE (Sept. Sev.) 284).*

403 Pescennius Niger. *Obv., head of Pescennius, laureate ;* IMP CAES C PESCEN NIGER IVSTI AV(g). *c. A.D. 193-4, Antioch (denarius, 2.86 gm., diam. 18 mm., BMCRE 304).*

453, 454

406

431, 432

433

392

393

394

395

396

397

398

399

400

401

402

403

404

405

406

407

408

409

410

411

412

413

414

404, 405 Caracalla and Geta, joint reign. *Obv.,
head of Divus Septimius;* DIVO SEVERO PIO.
Rev., eagle with wreath in beak on thunderbolt;
CONSECRATIO. *A.D. 211, Rome (aureus,
7.42 gm., diam. 20 mm., BMCRE 19).*

406 Caracalla, sole reign (for Julia Domna).
*Obv., bust of Domna, draped and with stephane,
on crescent, her hair in horizontally ridged waves;*
IVLIA PIA FELIX AVG. *A.D. 211-7, Rome
(antoninianus, 4.85 gm., diam. 21 mm.,
BMCRE 27).*

407 Caracalla, sole reign. *Obv., bust of Caracalla,
laureate, draped and cuirassed;* M AVREL
ANTONINVS PIVS AVG GERM. *A.D. 215,
Rome (sestertius, 26.10 gm., diam. 32 mm.,
Oxford).*

408 Caracalla, sole reign. *Rev., view of the Circus
Maximus, with arcaded front and arch to r.;
within, obelisk and quadrigae; in background,
temple, triple-tiered colonnade, and quadriga on
arch;* P M TR P XVI IMP II, COS IIII P P, S C.
*A.D. 213, Rome (sestertius, 30.37 gm., diam.
35 mm., BMCRE 251).*

409, 410 Elagabalus. *Obv., bust of Elagabalus, laureate, draped and cuirassed;* IMP CAES M AVR
ANTONINVS AVG. *Rev., Victory with wreath
and palm;* VICTOR(ia) ANTONINI AVG. *A.D.
218-9, Rome (aureus, 6.18 gm., diam. 20 mm.,
BMCRE 30).*

411, 412 Elagabalus (for Julia Soaemias). *Obv.,
bust of Julia Soaemias, draped, her hair in
horizontally ridged waves;* IVLIA SOAEMIAS
AVGVSTA. *Rev., Cybele, turreted, on throne,
holding branch, l. arm on drum; two lions by
feet of throne;* MATER DEVM, S C. *A.D. 218-
22, Rome (sestertius, 18.32 gm., diam. 30 mm.,
BMCRE 374).*

413 Elagabalus (for Julia Paula). *Obv., bust of
Julia Paula, draped, her hair in horizontally
ridged waves;* IVLIA PAVLA AVG. *A.D. 219-
20, Rome (dupondius or As, 10.98 gm., diam.
25 mm., BMCRE 421).*

414 Elagabalus (for Aquilia Severa). *Obv., bust
of Aquilia Severa, draped;* IVLIA AQVILIA
SEVERA AVG. c. *A.D. 220, Rome (denarius,
3.46 gm., diam. 20 mm., BMCRE 187).*

ably Syrian Antioch). The types used on
the coinage, whether of Rome or Antioch,
were devoid of distinction or special interest. Macrinus lasted barely more than a
year. Julia Domna had died shortly after
Caracalla. Her sister, Julia Maesa, was of
Emesa, where her grandson (not yet
fifteen) held the hereditary high-priesthood
of the god Elagabalus, worshipped as the
local Ba'al in the form of a black, conical
stone. Maesa's plot to replace Macrinus by
this young moral pervert (himself called
Elagabalus from the god he served, but
proclaimed as Marcus Aurelius Antoninus, 409, 410
'legal' successor of the Severi) succeeded
when Macrinus was defeated and afterwards killed in 218. With Julia Maesa and
his mother, Julia Soaemias, now both 'Aug- 411, 412
ustae', Elagabalus reached Rome in 219,
when he married Julia Paula. It was from 413
Rome that most of his coinage was issued
—Antioch produced a little [244]—and at first
this coinage of Rome was conservative,
stressing the consecration of Caracalla, the
loyalty of Elagabalus' forces, his victory
over Macrinus, and the high dignity of
Maesa and Soaemias. But from 220 restraint was abandoned. The cult of the
Ba'al of Emesa was introduced at Rome,
and Elagabalus chose a virgin bride for the
god, and for himself, in the person of Aqui- 414
lia Severa. Types of this period reflect the
change. Sol himself appears: his blazing
star is a frequent adjunct to other designs:
Elagabalus, 'invictus' like Sol, of whom he
is 'sacerdos', is shown at sacrifice to that god
whose black stone is seen carried in a
triumphal chariot; and Aquilia Severa is
honoured by coinage before her rejection
in favour of Annia Faustina and her

ultimate recall. Such were the lurid threads interwoven into the plainer stuff of the stock repertoire of older types. The final and fatal thread was the coinage in honour of Elagabalus' cousin Alexianus, named Caesar in 221, as Marcus Aurelius Severus Alexander—a youth so popular that, influenced by his mother Julia Mamaea, the praetorians assassinated Elagabalus in 222.

His coinage had been executed with very varying skill. At its best—on some of the gold and many sestertii—it was fine and careful; and antoniniani again afforded good scope for portraiture. Taken as a whole, however, there was a certain roughness and unevenness throughout, and it is noticeable that lettering, once a major beauty of imperial coinage, was tending to lose its harmonious balance and, indeed, to acquire an often clumsy size: it may be wondered if the technical departments of die-engravers and of letterers were by now working too independently of each other. A major point of interest in Elagabalus' coins comes from the observation of his changing features, progressing from an almost Caracallan form, neat and stern, to the final stage—thickened, lightly bearded, and plainly dissolute. Under Severus Alexander, his courteously constitutional successor, virtually all of whose coinage was struck at Rome,[245] a new serenity came over the coinage. This was due partly to the care taken in producing well-rounded flans,[246] partly to care in striking, and partly also to 434, 435 Severus Alexander's actual portraiture—a smoothly engraved head, short-haired, full of modesty, reserved, its 'expressiveness' confined to the widely open eye which looks candidly forward and sometimes even

upward. The same gentleness and dignity characterized the portraits of his mother Julia Mamaea and his wife Sallustia Barbia 436, 4 Orbiana. Reverse types under Alexander 438 tended to revert, strongly and openly, from the orientalism of Elagabalus to pure Roman traditions. Jupiter and Venus were 435, 4 to be associated with Alexander and Mamaea: Concordia with Orbiana. Aequitas, a routine enough personification, now perhaps had a special connotation, for Alexander totally discontinued the antoninianus which, introduced by Caracalla, began to fade out with Elagabalus. It is true that Alexander's aurei were no heavier than Caracalla's (c. 6.55 g., 1/50 of a pound), and that his denarii, scarcely more than 3 g. (officially 1/96 of a pound), and alloyed to fifty per cent or more, showed no intrinsic improvement. But at least the open duplicity of a double-denarius weighing less than two denarii was abolished.[247]

There were, however, some remarkable types for Alexander, and it is now possible, as a result of recent and admirable study,[248] to see how the individual working sections of the Roman mint—the *officinae*—produced the coinage in cyclical rhythm. Gold, silver and *aes* were struck upon a regular pattern of expressed need, with most of the *officinae* working for the emperor and a minority for his ladies. By means of this system it was possible to interject special types or issues at any given moment. These could be of standard denominations within the regular coinage-structure, as for example the fine asses showing Alexander's Nymphaeum in 226, or they could be medallic, and outside that structure: examples are provided by splendid pieces, dignified and restrained, celebrating a largesse, or Alexander's relationship with his mother, or his mother's high importance to the *felicitas* of the empire.[249] It was not to be long before *officinae* were visibly marked on imperial coinage; but even now their flexibility can be seen and appreciated.

Ever since the time of Augustus the empire had been threatened, more or less regularly, by two dangers—Parthia and Germany; and the age-long migration tendency from east to west built up pressures against which Roman frontier-armies on the Euphrates and on the Rhine and Danube had constantly to fight. In 234–5 Alexander failed to stem the German menace. He and his mother were murdered in 235 near Mainz, and power was transferred to Maximinus, a giant of a Thracian soldier. Maximinus was the first of nearly 20 emperors—apart entirely from usurpers in Gaul, Britain, and the east—to rule the empire in the next 50 years. The political basis of the empire, so strong until the second century, had disintegrated: the military basis, so strong under Septimius Severus, was now to be eroded by rivalry, by sheer personal unfitness, by frontier dangers, and by financial stress. These events are clearly mirrored in the coinage. The weight of the aureus, the anchor of the Roman monetary system, fell progressively: by the time of Gallienus (260–8) it scarcely adhered to any standard of weight at all, it was often accompanied by pieces of one-third, and even the fineness of gold was variable. From this it must be clear that, as military expenditure rose, gold became scarcer and its value increased. Silver, too, was grievously affected. Balbinus and

Pupienus, who succeeded Maximinus as joint Augusti to rule for three months in 238, reintroduced the antoninianus : after *c.* 245 the denarius scarcely appeared. The antoninianus itself was progressively debased until, by *c.* 270, its silver content was nominal. *Aes*, in its turn, also suffered. The smaller denominations were struck less and less, and the sestertius (for a time) more and more, Trajan Decius (249–51) even striking a double sestertius. Although we lack any contemporary analysis of monetary history (or even price-changes) of those times, the lesson is clear. Confidence in the coinage was collapsing. The precious metals, whenever available (and whenever spared from imperial taxation), were hoarded and so denied to the general pool of currency. Their value thus rose. And finally *aes* had thrust upon it an even less than purely token role which resulted in the production of vast numbers of almost pure copper antoniniani.[250]

For some decades after Alexander the coin-types of the 'legitimist' emperors lapsed into something like a routine dullness. Each in turn claimed the protection of heavenly *providentia*, looked to Jupiter and the other great gods as champions, restored *libertas*, distributed *liberalitates*, relied on the *fides* of the soldiers, and boasted of the *pax* won by *victoria*, leading to triumph, general *laetitia*, *aequitas* (especially in the economy), and *securitas*; and there were of course the now traditional types for heirs and imperial ladies. It was as if emperors who were insecure, and too often ephemeral, felt that those public announcement were best that adhered most closely to the great dynastic coinages of earlier

415 ▶

416 ▶

415, 416 Pertinax. *Obv., bust of Pertinax, laureate, draped and cuirassed ;* IMP CAES P HELV(ius) PERTINAX AVG. *Rev., Fortuna holding rudder on globe and cornucopiae ;* DIS CVSTODIBVS, S C. *A.D. 193, Rome (sestertius, 26.25 gm., diam. 33 mm., BMCRE 26).*

417 Didius Julianus (for Manlia Scantilla). *Obv., bust of Manlia Scantilla, draped ;* MANL SCANTILLA AVG. *A.D. 193, Rome (aureus, 6.56 gm., diam. 19 mm., BMCRE 10).*

418, 419 Didius Julianus. *Obv., head of Didius Julianus, laureate ;* IMP CAES M DID IVLIAN AVG. *Rev., Concordia holding aquila (in r. hand) and standard ;* CONCORD MILIT. *A.D. 193, Rome (aureus, 6.77 gm., diam. 19 mm., BMCRE 1).*

420 Didius Julianus (for Didia Clara). *Obv., bust of Didia Clara, draped ;* DIDIA CLARA AVG. *A.D. 193, Rome (sestertius, 23.70 gm., diam. 32 mm., BMCRE 40).*

417 ▶

418

419

420

425

426

427

421, 422 Septimius Severus. *Obv., head of Septimius, laureate ;* L SEPT SEV PERT AVG IMP III. *Rev., Hercules (with club and lion's skin) and Liber (with inverted cup and ribboned thyrsus) standing on either side of panther, which catches drops from the cup ;* DIS AVSPICIB(us) TR P II COS II P P, S C. *A.D. 194, Rome (sestertius, 24.27 gm., diam. 31 mm., BMCRE 505).*

423, 424 Septimius Severus (for Caracalla). *Obv., bust of Caracalla, draped and cuirassed ;* M AVR ANTONINVS CAES. *Rev., priestly emblems (lituus, axe, patera, jug, ladle, sprinkler) ;* SEVERI AVG PII FIL(ius). *A.D. 196-7, Rome*

(sestertius, 25.22 gm., diam. 33 mm., BMCRE 612).

425 Caracalla (for Julia Domna). *Obv., bust of Domna, draped, head bare ;* IVLIA AVGVSTA. *A.D. 211-2, Rome (aureus, 6.94 gm., diam. 19.5 mm., BMCRE V, p. 432, n). (For rev. see No. 428.)*

426, 427 Septimius Severus and Caracalla, joint reign. *Obv., bust of Caracalla, laureate, draped and cuirassed ;* M AVRELIVS ANTON AVG. *Rev., bust of Geta, draped and cuirassed ;* P SEPT GETA CAES PONT. *A.D. 198, Rome (aureus, 6.27 gm., diam. 19.5 mm., BMCRE 121).*

times. The chief interest in their coinages was to be found partly in the portraiture, partly in the technical and economic history of production. Portraiture, indeed, continued at a generally very high level. As long as the sestertius was struck (that is, until the reign of Gallienus), it was on this fine, large coin that the best portrait-work appeared: carefully studied, and admirably engraved in high yet sensitive relief, with an obvious desire to represent a man faithfully and humanely. The progressively dwindling output of smaller *aes* attained this standard less often. Aurei (usually produced with care) and antoniniani (of more variable technical quality) also showed good, clear portraits; but they were often good only because they were clear. In an age when recognition of the imperial features, short reign by short reign, was becoming more and more important, these gold and silver portraits (seen on coins which were the medium of military pay) were unequivocal, but they lacked the personality which the larger *aes* continued so brilliantly to express.

Amid the vast stream of standard types —multiplied as they were by the proliferation of an ever more debased silver coinage —there were however many occasions when a new message or a new emphasis was conceived and transmitted. These are too many to recount in detail in a short survey, but some examples may be given, and these suggest that the choice of types was not entirely governed, even now, by the dead hand of traditionalist bureaucracy. Balbinus and Pupienus, reviving the old concept of absolute parity in joint rule (they were both Augusti, and both *pontifex maximus*), went out of their way to point

to the *concordia* which bound them together. Ten years later, in 248, Philip and his son celebrated Rome's thousandth anniversary with magnificent games, and the coinage, as well as picturing many of the exotic animals which featured in those games, shows also the Wolf and Twins [251] and legends (also for Otacilia Severa and Philip II) proudly marking the *Saeculares Augg* (Augustorum) and the new *saeculum* now just beginning. The short reign of Trajan Decius was marked by stern efforts to repel barbarian pressures from Germany and the Balkans; by a new and splendid (but ephemeral) monetary denomination— the double sestertius; and by a series of coins commemorating 'good' emperors of the past, including that Trajan whose soldierly name he assumed.[252]

The accession in 253 of Valerian (who associated his son Gallienus in power with himself) found the Roman empire in a condition of military disintegration. As if barbarian threats to the northern frontiers were not enough, Persia was pressing dangerously in the east, where ultimately (in 260) Valerian was captured by the Persian Sapor. Usurpers, moreover, further weakened the strength of Rome. Already under Philip there had been shadowy figures—Pacatian, Jotapian, Silbannacus, Sponsianus—who left a ripple on the face of history and of coinage.[253] About 253–4 Uranius Antoninus set himself up briefly in the east at Emesa, coining in gold alone with types which, when they did not echo those of Rome, again celebrated the Emesan cult of the god Elagabalus.[254] Even greater trouble was to come from the west, where Postumus set himself up as the emperor of an

*, 468, 0, 472
6, 467

independent Gaul *c.* 259, to be followed by
Victorinus and the Tetrici, father and son,
with Laelian and Marius as sub-contenders.
The damage to Rome caused by the seces-
sion of Gaul, a rich provincial area, was
serious; and this can be judged by the profuse coinage, from such mints as Cologne,
Trier, Lyons, and Milan, which these Gallic
emperors issued.[255] Postumus' coinage is
of dramatic interest and indeed some splendour. It included a good deal of gold; a
mass of antoniniani of a silver-content
which, if now very low, compared with that
of Valerian; and a remarkable volume of
aes (including many sestertii), much of it
conspicuous for the absence of the s c
which still traditionally marked the dying
series of *aes* from the mint of Rome.

The Gallic provinces had normally in
the past possessed a robust sense of individualism; and Postumus expressed this
clearly. He was fighting, as Mars, for a
romanitas threatened by weakness in the
central government at Rome. Possibly he
was prepared to treat with that government: he himself assumed the role of a
Hercules (as Commodus had done before 0, 461
him: see p. 206), and by the agency
of Mercury, the *internuntius deorum*, he
could try to do a deal with that other god-
like figure, the emperor at Rome.[256] The
propagandist impact of his abundant coinage, with its unequivocal types, must have
been great, and all the greater for the skill
with which it was produced. His gold is 4, 459
of a mature and confident beauty, and in- 463*
cludes a facing portrait which is one of the
great glories of the Roman imperial series.
The antoniniani are, as usual, much more
variable, but these too show certain por-

traits and reverse designs which are in re-
freshingly sharp contrast to the issues of
the previous two decades. Even the sestertii, obviously produced by men of much
less skill, and not infrequently overstruck
on older coins, had a certain hard, linear
strength. With Postumus' successors in the 464*, 465* 466, 472
declining bid for an *imperium Galliarum*—
Laelian, Marius, Victorinus, and the two
Tetrici—splendour on the gold also declined, into a merely exquisite neatness; and
the workmanship of the antoniniani, sometimes good, was more often slipshod to a 468, 469
degree consonant with urgency of produc- 472
tion and a growing lack of skilled labour.

Much the same was true at this time of
Rome itself. The reign of Valerian in asso- 473, 474
ciation with Gallienus (253–60) showed a
continuation of former Roman idiom, with
gold that was careful rather than beautiful,
antoniniani that were often still bold, and
aes (with s c) of noticeably rough technique:
the best talents in the mint of Rome (still
with six *officinae*) were reserved for special
'medallions' or presentation pieces. Under
Gallienus as sole emperor (260-8), with the
empire increasingly rent, the mint of Rome
(now with 12 *officinae*) had to issue more and
more coin of diminishing intrinsic value:
his antoniniani, now of almost pure copper,
were finally produced with a carelessness
matching those of the Tetrici in Gaul.
Gallienus' gold, however, including fine 500*
medallions as well as aurei, showed an alto- 475
gether superior skill in the rendering of a
new portrait-idiom of markedly hellenistic
character, with fine, small, delicate features,
an abundance of softly dressed hair, and a
frequent emphasis upon the muscles of neck
and shoulder. A disintegrating empire and

428 Caracalla (for Julia Domna). *Rev., Domna seated, holding branch and sceptre ;* MAT AVGG MAT SEN M(at) PATR. *A.D. 211-7, Rome (aureus, 6.94 gm., diam. 20 mm., BMCRE V, p. 432, n.). (For obv. see No. 425.)*

429, 430 Maximinus I (for Maximus). *Obv., bust of Maximus, draped ;* MAXIMVS CAES GERM. *Rev., Maximus, in military dress, by two standards, holding baton and spear ;* PRINCIPI IVVENTVTIS, S C. *A.D. 236-7, Rome (sestertius, 22.49 gm., 37 mm., BMCRE 213).*

431, 432 Macrinus. *Obv., bust of Macrinus, laureate, draped and cuirassed ;* IMP C M OPEL SEV MACRINVS AVG. *Rev., Jupiter with thunderbolt and sceptre ;* PONTIF MAX TR P COS P P. *A.D. 217, (?) Antioch (aureus, 7.05 gm., diam. 21 mm., BMCRE 30).*

433 Macrinus (for Diadumenian). *Obv., bust of Diadumenian, draped ;* M OPEL ANT DIADVMENIAN CAES. *A.D. 217-8, (?) Antioch (aureus, 7.16 gm., diam. 20 mm., BMCRE 83).*

434, 435 Severus Alexander. *Obv., bust of Severus Alexander, laureate, draped and cuirassed ;* IMP C M AVR SEV ALEXAND AVG. *Rev., Jupiter with thunderbolt and sceptre ;* IOVI CONSERVATORI. *A.D. 222, Rome (aureus, 6.38 gm., diam. 21 mm., BMCRE 55).*

436, 437 Severus Alexander (for Julia Mamaea). *Obv., bust of Mamaea, draped, wearing stephane ;* IVLIA MAMAEA AVGVSTA. *Rev., Cupid reaching up to Venus with apple and sceptre ;* VENVS GENETRIX, S C. *A.D. 223, Rome (sestertius, 22.98 gm., 32 mm., BMCRE 154).*

438 Severus Alexander (for Sallustia Barbia Orbiana). *Obv., bust of Orbiana, draped, wearing stephane ;* SALL BARBIA ORBIANA AVG. *A.D. 225, Rome (As, 11.10 gm., 26 mm., BMCRE 298).*

439, 440 Maximinus I. *Obv., bust of Maximinus, laureate and draped ;* MAXIMINVS PIVS AVG GERM. *Rev., Victory holding wreath and palm by seated and bound captive ;* VICTORIA GERM. *A.D. 236-7, Rome (denarius, 2.44 gm., diam. 20 mm., BMCRE 186).*

431

432

433

434

435

436

437

438

439

440

441

442

443

444

445

446

447

448

449

450

451

452

453

454

455

456

457

458

459

460

461

441 Gordian I (with Gordian II). *Obv., bust of Gordian I, laureate, draped and cuirassed ;* IMP M ANT GORDIANVS AFR(icanus) AVG. *A.D. 238, Rome (denarius, 3.03 gm., diam. 19 mm., BMCRE 11).*

442 Gordian II (with Gordian I). *Obv., bust of Gordian II, laureate, draped and cuirassed ;* IMP M ANT GORDIANVS AFR AVG. *A.D. 238, Rome (denarius, 3.03 gm., diam. 19 mm., BMCRE 19).*

443 Pupienus. *Obv., bust of Pupienus, radiate, draped and cuirassed ;* IMP CAES M CLOD(ius) PVPIENVS AVG. *A.D. 238, Rome (sestertius, 22.30 gm., diam. 32 mm., BMCRE 43).*

444 Balbinus. *Obv., bust of Balbinus, radiate, draped and cuirassed ;* IMP CAES D CAEL(ius) BALBINVS AVG. *A.D. 238, Rome (antoninianus, 5.15 gm., diam. 25 mm., BMCRE 67).*

445, 446 Gordian III. *Obv., bust of Gordian III, radiate, draped and cuirassed ;* IMP CAES M ANT GORDIANVS AVG. *Rev., Aequitas holding scales and cornucopiae ;* AEQVITAS AVG. *A.D. 238-40, Rome (antoninianus, 4.17 gm., diam. 22 mm., BM).*

447 Gordian III (for Sabinia Tranquillina). *Obv., bust of Tranquillina on crescent, draped and wearing stephane ;* SABINIA TRANQVILLINA AVG. *A.D. 241, Rome (antoninianus, 4.40 gm., diam. 22 mm., BM).*

448, 449 Philip I (with Philip II). *Obv., bust of Philip I, radiate, draped and cuirassed ;* IMP PHILIPPVS AVG. *Rev., wolf and twins ;* SAECV-LARES AVGG, II *(2nd officina). A.D. 248, Rome (antoninianus, 4.12 gm., diam. 22 mm., BM).*

450, 451 Philip I (for Otacilia Severa). *Obv., bust of Otacilia, draped and wearing stephane ;*

OTACIL SEVERA AVG. *Rev., temple containing sceptred statue of Roma ;* SAECVLVM NOVVM. *A.D. 248, Rome (aureus, 4.52 gm., diam. 22 mm., BM).*

452 Trajan Decius. *Rev., personification of Dacia, with staff topped by ass's head ;* DACIA. *c. A.D. 249, Rome (aureus, 4.11 gm., diam. 21 mm., BM).*

453, 454 Trajan Decius. *Obv., bust of Decius, radiate, draped and cuirassed ;* IMP C M Q TRAIANVS DECIVS AVG. *Rev., Felicitas with caduceus and cornucopiae ;* FELICITAS SAECVLI, S C. *A.D. 249-51, Rome (double sestertius, 42.60 gm., diam. 35 mm., BM).*

455 Trebonianus Gallus. *Obv., bust of Gallus, radiate, draped and cuirassed ;* IMP CAE C VIB(ius) TREB GALLVS AVG. *A.D. 251-3, Rome (antoninianus, 3.78 gm., diam. 21 mm., BM).*

456 Aemilian. *Obv., bust of Aemilian, radiate, draped and cuirassed ;* IMP AEMILIANVS PIVS FEL(ix) AVG. *A.D. 253, Rome (antoninianus, 2.84 gm., diam. 21 mm., BM).*

457 Uranius Antoninus. *Obv., bust of Uranius, laureate, draped and cuirassed ;* L IVL(ius) AVR SVLP(icius) VRA ANTONINVS. *c. A.D. 253-4, Emesa (aureus, 5.79 gm., diam. 22 mm., BM).*

458, 459 Postumus. *Obv., bust of Postumus, with decorated helmet, cuirassed ;* POSTVMVS AVG. *Rev., trophy of arms between two seated captives, one bound ;* P M G(ermanicus) M(aximus) T(r) P COS III P P. *c. A.D. 261, (?) Lugdunum (aureus, 5.95 gm., diam. 22 mm., BM).*

460, 461 Postumus. *Obv., bust of Postumus, radiate, with the club and lion's skin of Hercules ;* POSTVMVS AVG. *Rev., bow, club, and quiver ;* P M TR P VIIII COS IIII P P. *c. A.D. 267, (?) Colonia Agrippinensis (Cologne) (antoninianus, 3.56 gm., diam. 20 mm., BM).*

dire economic pressures had not yet submerged the artistic traditions of engravers
475, 476 at Rome: the tragi-comic boast of *Ubique Pax* was rendered with taste and skill. *Aes*, by contrast, was (as under Valerian) rough and ready—and sparingly issued in any
478, 479 case: even more sparing under Claudius II (268–70), it petered out altogether with
480 Quintillus (270), whose coinage was chiefly remarkable for the great commemorative issues in honour of Claudius.

Rome, of course, was by no means the only mint working at this time for the 'legitimate' emperors based at Rome.[257] Already, for a long period, eastern coinage had been produced from time to time, that of Septimius Severus being notable (see
445, 446 448, 453 above, p. 216): Gordian III, Philip, Trajan Decius and Trebonianus Gallus had continued this policy of decentralization. Nor was decentralization seen only in eastern
455 coinage, for Trebonianus Gallus probably coined also at Mediolanum (Milan), giving expression to the increasing need for a source of monetary supply nearer to the Alps, the Rhine, and the Danube than Rome was. By the time of Valerian and Gallienus an even wider range of mints, for gold and for antoniniani (i.e. for military purposes above all), had been established: Rome, Milan, and a mint or mints in the east were now joined by Lugdunum (Lyons), Siscia (Sissek) in Pannonia, and possibly another mint (? Viminacium) in
478, 479 the Balkans; and Claudius II was to open yet another important new mint at Cyzicus in Asia Minor. It is evident that the problems of monetary supply (and the urgency of that supply) could now be effectively met only by a wider network of mints: the days were gone when a Hadrian or an Antoninus Pius could supply the whole empire from Rome alone. In general the separate identities of these supporting mints are shown by clearly distinct differences of style and fabric. Sometimes, too, identification is provided or suggested by the continuation, into a later and certain period of existence, of elements (e.g. mint-marks) which are now first seen. The types of these other mints closely followed the basic pattern established at Rome, the influence of which was always dominant: even at Alexandria, a mint striking Greek-style coinage in Greek denominational values for essentially un-Roman communities since Augustus' reign, it can be seen that the mint-officials usually looked over their shoulder to see what general themes and particular types Rome was emphasizing.

Under Aurelian (270–5) and his successors down to the monetary reform of Diocletian in 294[258] this system of decentralized mints was maintained with little change, though Aurelian added the mints of Serdica and Tripolis, and moved the production of coinage from Milan to Ticinum (T).[259] More important was the monetary reform which occurred under Aurelian. Hitherto, as has been seen, the double denarius (or 'antoninianus') introduced on a strongly alloyed standard by Caracalla in 215 (see above, p. 218) had steadily declined in silver content until it became almost pure copper under Gallienus, by which time also *aes* was (in sympathy) almost defunct and even gold—now the only reliable measure of value—very variable in its weight. The chief indication of Aurelian's reform (apart from the reintroduction of excellent technique, of steady weights for gold, and of a wider range of supporting *aes*) lies in the formula appearing on many of his antoniniani, which, now still very base, and containing only about 4 per cent of silver, are marked xxi (or xx.i or xx) or, in Greek numerals, ka (or k.a). The frequent appearance of the punctuated versions (xx.i, k.a.) shows that the formula expresses, not the figures 21, but either an equivalence, i.e. 20 and (=) 1, or (since x had indicated 'denarius' since its earliest inception : see above, p. 46) 2 denarii = 1 unit. If the antoninianus of Caracalla was (and had remained) a double denarius, then the continuation—and the restoration—by Aurelian of a radiate-head and silvery-looking piece marked xx.i seems to indicate that he was emphasizing the continuation of Caracalla's double denarius, though of course at a far lower intrinsic value.[260] In other words, Aurelian, after the currency disasters of the 260s, was restoring the status quo as nearly as possible to what it had been under Valerian, and his 'reform' was more probably an attempt to recapture past stability rather than an innovation.[261]

Aurelian's coinage, from dies carefully engraved and well struck, introduced a new, hard, clear style of portraiture that was to endure with modifications, for some three decades. The imperial features were heavily stylized, with less attempt at individualism, perhaps, than at the rendering of a stern and furrowed face beneath the closely cut hair which covers an often very long head. On the gold and the antoniniani the reverse types were in general unremarkable, as also on most of the *aes*, though (?) sestertii of Rome showed fine portraits of the empress Severina and Asses from Serdica stressed the emperor's role as the protégé of *Sol Dominus Imperii Romani*. This *aes* now lacked the hitherto regular s c. At the mint of Rome the number of *officinae* fluctuated. There was, as is known, serious trouble at one moment with the *monetales* of Rome under Aurelian.[262] But his most serious trouble lay in the increasingly dangerous pressures upon the imperial frontiers, including those of the east, where Zenobia, queen of Palmyra, engineered the assumption of the title Augustus by her son Vabalathus in a rebellion which, successful in capturing Antioch and its mint, ended only by Aurelian's personal command in the capture of the city.

The coinage of his successors down to Carinus showed few new elements, though that of Probus (276–82) was remarkable both for its abundance and more varied reverses and also for the much more frequent use of armoured portraits for the emperor, whose armies were active for Rome in Gaul, on the Rhine, in the Balkans, and in the east. Carus did not hesitate to appear on coinage as 'Deus et Dominus'. Essential change was to come with Diocletian, chosen as emperor by the military in 284. A soldier and an administrator of equal strength and competence, Diocletian during his long reign transformed the empire from a state of weakness to one of stability. Recognizing the magnitude of his task he appointed Maximian as his Caesar in 285, assuming the title *Jovius* himself and giving that of *Herculius* to Maximian : in declaring their respective protector-gods he declared also their relative positions. One year later Maximian became co-Augustus,

462 Philip II (with Philip I). *Obv., bust of Philip II, laureate, draped and cuirassed;* IMP M IVL PHILIPPVS AVG. *A.D. 248, Rome (sestertius, 21.20 gm., diam. 28 mm., BM).*

463 Postumus. *Obv., bust of Postumus, nearly frontal, cuirassed;* POSTVMVS AVG. *A.D. 259-68, (?) Colonia Agrippinensis (aureus, 6.67 gm., diam. 21 mm., BM).*

464,465 Victorinus. *Obv., bust of Victorinus, laureate and cuirassed;* IMP CAES VICTORINVS P F AVG. *Rev., bust of Sol, radiate and draped;* INVICTVS. *A.D. 268-70, Gaul (aureus, 4.72 gm., diam. 19 mm., BM).*

466 Laelian. *Obv., bust of Laelian, laureate and cuirassed;* IMP C LAELIANVS P F AVG. c. *A.D. 268, (?) Moguntiacum (Mainz) (aureus, 6.63 gm., diam. 20.5 mm., BM).*

467 Marius. *Obv., bust of Marius, radiate, draped and cuirassed;* IMP C MARIVS P F AVG. c. *A.D. 268, Gaul (antoninianus, 2.41 gm., diam. 16 mm., BM).*

468,469 Victorinus. *Obv., bust of Victorinus, radiate and cuirassed;* IMP C VICTORINVS P F AVG. *Rev., Pietas sacrificing at altar;* PIETAS AVG. *A.D. 268-70, Gaul (antoninianus, 3.10 gm., diam. 23 mm., BM).*

470,471 Tetricus I. *Obv., bust of Tetricus I, laureate and cuirassed, with spear and shield;* IMP TETRICVS AVG. *Rev., Spes holding up flower and raising skirt;* SPES PVBLICA. *A.D. 270-3, Gaul (aureus, 3.84 gm., diam. 20 mm., BM).*

472 Tetricus I (for Tetricus II). *Obv., bust of Tetricus II, radiate, draped and cuirassed;* C PIV ESV TETRICVS CAES. *A.D. 270-3, Gaul (antoninianus, 3.46 gm., diam. 20 mm., BM).*

473,474 Valerian with Gallienus. *Obv., bust of Valerian, laureate and cuirassed;* IMP C P LIC(inius) VALERIANVS P F AVG. *Rev., Apollo with laurel-branch and lyre;* APOLINI (*sic*) CONSERVA(tori), S C. *A.D. 253-9, Rome (sestertius, 16.04 gm., diam. 28 mm., BM).*

475,476 Gallienus (sole reign). *Obv., head of Gallienus crowned with reeds;* GALLIENAE AVGVSTAE *((?) form of vocative). Rev., Victory in galloping biga;* VBIQVE PAX. *A.D. 259-68, Rome (aureus, 5.99 gm., diam. 21 mm., BM).*

477 Gallienus (for Salonina). *Obv., bust of Salonina, draped, her hair waved and plaited;* CORNELIA SALONINA AVG. *A.D. 259-68, Rome (sestertius, 26.10 gm., diam. 32 mm., BM).*

466

467

468

469

470

471

472

473

474

475

476

477

478

479

480

481

482

483

484

485

486   487

488   489

490   491

492   493

494

495

496

497

498

499

478, 479 Claudius II (Gothicus). *Obv., bust of Claudius, radiate and cuirassed ;* IMP C M AVR CLAVDIVS AVG. *Rev., trophy of arms between two captives, seated and bound ;* VICTORIAE GOTHIC. *A.D. 268-70, Cyzicus (antoninianus, 2.94 gm., diam. 21.5 mm., BM).*

480 Quintillus. *Obv., bust of Quintillus, radiate and draped ;* IMP C M AVR CL(audius) QVIN-TILLVS AVG. *A.D. 270, Rome (antoninianus, 2.93 gm., diam. 19 mm., BM).*

481 Aurelian. *Rev., Sol, radiate, with laurel-branch and bow, trampling down an enemy ;* ORIENS AVG, △ (= 4th officina), XXIR(oma). *A.D. 270-5, Rome (antoninianus, 4.41 gm., diam. 22 mm., BM).*

482 Aurelian. *Rev., Mars advancing with spear and trophy ;* P M TB (*sic*) P VII COS II P P. *A.D. 270-5, (?) Rome (aureus, 6.23 gm., diam. 22 mm., BM).*

483, 484 Aurelian. *Obv., bust of Aurelian, radiate and cuirassed ;* IMP AVRELIANVS AVG. *Rev., bust of Severina, draped, on crescent, with steph-ane on her head ;* SEVERINA AVG. *A.D. 270-5, (?) Rome (sestertius, 13.19 gm., diam. 28 mm., BM).*

485 Vabalathus. *Obv., bust of Vabalathus, lau-reate and draped ;* VABALATHVS VCRIMDR. *A.D. 270-1, Antioch (antoninianus, 3.52 gm., diam. 23 mm., BM).*

486 Tacitus. *Obv., bust of Tacitus, radiate and cuirassed, with spear and shield ;* IMP C M CL TACITVS P AVG. *A.D. 275-6, Siscia (aureus, 6.94 gm., diam. 23 mm., BM).*

487 Florian. *Obv., bust of Florian, radiate, draped and cuirassed ;* IMP C M AN(nius) FLORIANVS AVG. *A.D. 276, Lugdunum (antoninianus, 3.17 gm., diam. 22 mm., BM).*

488, 489 Probus. *Obv., bust of Probus, helmeted and cuirassed, with spear and shield ;* IMP PROBVS AVG. *Rev., bust of Sol, radiate and draped ;* SOLI INVICTO COMITI AVG. *A.D. 276-82, Rome (aureus, 6.19 gm., diam. 20 mm., BM).*

490, 491 Probus. *Obv., bust of Probus, radiate and in consular robe, holding eagle-tipped sceptre ;* IMP C M AVR PROBVS P AVG. *Rev., personi-fication of the city of Siscia seated between two river gods and holding diadem ;* SISCIA PROBI AVG ; XXIQ (= 5th officina) in exergue. *A.D. 276-82, Siscia (antoninianus, 4.25 gm., diam. 24 mm., BM).*

492, 493 Carus. *Obv., bust of Carus, laureate and cuirassed ;* DEO ET DOMINO CARO AVG. *Rev., Victory on globe with wreath and palm ;* VICTORIA AVG. *A.D. 282-3, Siscia (aureus, 4.87 gm., diam. 20 mm., BM).*

494 Carinus (with Carus). *Obv., bust of Carinus, radiate and cuirassed ;* IMP C M AVR CARINVS P F AVG. *c. A.D. 283-5, Siscia (antoninianus, 3.92 gm., diam. 21 mm., BM).*

495 Numerian (with Carus). *Obv., bust of Num-erian, radiate and cuirassed ;* IMP C NVMERIA-NVS AVG. *c. A.D. 283-4, Lugdunum (antoni-nianus, 4.28 gm., diam. 22.5 mm., BM).*

496, 497 Diocletian with Maximian Herculius. *Obv., bust of Diocletian, laureate and draped ;* IMP C C VAL DIOCLETIANVS P F AVG. *Rev., bust of Maximian, laureate, with club and lion's skin ;* IMP C MAXIMIANVS AVG. *A.D. 285, (?) Lugdunum (aureus, 5.33 gm., diam. 20 mm., BM).*

498, 499 Diocletian (for Galerius as Caesar). *Obv., bust of Galerius, radiate, draped and cuirassed ;* GAL VAL MAXIMIANVS NOB CAES. *Rev., prince, in military dress, with standard and sceptre ;* PRINCIPI IVVENTVT ; XXIΓ (= 3rd officina) in exergue. *After A.D. 294, Rome (antoninianus, 3.60 gm., diam. 24 mm., BM).*

and finally, in 293, the two Augusti were joined by two new Caesars, Galerius and Constantius, in a new imperial partnership of four to govern and protect the empire. Aurei down to this time, after beginning at a weight of 70 to the pound of gold (and marked o, i.e. 70, at Antioch), increased to a rate of 60 (at Antioch).[263] Antoniniani, still often with XXI, and of billon with a minimum of silver, continued as before, accompanied by smaller, laureate billon pieces and by a very few *aes* pieces. The mints at work were Lugdunum (4 *officinae*), Treveri (2), Rome (7), Ticinum (6), Siscia (3), Heraclea (5), Cyzicus (6), Antioch (10), and Tripolis (2): the addition of Treveri and Heraclea, and the scale of production at Antioch, clearly reflect military needs. In general character the coinage of these mints down to 293 continued along the lines set by Aurelian, with a hard, clear style and many conventional types. But new conceptions were creeping in, and not least on the gold, where, after a conventional start, a newly modified portrait-style developed, with heads (instead of armoured busts) that were now larger, in higher and well modelled relief, and with a more sensitive indication of personal individuality.

Among the major problems of these years was the alienation of Britain from the rest of the empire; Carausius, setting himself up as Augustus in 287, and straddling the Channel with his footholds at Bononia (Boulogne) and Rotomagus (Rouen), exerted so strong a power that he was able to pose as an imperial partner of Diocletian and Maximian, his 'fratres', and to maintain his position for six years until Allectus (293–6), also a usurper, killed and displaced

him. Carausius issued abundant coinage,[264] much of it from London (ML) and C(amulodunum ?, Colchester), some also from RSR (Richborough ?) and across the Channel, a very little from BRI(conium ?, = Viriconium, Wroxeter), and a mass that bore no mint mark. A great deal of this coinage was rough in the extreme, but it is of special interest because of its range, its adherence to the norms of the coinage of Diocletian and Maximian (for example, with XXI at first on many antoniniani), its inclusion of some gold (on a light standard), its anticipation of Diocletian's later 'reformed' *argenteus*, and the novelty and vigour of many of its types. Among the latter is a comprehensive legionary series, with some fine 'Adventus' types, the famous 'Expectate Veni' (with Britannia welcoming Carausius),[265] the Wolf and Twins with 'Romano (rum) Renov(atio)', and 'Rest(itutum) Saec (ulum)': with these may be classed Carausius' facing portrait (modelled on that of Postumus; see above, p. 233), the triple portrait of Carausius with his 'colleagues' Diocletian and Maximian, the obverses (London and ? Colchester) impudently struck in the names of Diocletian and Maximian alone, and even the recently found medallions of Carausius, admirable in workmanship. By contrast the coinage of Allectus (293–6)—with gold, antoniniani and halves, but no argentei—from London and ? Colchester is less remarkable: it was neat, but it lacked the rough vigour of Carausius.[266]

In 294 Diocletian and his partners carried out a reform of the coinage more radical than any that had ever been attempted before. Aurei continued at 60 to the pound, being accompanied not infrequently by larger or smaller multiples. The argentei introduced by Carausius were officially adopted—silver coins at a weight of 3 g. or just over, which were a revival of the old 'Neronian' denarius. These were supported by large copper coins, now known as 'folles', which contained a small percentage of silver and weighed *c.* 10 g. Some smaller pieces were also produced. Issued initially from a range of nine mints stretching from end to end of the empire, this reformed coinage was remarkable for a feature which had never previously been seen in the coinage of Rome : the reverse types of the argentei and the folles, at any rate to begin with, were standardized throughout the range of mints—XCVI (= 1/96 of a pound of silver) or a camp-gate or the imperial colleagues at sacrifice for the argentei,[267] and GENIO POPVLI ROMANI (with few and special exceptions) on the folles. The Genius of the Roman people was in fact their guardian and romanizing spirit, and it is a measure both of Diocletian's vision and also of his bureaucratic power that he was able to insist on the near-universal use of this 'civilian' type with its appeal for universal *romanitas*. The argentei, by contrast, bore mainly military types appropriate to those who received them in military pay. Again by contrast, the gold (not struck at all mints) concentrated upon the gods (and especially the tutelary gods Jupiter and Hercules) and upon the four tetrarchs— their partnership, their mutual sense of duty, and their military efforts on behalf of the empire. Nowhere is this better seen than in the superb series of gold multiples surviving from the Arras hoard, of which

those which commemorate Constantius' recovery of Britain from Allectus (enabling a mint to be opened at London) are perhaps of outstanding interest.[268] It is evident that the great mint artists—and not merely at Rome, but at Treveri (Trier) and elsewhere —were still admirably employed in the production of large and special pieces as well as for normal aurei. However, the general standard of technique was excellent on the whole range of Diocletian's reformed coinage, folles included. Most mints continued to operate on the *officina* system, seen in the careful addition of *officina* marks;[269] and the network of mints, the near-uniformity of types for silver and the folles, the meticulous technique (amounting often to real beauty, especially on the gold and its multiples), and the sheer abundance of production must, in combination, have endowed the new coinage with a great importance in its own time. Today its contribution to the understanding of the political notions of that time is considerable.[270]

As a currency, nevertheless, it was not stable, and it is now apparent that Diocletian's Edict on Maximum Prices in 301 was accompanied by a measure which doubled the values of the argenteus and the follis in relation to gold.[271] At the same time a new and significant type appeared on the folles —*Sacra Moneta* with variants, emphasizing by 'sacra' the inviolability of the new valuation. In fact, Diocletian and his colleagues were still burdened by one overwhelming currency problem. During the earliest empire a bimetallic system had prevailed, with gold and fairly pure silver in a stable, mutual relationship, supported by token *aes*. When silver was increasingly

253

debased, and especially when the antoninianus became almost pure copper in the middle of the third century, 'silver'—still in fixed mutual relationship with gold—to all intents and purposes became part of a dying token *aes* system. Diocletian and his colleagues produced abundant gold, and some (though not enough) real silver : their massive issues of copper folles with *c.* 4 per cent of silver simply perpetuated the problem of the antoninianus, which, though still produced in copper, now played only a minor part as a fractional piece. [272]

In this, then, Diocletian failed. But he had stabilized the frontiers, and elaborated a system of collegiate military rule, with each ruler based in a different, vital part of the empire—he himself at Nicomedia or Antioch, Galerius at Sirmium or Serdica, Maximian at Aquileia or Milan, and Constantius at Treveri. This firm division of government was reflected in the firm and nearly uniform network of mints, each group closely controlled (with its necessary coinage metals) by one of the four military rulers. But Diocletian's reign had begun in 284, and he decided that 20 years should be the limit. Accordingly he retired in 305, forcing retirement at the same time upon an openly reluctant Maximian.

500

501

502
503

500 Gallienus. *Obv., bust of Gallienus in lion's skin head-dress ;* GALLIENVS AVG. *A.D. 259-68, (?) Mediolanum (aureus, 5.77 gm., diam. 20 mm., BM).*

501 Diocletian. *Obv., head of Diocletian ;* IMP C C VAL DIOCLETIANVS P F AVG. c. *A.D. 294, Nicomedia (10-aureus piece, 53.5 gm., diam. 37 mm., BM). (For rev. see No. 504.)*

502, 503 Carausius. *Obv., bust of Carausius, laureate and cuirassed ;* CARAVSIVS P F AVG. *Rev., Hercules holding club, lion's skin and bow ; quiver on shoulder ;* CONSERVATORI AVGGG ; ML *in exergue. A.D. 287-93, Londinium (aureus, 4.30 gm., diam. 18 mm., BM).*

504 Diocletian. *Rev., Jupiter with wreath-bearing Victory on globe and sceptre ;* IOVI CONSERVATORI ; SMN *in exergue.* c. *A.D. 294, Nicomedia (10-aureus piece, 53.5 gm., diam. 37.5 mm., BM). (For obv. see No. 501.)*

505, 506 Carausius. *Obv., bust of Carausius, laureate and in consular robe, holding eagle-tipped sceptre ;* IMP C M AV CARAVSIVS P F AVG. *Rev., Victory in biga ;* VICTORIA CARAVSI AVG ; I N P C D A *(meaning unknown) in exergue.* c. *A.D. 287, uncertain mint (bronze, 21.62 gm., diam. 36 mm., BM).*

504

505

506

VIII. THE FINAL STAGE: FROM CONSTANTINE I TO ROMULUS AUGUSTULUS

Diocletian had taken good care to preserve the quadruple structure of imperial rule after his retirement with Maximian. The new Augusti were Constantius (west) and Galerius (east), the former Caesars : Severus (west) and Maximinus (east) became the new Caesars. But without Diocletian's dominant strength the structure was too weak to withstand rivalries. Constantius died at York in 306, being succeeded by Severus as Augustus and Constantine (son of Constantius) as Caesar. In the same year Maximian's son Maxentius, excluded from the Tetrarchy, set himself up as emperor in Rome and Italy, and Maximian was soon persuaded to resume imperial power as colleague to his son. Their forces defeated and captured Severus in 307, after which Constantine assumed the status of the western Augustus. By 308 Galerius and Constantine had been joined as Augusti by Licinius and Maximinus : Galerius' death occurred in 311, Maxentius was killed in 312, and Licinius defeated Maximinus in 313. Constantine in the west and Licinius in the east were thus left finally to share the empire : Crispus and Constantine II (sons of the former) and Licinius II were made Caesars in 316–17. In 324 Constantine fought and defeated the

Licinii, and emerged as sole emperor, to rule until his death in 337. Stability thus emerged after twenty years of costly, complex and turbulent rivalry.[273]

The imperial monetary system was not proof against these great strains. Gold was struck in some abundance, especially at mints over which a given emperor exercised specially close control,[274] but it is likely that supplies of precious-metal bullion sometimes showed an uncomfortable diminution. For a good many years after 305 the coinage of silver argentei was very slight, and it was in 309 that Constantine reduced the weight of gold coins from the Diocletianic 1/60 of a pound to the new solidus level of 1/72 of a pound—a standard which, while for a time it ran in parallel with the older and heavier one still retained in the eastern part of the empire by Licinius, ultimately became universal. Reduction in the weight of the gold coins of the west may, of course, have been in part Constantine's answer to inflationary price increases; and the same may be true of what happened to the *aes*. The follis, originally struck by Diocletian at a weight of *c.* 10 g., and containing a small percentage of silver,[275] slid—sharply at first in 307, and then less violently—to a weight of between 5.0 and 3.0 g. by 313, becoming stable thereafter around the lower figure, which was accompanied by a much reduced size.[276] These small, light folles came to be struck in very great quantity after 313. A wide network of prolific mints covered the empire, from London in the north-west to Alexandria in the south-east.[277] Each of these mints, down to the defeat of Licinius in 324, struck coinage in the names of all legitimate imperial partners. After 324 Constantine, as sole emperor, coined in the names of himself and his Caesars.

A coinage so abundant, so widespread, and so generally uniform in its weight-standards constituted a tribute to the imperial civil service of the early fourth century. The general direction of monetary policy lay no doubt with the senior emperor at any given time; but his directives were swiftly transmitted to the imperial procurators in charge of the individual mints, and swiftly and accurately carried out by them, so that all areas of the empire were adequately provided for.[278] Under Diocletian's Tetrarchy, as has been seen, this centralized direction led to a surprisingly great uniformity of types on the *aes* and the silver, with the Genius type prominent on the *aes*. After 305, when the tetrarchic system began to break up, *aes* types became much more variable at the will of each partner or ruler. Genius was still prominent, among a wide number of other types, but in the east it was no longer the Genius of the Roman people that was emphasized, but the Genius of an emperor, or of a Caesar. There was widespread commemoration of the twin achievements of Diocle-

tian's partnership with Maximian, seen in the *Providentia Deorum Quies Augg* 'retirement' type. There was commemoration, too, of emperors who died—of Constantius I, of Galerius, and even (by Maxentius) of his young son Romulus; and Galerius' mints struck abundantly to honour his wife Valeria in her lifetime. Maximinus struck a few outstanding types of military purport and threat. In the west, Constantine's opposition to Maxentius was marked by the emerging emphasis on the *Soli invicto comiti* and *Marti conservatori* types : Mars and the sun-god would see him through. In the east, controlled by the Jovian dynasty,[279] the choice concentrated (apart from Genius) upon *Iovi conservatori* and *Virtuti exercitus*.

Aes types after 313 briefly continued to emphasize Sol, Mars, and Genius, but it was not long before a new system of successively dominant types was introduced —*Claritas Reipublicae* (a Sol type) *c.* 317, *Victoriae Laetae Princ Perp* (two Victories) *c.* 319, *Virtus Exercit* (trophy and two captives) *c.* 320, *Beata Tranquillitas* (altar) *c.* 321, *Caesarum Nostrorum Vot V* or *X c.* 320 and 323, and *Sarmatia Devicta* (Victory and captive) *c.* 323–4. With Licinius defeated, Constantine thereafter concentrated on *Providentia Augg* or *Caess* and *Securitas Reipublicae c.* 324, and on *Gloria Exercitus, Urbs Roma* (wolf and twins), and *Constantinopolis* (Victory on prow) *c.* 330—the two latter to celebrate the establishment of Constantinople as the empire's Christian capital in that year.[280] This system of successive blocks of major types was to prevail after Constantine's death.

The *aes* types, then, were the vehicle of simple messages, political, dynastic and military: they included also a number in memory of former imperial persons and in honour of such imperial ladies as Helena, Constantine's mother (d. 324), and Fausta his wife (put to death 326), each styled 'nobilissima femina' and 'Augusta'. Such silver as appeared—and it was sparing—was not much different. It was on the gold solidi and their multiples and fractions, and on the now developing series of *aes* multiples, that real variety and flexibility were to be seen. In some cases older types were refined or elaborated: the ample series of Constantinian gold multiples shows such examples as *Equis Romanus, Gloria Constantini Aug*, the confronting heads of Constantine II and Crispus, *Senatus* (superbly engraved and worked in low, flat relief), wreathed *Vota* legends,[281] and *Princeps Iuventutis*. As had for long been usual, the care given to engraving and striking in the production of gold (solidi as well as multiples) was markedly greater than that shown for *aes*, or even for silver; and these types reveal a new conception of imperial monetary art—well contained and disciplined, but not just neat; spacious, but never loose; decorative without being extravagant, the generally low and flat relief (lower than under Diocletian) permitting great subtlety of engraving and of line. Nor were the tendencies confined to treatment. The actual range of types was imaginatively extended, and a glance back at (say) the coinage of Gallienus or Probus will show the totally new lines of choice opened up under and after Diocletian, leading to such new concepts as the four seasons at play, or Constantine as 'rector totius orbis' holding the zodiac, or the splendidly simple

CAESAR in wreath, or Sol above a bird's-eye view of a camp, or the Christian standard piercing a serpent.[282]

The art of portraiture, too, was reaching out to new ranges of conception and treatment. From the middle of the third century imperial coin-portraiture had lacked any fundamental variation. The Aurelianic concept was not essentially different from the Diocletianic: portraits might be totally simple and unadorned, as under the Tetrarchy, or seen in panoply, with cuirass and spear and shield, and they might be small, constrained, and neat, or more widely spread; but they were all characterized by a certain mode of presentation—upright, hard and objective. There were, of course, exceptions: Maxentius—the odd man out politically—had received some facing portraits, interesting iconographically rather than artistically; and the two Licinii, father and son, were to repeat the experiment on coins which to the modern eye appear frankly ugly. From 313, however, Constantine's massive growth in stature produced new portrait forms—perhaps, indeed, one should say encouraged new forms, for, as his power increased, so also did his *auctoritas*, that majestic and mysterious blend of the human and the divine which Augustus, long before, had possessed to a degree which inspired a great variety of highly sensitive portraits, most of them seeking subjective depth. The progress of Constantinian portraiture was not systematic, depending as it did on the existence of particular models and particular engravers in the various mints; and there was naturally a slow development of some long-traditional forms, such as 'plain' and helmeted

545
546

542

528
527

483
501*

518

540*, 543

261

heads. But 'plain' heads, transformed in any case by the replacement of laurel wreath by imperial diadem, ended in serenely delicate, strongly sensitive majesty; and the same feeling of greatness—reserved but not remote, and set apart not by passion but by superhuman quality, is transmitted by Constantine in his imperial vestments, or by Constantine's three-quarter facing portrait set against a halo of divinity, or by Constantine's profile tilted up as if in prayer.

539* The flow of coinage in the Constantinian period was very great (as it was to be also under his immediate successors), and poured out from a total of 17 mints at one time or another. In some eastern mints the number of *officinae* could be high—up to 10, or even more : one reason for this is presumably to be found in the fact that the local city or regional coinages of the eastern empire, previously abundant, had died out by the end of the third century. Imperial monopoly of a uniform system of empire-wide mints was thus absolute, and it was as a corollary of this that the laws against forgery and counterfeiting were likewise systematized.[283] The counterfeiting of gold, for long past regarded as sacrilege, had always been severely punished, and that of silver had continued to be covered by the old republican Cornelian Law. It was with *aes*—theoretically containing a small percentage of silver—that fourth-century legislation was newly concerned. And there was need for concern. In the later third century a spate of little 'radiate' coins, imitating the already debased antoniniani of the period, had occurred in Gaul and Britain especially. These had been checked with Diocletian's reform of the currency;

507, 508 Carausius (jointly for Diocletian and Maximian Herculius). *Obv., busts of Diocletian (nearest), Maximian (central), and Carausius (furthest) radiate and cuirassed, side by side, r. hands raised ;* CARAVSIVS ET FRATRES SVI. *Rev., Moneta holding scales and cornucopiae ;* MONETA AVGGG ; S P *(in field) ;* C *(in exergue). A.D. 287-93, Camulodunum (antoninianus, 4.65 gm., diam. 24 mm., BM).*

509 Carausius (for Diocletian). *Obv., bust of Diocletian, radiate and cuirassed ;* IMP C DIOCLETIANVS AVG. *A.D. 287-93, Londinium (antoninianus, 4.19 gm., diam. 22.5 mm., BM).*

510 Carausius (for Maximian Herculius). *Obv., bust of Maximian, radiate and cuirassed ;* IMP C MAXIMIANVS P F AVG. *A.D. 287-93, Londinium (antoninianus, 4.41 gm., diam. 22.5 mm., BM).*

511, 512 Allectus. *Obv., bust of Allectus, laureate and cuirassed ;* IMP C ALLECTVS P F I(nvictus) AVG. *Rev., Mars holding spear and shield ;* VIRTVS AVG ; MSL *in exergue. A.D. 293-6, Londinium (aureus, 4.72 gm., diam. 20 mm., BM).*

513 Diocletian. *Rev., Genius of the Roman People, holding patera and cornucopiae ;* GENIO POPVLI ROMANI ; LON *in exergue. c. A.D. 297, Londinium (follis, 9.37 gm., diam. 29 mm., BM).*

514 Galerius Maximian. *Rev., personification of Carthago holding fruits in both hands ;* SALVIS AVGG ET CAESS FEL(ix) KART ; △ (= 4th officina) *in exergue. c. A.D. 298-303, Carthago (follis, 8.80 gm., diam. 29 mm., BM).*

515, 516 Constantius I as Caesar. *Obv., head of Constantius, laureate, draped and cuirassed ;* FL VAL CONSTANTIVS NOBIL CAES. *Rev., armed horseman riding towards suppliant woman (Britannia) in front of city-gate ; below, galley and* LON ; REDDITOR LVCIS AETERNAE ; PTR *in exergue. c. A.D. 296-8, Treveri (10-aureus piece, 52.88 gm., diam. 38 mm., Arras).*

507

508

509

510

511

512

513

514

515   516

517

518

519

520   521

522

523

524

525

526

527

528

529

530

531

532

533

534

535

536

537

538

517 Maximianus Herculius. *Rev., Moneta holding scales and cornucopiae ;* SACR MONET AVGG ET CAESS NOSTR *; star and* VI (= *6th issue*) *in field ;* AQP(rima officina) *in exergue.* c. *A.D. 303, Aquileia (follis, 9.40 gm., diam. 27 mm., BM).*

518, 519 Maxentius. *Obv., facing bust of Maxentius, draped and cuirassed ;* MAXENTIVS P F AVG. *Rev., wolf and twins ;* TEMPORVM FELICITAS AVG N *;* POST *in exergue. A.D. 308-12, Ostia (aureus, 5.56 gm., diam. 19 mm., BM).*

520, 521 Diocletian (in retirement). *Obv., bust of Diocletian in consular robe holding olive-branch and roll ;* D(omino) N(ostro) DIOCLETIANO BEATISSIMO SEN(iori) AVG. *Rev., Providentia extending hand to Quies holding branch and sceptre ;* PROVIDENTIA DEORVM QVIES AVGG *;* S F *in field ;* PTR *in exergue. A.D. 305-7, Treveri (follis, 11.56 gm., diam. 29 mm., BM).*

522 Galerius Maximian (for Valeria). *Obv., bust of Valeria on crescent, draped, wearing stephane ;* GAL(eria) VALERIA AVG. *A.D. 308-11, Siscia (follis, 6.74 gm., diam. 25 mm., BM).*

523, 524 Maximinus II as Caesar. *Obv., head of Maximinus, laureate ;* GAL VAL MAXIMINVS NOB CAES. *Rev., Concordia, modius on head, holding sceptre ;* CONCORD IMPERI *;* S $\frac{A}{P}$ *in field ;* ALE *in exergue.* c. *A.D. 306-7, Alexandria (follis, 8.68 gm., diam. 21 mm., BM).*

525, 526 Constantine I (for Crispus). *Obv., head of Crispus, helmeted and cuirassed ;* CRISPVS NOB CAES. *Rev., two Victories holding up shield inscribed* VOT(a) P(opuli) R(omani) *above altar ;* VICTORIAE LAET P(rincipis) P(erpetui); PTR *in exergue. A.D. 319, Treveri (follis, 3.68 gm., diam. 20 mm., BM).*

527 Constantine I. *Rev., labarum, crowned by christogram, piercing serpent ;* SPES PVBLIC *;* A *in field ;* CONS *in exergue. A.D. 327, Constantinopolis (follis, 2.96 gm., diam. 20 mm., BM).*

528 Constantine I (for Constantine II). *Rev., Sol, raising r. and holding globe, standing in centre of (?) camp-plan ;* VIRT(us) EXERC(itus) *;* TSB *in exergue. A.D. 319, Thessalonica (follis, 3.16 gm., diam. 19 mm., BM).*

529, 530 Constantine I (for Constantius). *Obv., bust of Constantius, laureate, draped and cuirassed ;* FL(avius) IVL CONSTANTIVS NOB C(aesar). *Rev., two standards between two soldiers, each with spear and shield ;* GLORIA EXERCITVS *;* CONSS (= *6th officina*). *A.D. 330-3, Constantinopolis (follis, 2.28 gm., diam. 19 mm., BM).*

531, 532 Constantine I (for Crispus). *Obv., head of Crispus, laureate ;* CRISPVS NOB CAES. *Rev.,* BEATA TRANQVILLITAS *around three stars above globe set on altar inscribed* VOTIS XX *;* C R *in field ;* PLG *in exergue.* c. *A.D. 322-3, Lugdunum (follis, 3.31 gm., diam. 19 mm., BM).*

533, 534 Constantine I. *Obv., bust of Roma, helmeted and draped ;* VRBS ROMA. *Rev., two stars and* ∴ (*issue mark*) *above wolf and twins ;* SMNA *in exergue.* c. *A.D. 330-5, Nicomedia (follis, 2.57 gm., diam. 18 mm., BM).*

535, 536 Constantine I. *Obv., bust of Constantinopolis, draped, with laureate helmet and spear ;* CONSTANTINOPOLI. *Rev., Victory with spear and shield on ship's prow ;* CONSIA *in exergue.* c. *A.D. 330-3, Constantinopolis (follis, 2.59 gm., diam. 20 mm., BM).*

537, 538 Constantius II and Constans. *Obv., veiled bust of Constantine I ;* [DIVO CONST]ANTINO PIO. *Rev., soldier with spear and globe ;* AETERNA P[IETAS] *; christogram in field ;* PLG *in exergue.* c. *A.D. 337-41, Lugdunum (follis, 1.54 gm., diam. 14.5 mm., BM).*

but imitations were not absent in the first half of the fourth century, as is clearly shown by clay coin-moulds found in Egypt. The inviolability of the imperial coinage had to be preserved.[284]

Under Constantine a wide and firm stability had been achieved. After his death in 337 this was broken by dynastic quarrels which effectively split the Roman empire into those western and eastern sections which, in time, allowed the Byzantine Empire to survive after the Western Empire had collapsed. Of Constantine's sons, Constantine II ruled the western provinces until he was killed in 340; Constans, already ruling in the central provinces, took those western provinces until he himself was killed in 350; Constantius II was emperor of the eastern provinces until he died in 361. After 350 Constantius' hold upon the west was often threatened. The revolts of Nepotian and of Vetranio in 350 were not serious, but that of Magnentius in the same year was much more so, extending finally (with Decentius as his Caesar from 351) from an initial base in Gaul, with mints at Trier, Amiens, Lyons and Arles, to Italy, Rome itself, and Pannonia before their deaths in 353. Constantius II was forced ultimately, after Constantius Gallus' death, to acknowledge Julian as joint ruler in Gaul; and it was Julian who became sole emperor, after Constantius died, for the brief period 361–3, being followed by the ephemeral Jovian (363–4). The monetary system during this period from 337 to 364 saw little change at first: gold solidi were struck in quantity throughout, and the output of silver increased.[285] But in addition to the silver pieces of roughly normal Constantinian weight and size, silver coins of twice that weight came to be produced.[286] The *aes*, moreover, underwent reconstruction. A range of new *aes* types from 346 marked the 1100th anniversary in 348 of the foundation of Rome, and these new types appeared on revised denominations which affected the subsequent issues of Magnentius and Julian. Under Constantine the follis had sunk to very low size and weight. Now this lowest denomination became larger and heavier, at about 4.50 g., and it was accompanied by a double, of approximately the size of a reduced Tetrarchic follis, and destined to continue for a time.[287]

The system of successive 'blocks' of *aes* types, running for some years, which had emerged under Constantine and which was in general to continue for some years to come, can well be seen in the case of such an important and prolific mint as Trier.[288] After Constantine's death in 337 there was at first a prolongation of the types then current—*Gloria Exercitus, Urbs Roma,* and *Constantinopolis* (see above, p. 260)—with the addition of some in memory of Constantine, like *Aeterna Pietas,* and others in the name of imperial ladies, like *Pax Publica* and *Pietas Romana.* About 341 a new *aes* type appeared, to be used exclusively down to *c.* 346—*Victoria Dd Augg Q Nn,*[289] two Victories standing with upheld wreaths, struck in parallel for the new imperial colleagues Constantius II and Constans. From *c.* 346 down to the earlier 350s the 1100th anniversary of the foundation of Rome prompted a great series of new types with the single theme of *Fel. Temp. Reparatio*: the designs include the emperor taking a youth from a forest hut, a phoenix on a

537, 538

553

548, 549

541·

554

530,5
535, 5
537, 5
547
548, 5
551

globe, the emperor holding a phoenix in a ship steered by Victory, and a Roman soldier spearing a foeman as he falls from his horse.[290] No more comprehensive statement could have been devised to emphasize Rome's age-long protection of the civilized world against the forces of barbarism, or the hopes for a future which each succeeding century renewed. Nor was such a statement vain or wasted. The whole vast empire, from end to end, was a busy, sophisticated and complex unit, well integrated as between urban industries and agriculture; and its whole safety depended on the continuing defence of the northern and eastern frontiers against those pressures which had by now threatened them for over three centuries. What was at stake, in truth, was the Roman way of life throughout the empire. These *aes* types, flooding through the empire from many mints, made the message clear.

Magnentius' revolt was well mirrored in the Trier issues with a range of new types: *Felicitas Reipublice, Gloria Romanorum, Victoriae Dd Nn Aug et Cae(s)*, and—most interestingly—*Salus Dd Nn Aug et Caes*, with a large and finely designed christogram as the type, between alpha and omega. Public happiness, and glory and victory in war, depended on Christian *salus* working through Magnentius. Magnentius' death was succeeded by a return to the fallen horseman variety (now perhaps especially appropriate) of *Fel. Temp. Reparatio*, until this gave way to *Spes Reipublice* in the later 350s.

Throughout these years from Constantine's death onwards the types of *aes* had thus consisted of general statements, variously presented, of a few themes of overwhelming general importance, and the whole emphasis lay upon the emperor, military security, and the public weal—the intertwining of those threads on which alone the safety of the empire depended. Topicalities had long since been abandoned: they were dying in the third century and (though still not wholly absent) in the early fourth, and from *c.* 340 they had given way to generalized pronouncements of a kind which was really necessitated by a world-wide network of mints. Gold and silver, each struck in abundance,[291] followed the same path, with types which, if more elaborate and better designed and struck, concentrated primarily upon the emperor and Rome's military glory. The chief interest in these precious-metal coinages lies in the portraiture which, year by year, reign by reign, and mint by mint, displays the same neat, well-controlled, and technically fine characteristics—the fruit, no doubt, of the hereditary caste-system which (in an age when each man's status was more and more categorized) applied to the moneyers' profession.[292] As under Constantine, the imperial features are on the whole delicate, introspective and remote, this remoteness being somehow emphasized by the general tendency to represent the head as being tall and narrow—an idiom which, whether or not it arose simply from the optic mechanisms of the engravers,[293] curiously anticipates the Gothic idioms of a much later age. Exceptions there are, of course. Constantius II was represented on a considerable range of gold solidi by a near-facing portrait of pre-Byzantine form, showing him helmeted and cuirassed, with spear and shield, alert if he were not still

552

550

555

remote. Vetranio's brief coinage returned momentarily to the hard, semi-realistic forms of the Tetrarchy. Magnentius and his son, abandoning wreath or diadem, have portraits which, if often delicate, are as often tinged with a rough and rugged strength clearly suggestive of force of personality. And Julian, the apostate emperor of 361–3, inheritor at first of the somewhat bloodless portrait-form of Constantius II, was not long in introducing a more robust, heavier, and bearded idiom of portraiture which, with his famous bull reverse on his larger *aes*, gives to his short coinage a flash of novel interest.[294]

After Jovian's death in 364 Valentinian I was chosen to succeed him : he himself elected to rule the western section of the empire, appointing his younger brother Valens to take control of the eastern part. In 367 Valentinian made his eight-year-old son Gratian titular Augustus. For some years imperial energies were fully employed in the defence of the Rhine and Danube frontiers, with the redoubtable Count Theodosius playing a leading military part and his son, also Theodosius (the future emperor), emerging to prominence. Upon Valentinian's death in 375 Valens became senior Augustus, with Valentinian II (the young son of Valentinian I) as the newest junior; but Valens himself was killed in 378, whereupon Gratian, now western ruler, appointed Theodosius to rule in the vulnerable Balkans with general control over the east. By 383 crisis was mounting. Relations between Gratian and Theodosius had deteriorated : Theodosius appointed his son Arcadius to be Augustus (of whom, with Valentinian II, there were now four);

554
541·
556
557, 558
559, 560
561, 562
564, 565
566, 567

539 Constantine I. *Obv., head of Constantine I, diademed.* c. *A.D. 326-7, Siscia (1 1/2-solidus piece, 6.81 gm., diam. 24 mm., BM). (For rev. see No. 542.)*

540 Licinius I. *Obv., facing head of Licinius I, draped and cuirassed ;* LICINIVS AVG OB D(iem) V(annorum) FILII SVI. c. *A.D. 321-2, Antioch (aureus, 5.27 gm., diam. 20 mm., BM).*

541 Julian. *Obv., head of Julian, diademed, draped and cuirassed ;* FL CL IVLIANVS P P AVG. c. *A.D. 361-3, Thessalonica (solidus, 4.35 gm., diam. 20 mm., BM). (For rev. see No. 544.)*

542

543

544

542 Constantine I. *Rev., Constantine, with trophy, dragging one bound captive by the hair and spurning another with his foot;* GLORIA CONSTANTINI AVG ; SIS *in exergue.* c. *A.D. 326-7, Siscia (1 1/2-solidus piece, 6.81 gm., diam. 25.5 mm., BM). (For obv. see No. 539.)*

543 Licinius I (for Licinius II). *Obv., facing head of Licinius II, draped and (?) cuirassed ;* D N VAL LICIN LICINVS NOB C. c. *A.D. 321-2, Nicomedia (aureus, 5.27 gm., diam. 21 mm., BM).*

544 Julian. *Rev., soldier, with trophy, dragging bound captive by the hair ;* VIRTVS EXERCITVS ROMANI ; TES *and wreath in exergue.* c. *A.D. 361-3, Thessalonica (solidus, 4.35 gm., diam. 20.5 mm., BM). (For obv. see No. 541.)*

and Magnus Maximus, rising in Britain— 563 where he temporarily re-opened the London mint,[295] attacked Gaul, where Gratian was killed. Theodosius, however, relentlessly extended his imperial mastery, and by the time of his death in 395 Maximus had been killed (388); Valentinian II was dead by his own hand (392); Eugenius—briefly put in his place—was killed (392–4); and Honor- 568, 569 ius had joined his brother Arcadius as co-Augustus under Theodosius, who had thus built his own dynasty upon the ruins of that of Valentinian I. The spheres of power were now divided afresh, with Honorius dominant in the west and Arcadius in the east.

These events, however complex, must be sketched if only to explain certain aspects of the coinage of the times.[296] Gold was struck in quantity, with multiples and fractions; and silver too, in light and heavy miliarensia and in smaller siliquae : great armies had to be paid, whether for imperial defence or for purely personal support. *Aes* had a variable development. The larger denomination introduced under Constantius II was for a time retained at *c.* 5.45 g. or lower, with the smaller at *c.* 2.75-2.25 g., but ultimately a yet smaller coin of a little over 1.0 g. became dominant. Value-relationships both between metals, and also between *aes* denominations, remain obscure.[297] The *aes* was of great abundance. In any given period, the legitimate co-rulers each coined for the others (as well as for themselves) in any given mint, of which there were up to 15 in regular operation, with clear mint marks and—in the case of much *aes*—prominent *officina* marks as well.[298] But there were observable distinctions between the colleagues, carefully worked out with the passage of time. In the past the choice between a broken and an unbroken obverse legend (e.g. *Imp Diocleti-anus P F Aug, Imp C Severus P F Aug*) had been largely a matter of convenience, depending on the size of the head and the length of the inscription. Between 364 and 395, however, it gradually became convention that a broken legend signified the senior Augustus: thus at Thessalonica between 383 (when Theodosius occupied the mint there) and 388, the 'broken' seniority went to Theodosius himself, the truly senior Valentinian II being assigned (at first with Arcadius) 'unbroken' juniority.[299] Finally, it is to be noted of this period that whereas the *aes* of Constantine II, and particularly the *Fel. Temp. Reparatio* 'fallen horseman' type (see above, p. 269), had been very widely copied, *aes* between 364 and 395 was subject to only very infrequent imitation: presumably the laws against such practice were more effectively enforced.[300]

However fundamentally unstable the imperial structure of a divided empire might be, and however precarious the integrity of the northern frontiers,[301] the coin-types of the period 364–95 assumed and maintained an immutability, almost a monotony, that seemed to speak for a combination of continuity and security. They were woven principally around the emperors: we see the emperor as 'Restorer of the State', 'Glory of the Romans', 'Conqueror of Barbarians', 'Prince of the Youth', 'Salvation of the State'; and in types showing two seated emperors [302] we see them as the twin instruments of imperial Victory and as 'Born for the good of the State'. Such in particular was the general message of the gold, which included also multiples emphasizing certain themes like an imperial progress or visit—*Felix Adventus Aug N*. Silver was devoted above all to the celebration of the quinquennial imperial vows (see above, p. 261), but there was ample room too for the themes of imperial victory, imperial concord, the valour of the army, and the central concept of the firmly seated city of Rome. The ubiquitous *aes* in turn celebrated Roman glory, the safety and well-being of the State, imperial victory and imperial concord. Types such as these, appearing with majestic predictability, mint by mint and year by year, must have done much to quiet all but the more violent doubts felt about either imperial efficiency or frontier security. Imperial efficiency would have been, indeed, even less good than it was if the opportunity had not from time to time been found of buying off 'barbarian' leaders with gold, often in the form of the great medallions later to be found in extraordinarily varied areas of central and even northern Europe.[303] Moreover, the illusion of stability was certainly strengthened by the essential purity of the precious-metal coinages. This was, of course, to the government's advantage in view of its insistence upon tax-payment in the precious metals,[304] but it was also a guarantee to the individual possessor of gold or silver coin that he possessed a store of true value: the formulae OB(*ryzum aurum*, = purified or standard gold) and PS or PV(*sulatum argentum*, = refined silver) commonly called attention, as adjuncts to a mint-mark, to these high standards of purity.[305]

Although the coinage from Valentinian to Theodosius I has an inherent monotony (or near-monotony) of type, the gold and the larger silver possess a certain firmness in the proportions of design and a certain technical excellence which results in a pleasing impression of jewelled neatness and clarity. Portraits are generally of robust size, with well-rounded modelling in good relief; and the 'spirituality' and remoteness which had characterized the portraiture of Constantius II and Constans gives way to something more realistic and indeed more valorous. 'Dominus Noster'—now invariable in place of the 'Imperator' of former days—is with few exceptions seen as a virile man of flesh and blood : only in the case of Eugenius, elderly and bearded, is the austere note of angular and vertical treatment preserved at all conspicuously. Some of the smaller silver is carefully struck : much, however, is more careless, with a marked irregularity in the shape of the flan; and this is even more true of the *aes*, which gives an obvious feeling of the hasty production of what was intrinsically of small value.

This was a period in which Christianity had become the official state religion, and the removal from the coinage of the old range of pagan deities—begun under Constantine I and confirmed by his sons—is now complete, for Victoria (winged and ubiquitous) had become God's angel. Nevertheless paganism died hard. Christian symbolism on coinage was sparse and muted : at its strongest it could appear as a hand from above crowning Arcadius (a concept susceptible equally of pagan interpretation), and in fact it was generally restricted to the *labarum*, or ☧ standard, in the triumphant emperor's hands, or to the inclusion of some form of the Christogram as an adjunct to the main type. By contrast, it has been suggested, the pagan faction of the time was responsible for the production of a surprising series of anonymous *aes* coins with Egyptian religious types of Isis, Serapis, and Anubis—the last flicker of opposition to Christianity to be reflected on the imperial coinage.[306]

The death of Theodosius I in 395 was followed, as already noted, by the fresh territorial partition of the empire between Honorius in the west and Arcadius in the east : Rome and Constantinople were now to be, in a real sense, twin capitals of empire. But they were capitals of increasingly disparate strength. Palace intrigue and plot might be equally rife in both, and indeed the eastern dynasty was often precarious enough until the advent of Anastasius in 491. But the western succession was no less precarious, and there now failed in the west that stamina and cohesion which had been so strong through four centuries of military autocracy. The decline of the west, and its steady separation from the empire of the east, is well shown by the history of the previous great network of imperial mints. Lugdunum and Arelate in Gaul, and Aquileia, Siscia and Alexandria too, ceased to coin in the 420s. The great mint of Trier closed *c.* 450. In the east the whole great block of busy mints—Thessalonica, Heraclea, Constantinople itself, Nicomedia, Cyzicus, and Antioch—coined only for the eastern empire after 455. Coinage for the west was restricted finally, and pathetically, to a trickle of issues from Milan, Rome and

Ravenna for a few years in the period of the 450s and 460s.

Honorius's reign lasted until 423. There followed a series of ephemeral emperors, often ruling for no more than a year or two, unable to repair the failing strength of an empire increasingly pressed and eroded by the surrounding waves of barbarism, potent and unwearied, until with Romulus Augustulus (475–6) Rome fell, submerged by those waves. Names famous more for their transience than for anything else pass in rapid procession, with those of imperial ladies, including Constantius III (421) and his wife Galla Placidia; Priscus Attalus 670 (409–10, 414–15); Valentinian III, seemingly stable between 425 and 455, with his wife Licinia Eudoxia and his sister Justa Grata Honoria; Majorian (457–61); Libius Severus (461–5); and Anthemius, Olybrius, Glycerius and Julius Nepos all between 467 and 475. Currency was fitful, and types were restricted. *Aes* and silver were sparse : gold, still the sheet-anchor of security in value, less so. The types continued the themes of imperial victory, the well-being of the State, the *vota* undertaken for imperial success, and the permanent invincibility of Rome, now and for ever; and, in a period when payment for services rendered was of supreme importance, medallions for presentation and reward were still produced, in silver as well as gold. Portraiture was by now frozen in its later fourth-century idiom : the emperor could still appear fully armed for battle, or simply diademed, wide-eyed, and waiting.

571, 572 With Romulus Augustulus the waiting was over, and the end had come. The Byzantine empire was to last for another

545 Constantine I (for Helena). *Obv., bust of Helena, diademed and draped;* FL HELENA AVGVSTA. *c. A.D. 324-5, Siscia (follis, 3.66 gm., diam. 19.5 mm., BM).*

546 Constantine I (for Fausta). *Obv., bust of Fausta, draped;* FL MAX FAVSTA AVG. *c. A.D. 324-5, Lugdunum (follis, 3.27 gm., diam. 20.5 mm., BM).*

547 Constantius II and Constans (for Theodora). *Obv., bust of Theodora, laureate and draped;* FL MAX THEODORAE AVG. *c. A.D. 337-41, Treveri (follis, 1.41 gm., diam. 15 mm., BM).*

548, 549 Constantius II. *Obv., bust of Constantius, diademed, draped and cuirassed;* CONSTANTIVS P F AVG. *Rev., two Victories holding up wreaths over star;* VICTORIAE DD (dominorum) AVGG (Augustorum) Q(ue) NN (nostrorum); TRP *in exergue. c. A.D. 341-6, Treveri (follis, 2.03 gm., diam. 15 mm., BM).*

550 Constantius II. *Rev., soldier with shield spearing fallen horseman;* FEL TEMP REPARATIO; Γ *in field;* CONSB * *in exergue. c. A.D. 346-50, Constantinopolis (aes, 6,49 gm., diam. 26 mm., BM).*

551 Constans. *Rev., soldier with spear leading barbarian by the hand from hut under tree;* FEL TEMP REPARATIO; TRS *in exergue. c. A.D. 346-50, Treveri (aes, 3.81 gm., diam. 22 mm., BM).*

552 Constans. *Rev., Constans, holding phoenix and labarum, in ship steered by Victory;* FEL TEMP REPARATIO; A *in field;* TRS *in exergue. c. A.D. 346-50, Treveri (aes, 4.57 gm., diam. 22 mm., BM).*

553 Constans. *Obv., bust of Constans, diademed, draped and cuirassed;* FL IVL CONSTANS PIVS FELIX AVG. *A.D. 337-50, Thessalonica (silver multiple, 12.81 gm., diam. 39 mm., BM).*

276

545

546

547

548

549

550

551

552

553

554

555

556

557

558

559

560

561

562

563

564

565

566

567

568

569

570

571

572

554, 555 Magnentius. *Obv., draped bust of Magnentius ;* D N MAGNENTIVS P F AVG. *Rev., christogram between alpha and omega ;* SALVS DD NN AVG ET CAES ; TRP *in exergue. A.D. 351-3, Treveri* (aes, *7.80 gm., diam. 26 mm., BM).*

556 Julian. *Rev., bull ; two stars above ;* SECVRITAS REIPVB(licae) ; CONSPΓ *and palm-branch in exergue. A.D. 361-3, Constantinopolis* (aes, *8.71 gm., diam. 28 mm., BM).*

557, 558 Valentinian I. *Obv., bust of Valentinian, diademed and cuirassed ;* D N VALENTINIANVS P F AVG. *Rev., laurel-wreath enclosing* VOTIS X MVLTIS XV ; S(acra) M(oneta) KAP *below. A.D. 367-75, Arelate* (silver heavy miliarense, *5.24 gm., diam. 26 mm., BM).*

559, 560 Valens. *Obv., bust of Valens, diademed, draped and cuirassed ;* D N VALENS P F AVG. *Rev., Valens with labarum and globe by bound and kneeling captive ;* TRIVMFATOR GENT(ium) BARB(ararum) ; TRPS· *in exergue. A.D. 367-75, Treveri* (silver triple light miliarense, *13.48 gm., diam. 37 mm., BM).*

561, 562 Gratian. *Obv., bust of Gratian, diademed, draped and cuirassed ;* D N GRATIANVS P F AVG. *Rev., Valens with labarum and shield ;* VIRTVS EXERCITVS ; TRPS· *in exergue. A.D. 367-75, Treveri* (silver light miliarense, *4.23 gm., diam. 23 mm., BM).*

563 Magnus Maximus. *Obv., bust of Magnus Maximus, diademed, draped and cuirassed ;* D N MAG MAXIMVS P F AVG. *A.D. 383-8, Londinium* (silver siliqua, *1.77 gm., diam. 19 mm., BM).* *(Rev. marked* P(u)S(ulatum).)

564, 565 Theodosius I. *Obv., bust of Theodosius, diademed, draped and cuirassed ;* D N THEODOSIVS P F AVG. *Rev., Constantinopolis with sceptre and globe enthroned on prow ;* CONCORDIA AVGGGG (*i.e. of the three Augusti*) A (*1st officina*) ; CONOB(ryzum) *in exergue. A.D. 378-83, Constantinopolis* (solidus, *4.38 gm., diam. 21 mm., BM).*

566, 567 Arcadius. *Obv., bust of Arcadius, diademed, draped and cuirassed ; above, hand lowering wreath ;* DN ARCADIVS P F AVG. *Rev., emperor holding standard and shield by kneeling captive ;* GLORIA ROMANORVM ; * ANTS *in exergue. A.D. 383-8, Antioch* (aes, *6.21 gm., diam. 24 mm., BM).*

568, 569 Honorius. *Obv., head of Honorius, diademed, draped and cuirassed ;* D N HONORIVS P F AVG. *Rev., emperor, holding standard and Victory on globe, spurning fallen enemy with his foot ;* VICTORIA AVGGG ; M D (= *Mediolanum) in field ;* COMOB *in exergue. A.D. 394-5, Mediolanum* (solidus, *4.46 gm., diam. 21 mm., BM).*

570 Valentinian III. *Obv., bust of Valentinian, diademed, in imperial mantle ; r. hand raised ; cross in l. ;* D N FLA VALENTINIANVS P F AVG. *A.D. 425-55, Rome* (solidus, *4.45 gm., diam. 22 mm., BM).*

571, 572 Romulus Augustulus. *Obv., head of Romulus, diademed and draped ;* D N ROMVLVS AGVSTVS (*sic*) P F AVG. *Rev., cross in wreath above* COMOB. *A.D. 475-6, Ravenna* (one-third of a solidus, *1.44 gm., diam. 15 mm., BM).*

thousand years; but the life of Rome, since its foundation as a small central Italian city-state, had endured unbroken for more than twelve hundred, and Roman coinage, as an expression of statehood, had been unchecked for nearly eight hundred. That coinage, at most periods regular, abundant, and solidly based on precious-metal values, had been one of the strongest threads in binding together a vast empire into an economic unity, and one of the brightest factors in illuminating the central and very real *romanitas* of that empire as it began to grow and finally reached its flower. The influence of that long tradition was now to be seen, vigorous and clear, on the coinages of the invaders—Vandals, Visigoths, Suevi, Burgundians, Merovingians and others—who, after the fall of the Roman empire, filled the great vacuum that Rome had left.

NOTES ON THE TEXT

I. THE EARLIEST COINAGE OF THE ROMAN REPUBLIC

1. Cf. Seltman, *GC²*, p. 42. For the general development of Greek coinage, see now G. K. Jenkins, *Ancient Greek Coins*, London, 1972.
2. Cf. Thomsen, *ERC* i, pp. 19, 25 ff. The whole of the relevant chapter (pp. 19 ff.) is indispensable for its assemblage of ancient written sources for the early coinage of Rome.
3. Cf. Thomsen, *ERC* i, pp. 20 ff.
4. Thomsen, *ERC* i, p. 19; see also below, p. 19.
5. Thomsen, *ERC* iii, p. 201.
6. Cf. Thomsen, *ERC* iii, p. 200, on Pliny, *NH* 33.42.
7. See Thomsen, *ERC* iii, pp. 179 ff.
8. Cf. Noe, *The Coinage of Metapontum*, p. 12.
9. Cf. Seltman, *GC²*, pp. 1 ff.
10. Amphora/Spearhead; Anchor/Tripod; Corn-ear/Tripod; Bull/Bull; Shield/Shield; Sword/Scabbard; Trident/Caduceus. See Thomsen, *ERC* iii, pp. 187 ff., and Crawford, *RRCH*, p. 11.
11. Thomsen, *ERC* iii, pp. 187-91, 207 ff.
12. Thomsen, *ERC* iii, pp. 143 ff.
13. *Digesta* I, 2, 2, 30 f.
14. s.v. Μονῆτα.
15. *NH* 33.42-7.
16. Livy, *Epit.* xv, put it in 268.
17. *ERC* i, pp. 210 ff., for the discussion of past treatment of the major crux—the date of the first denarii.
18. See below, pp. 39–40.
19. Except some of the Italian school, for whom an early date for the denarius arouses, perhaps, some fundamental feelings of national prestige.
20. H. Mattingly and E. S. G. Robinson, 'The Date of the Roman Denarius', *Proc. Brit. Acad.* 1932, pp. 211 ff.
21. See Buttrey in *Congr. Internaz. Num., Roma, 1961*, ii, pp. 261 ff.
22. Crawford, *RRCH*, p. 4 f., and hoards nos. 1-70 (pp. 43 ff.) and 71-109 (pp. 60 ff.).
23. See Thomsen, *ERC* i, p. 49; iii, pp. 78 ff.
24. For Livy's references see Thomsen, *ERC* i, p. 30 f.
25. Thomsen, *ERC* i, pp. 59 ff.
26. Thomsen, *ERC* iii, p. 243 ff.
27. A unique fraction exists, of 0.65 g.
28. Cf. Thomsen, *ERC* iii, pp. 83 ff., 93 ff.
29. Reasons for the slightly heavier weight are unknown; cf. Thomsen, *ERC* iii, p. 232 f.
30. Above, p. 19.
31. Cf. Thomsen, *ERC* iii, pp. 116 ff.
32. The Roma/Victory issue bore a sequence of Greek letters, an issue-marking device drawn from the Egyptian coinage of the Ptolemies, with whom Rome established a connection in 273 B.C.: cf. Sydenham, *CRR*, pp. xix and 2 f., though dated too late.
33. For these two *aes* series see Thomsen, *ERC* i, pp. 68-71, 75; for their weights, *id.* iii, p. 234 f. For the nomenclature of the Roma/Roma series, seen as Diana/Diana in Thomsen, *ERC* i, cf. his vols. ii, pp. 153 ff. and 160 f., and iii, p. 12, n. 10.

[34] See Thomsen, *ERC* i, pp. 52 ff. Note that sporadic struck bronze, with ROMANO, had been issued previously from *c.* 289 B.C.; cf. Thomsen, *ERC* iii, p. 52, and Crawford, *RRCH*, p. 11.

[35] Thomsen, *ERC* i, pp. 72-80; iii, p. 234.

[36] And they were quite certainly not neglected : the many series of *aes grave* running from As to uncia or even semuncia could hardly have looked to anything except an internal economy operating at very varied levels.

[37] Cf. Mattingly, *RC²*, p. 91 f.

[38] Thomsen, *ERC* i, pp. 90 ff.

[39] Thomsen, *ERC* ii, p. 260.

[40] Thomsen, *ERC* ii, p. 270, with note 235 : the closure under Nero in A.D. 64, freely advertised on his coins, should however have been included.

[41] Thomsen, *ERC* i, pp. 91 ff. The very rare units of *c.* 4.50 g. (Thomsen, *ibid*, fig. 144) marked XXX (= 30 sestertii ?) once suspected, are now accepted : see Thomsen, *ERC* ii, pp. 261 ff., and Mattingly, *RC²*, p. 17.

[42] See Thomsen, *ERC* i, p. 19 f., and ii, pp. 243 ff., on Pliny, *NH.* 33.47.

[43] See Thomsen, *ERC* iii, p. 265.

[44] Thomsen, *ERC* i, p. 80 f. Note that a great five-As multiple (marked v) was also produced with types of the As: Thomsen, *ERC* i, p. 78 f., figs. 87-8.

[45] Thomsen, *ERC* i, pp. 80 ff.; ii, pp. 15 ff.; iii, p. 169 f.

[46] Thomsen, *ERC* i, pp. 82, 84-5, 88.

[47] These in fact furnish the whole material for the three masterly volumes of Thomsen's *ERC*. Even so, some scholars of the Italian school hold fast to the view that Pliny's silver struck in 289 was not the ROMANO didrachm, but the denarius.

[48] *RC²*, pp. 6 ff.

II. THE INTRODUCTION AND SUPREMACY OF THE DENARIUS, *c.* 211-100 B.C.

[49] For these Spanish preliminaries see Sutherland, *The Romans in Spain*, pp. 22 ff.

[50] See especially Thomsen, *ERC* i, pp. 19 (with Pliny, *NH* 33. 42-46), 35 (with Festus, *De verborum significatu*, p. 347 M), 210 ff. (a synopsis of theories expounded since 1793), and ii, pp. 73-391.

[51] Crawford, *RRCH*, p. 1.

[52] *Id.,* p. 4 f., with hoards nos. 62, 68, 96 and 99.

[53] Thomsen, *ERC* ii, pp. 356 ff.

[54] Mattingly, *RC²*, p. 17. Mattingly's earlier preference for 187 is seen in the arrangement and chronology followed by Sydenham, *CRR*, pp. xxv ff., 14 ff.

[55] The *obv.* head may be Roma, or Roma-Bellona. The *rev.* refers to the legendary help received from the Dioscuri in the Roman victory over the Etruscans at Lake Regillus in 496 B.C. : their help was not less to be desired in 212 B.C.

[56] Livy xxvi, 10, 11 f., speaking of the gold preserved in the treasury for extreme emergencies (*ad ultimos casus*).

[57] The Mars/Eagle gold is discussed at length by Thomsen, *ERC* ii, pp. 218 ff., 282 ff., 303 ff., with preference (cf. *ERC* i, p. 95 f.) for valuation in sestertii. Valuation in Asses was preferred (against the evidence, not necessarily reliable, of Pliny *NH* 33. 47) by Mattingly, *RC²*, p. 16, and by Sydenham, *CRR*, p. xxvi, though both these scholars dated the Mars/Eagle gold much too late, *c.* 169 B.C. : it is accepted also by Crawford, *JRS* 1964, p. 31.

[58] See above, p. 46 and note 53.

[59] Thomsen, *ERC* i, pp. 47, 92; ii, pp. 331 ff. Half-victoriates were struck; one double-victoriate is known.

[60] See note 56 above.

[61] None of the silver coins in the Morgantina hoard (above, note 53) bore a symbol.

[62] See the fundamental discussion in Thomsen, *ERC* ii, pp. 320 ff., and the later conspectus of Crawford, *RRCH*, p. 12 f. (Table II) : Crawford's Tables IV-V (pp. 16 f.) show the approximate chronological sequence of the victoriate as a whole.

[63] Cf. the passages collected in Thomsen, *ERC* i, p. 42 f.

64 Often called Diana, the charioteer wears a small crescent above her forehead.

65 The ancient references, literary and epigraphical, are conveniently collected in Pink, *The Triumviri Monetales and the structure of the coinage of the Roman Republic*, pp. 7-9, and discussed in his pp. 49 ff. The actual arrangement of the coinage by Pink is often open to question. See also Mattingly, *RC²*, pp. 29 ff., and Pink in *ERCHM*, pp. 55 ff.

66 For an approximate sequence of symbols, monograms and abbreviated names on Roman coinage from *c.* 211-150 B.C. (substantially correcting both the sequence and the chronology of Sydenham, *CRR*) cf. Crawford, *RRCH*, Tables VI-IX (pp. 18 ff.). For the later coinage of Athens cf. M. Thompson, *The New Style Silver Coinage of Athens*: the precise date of its introduction is still argued. The term 'family coinage' of Rome, based on the supposition that the *tresviri monetales* were coining by some sort of family right, is of course grossly wrong.

67 See Pink, *The Triumviri Monetales*, pp. 60 ff.; also Mattingly, *RC²*, p. 30 f.

68 Cf. Mattingly, *RC²*, p. 19 f.; Crawford, *RRCH*, p. 5.

69 Crawford, *RRCH*, especially Tables VI-X (pp. 18 ff.).

70 For Count de Salis' work see Grueber, *BMCRR* i, pp. xii ff. : Grueber followed his 'Roman' and 'Italian' classifications without question. Elaboration came with Mattingly (cf. *RC²*, pp. 18 ff., and *Proceedings of the Brit. Acad.*, xxxix, pp. 239 ff.; xlix, pp. 339 ff.) and with Sydenham, *CRR*.

71 *BMCRR* i, p. xiv.

72 See O. Ravel, *NC* 1945, pp. 117 ff., and Sutherland, *ANSMN* iv, pp. 1 ff.

73 See Crawford, *RRCH*, p. 3, and Pink, *The Triumviri Monetales*, p. 13 f.

74 As, Janus-head; semis, Saturn-head; triens, Minerva-head; quadrans, Hercules-head; sextans, Mercury-head; uncia, Bellona-head; semuncia, Mercury-bust.

75 Grueber, *BMCRR* i, p. xli, suggested 'about B.C. 140'. Later, Sydenham (*NC* 1934, pp. 81 ff.; and *CRR*, pp. xxviii f.) argued for

the agency of Tiberius Gracchus in 133 B.C., and Mattingly (*NC* 1934, pp. 88 ff.; *Proceedings of the Brit. Acad.* xxxix, pp. 239 ff.; *RC²*, p. 19) for that of Caius Gracchus *c.* 122 B.C. Buttrey (*ANSMN* vii, pp. 57 ff.) has recently shown that the revaluation was not strictly a monetary reform, and that it did no more than formalize an existing situation in which bronze values had fallen sharply : hence the swift abandonment of the explicit but short-lived mark XVI for the simpler X (still differentiated from the original x) or even x itself. His suggested date, 'in the 140s or 130s', is modified upwards by Crawford, *RRCH*, p. 5, for whom 140 B.C. is a *terminus ante quem*.

76 The cult of Juno Caprotina was associated with Lanuvium, and so too the *gens Renia*.

77 The sequence of *monetales*, here and elsewhere, is based on the hoard-tables of Crawford, *RRCH*, pp. 22 ff. (Tables X ff.).

78 See Alfoldi, 'The main aspects of political propaganda in the coinage of the Roman Republic', in *ERCHM*, pp. 63 ff., and especially pp. 70 ff., where the type-change *c.* 150 B.C. is seen as a sign of break from the *severitas* of the elder Cato's time.

79 Of the moneyers noted above in connexion with changing denarius-types, Cn. Gellius struck semis, triens and quadrans; Aufidius Rusticus semis and triens; C. Renius, Curiatius Trigeminus, Aurelius Cota, and Pompeius Fostlus semis and quadrans; Veturius quadrans alone; and the rest no bronze at all. The As was produced only very occasionally. Cf. Sydenham, *CRR*, pp. 49 ff. (with dating to be corrected).

80 For the defeat of Bituitus and the agency of L. Licinius Crassus and Cn. Domitius Ahenobarbus at Narbo, cf. *BMCRR* i, p. 184, note 1; and for the probable date of the foundation of Narbo, Crawford, *RRCH*, p. 5, and Mattingly, *RC²*, p. 19. For *serrati* as a barbarian preference, Tacitus, *Germania* 5. Plated denarii are discussed at length by Lawrence and Sydenham, *NC* 1940, pp. 184-202, and by Sydenham, *CRR*, p. xliii f.; see *id.*, pp. xl ff. for *serrati*.

[81] See Pink, *The Triumviri Monetales*, pp. 57 f., 64 f. The implication of such special coinages must be that the *monetales*, normally able to call upon coinage-silver, without question, up to a certain level, sometimes had to exceed that level, after receiving special authority to do so.

[82] Cf. Crawford's valuable analysis in *Papers of the Brit. Sch. at Rome* 1966, pp. 18 ff.

[83] Cf. Mattingly's convenient summary in *RC²*, pp. 30 ff.; also Pink, *The Triumviri Monetales*, pp. 58 ff.

[84] That is, 'for the purchase of corn; authorized by the Senate'.

[85] Cf. Pliny, *NH* 33.3.13. The quinarii of Cloulius bore die-sequence letters, and were issued in quantity.

III. REPUBLICAN COINAGE IN THE TIME OF THE IMPERATORES, *c.* 100-48 B.C.

[86] Thus, C. Paapi(us) C.(f.) Mutil(us), Ni(merius) Luvci(lius) Mar(ci filius ?), and Mi(nius) Ieius Mi(nii filius) in Oscan, and Q. Silo in Latin : also 'Embratur' (= Imperator). See in general *BMCRR* ii, pp. 317 ff. For the sequence of these 'Italic' issues see Crawford, *NC* 1964, pp. 145 ff.

[87] Appearing variously as L. PISO L. F.; L. PISO FRVGI (FRVG, FRV); L. PISO L. F. FRVGI; L. PISO, and PISO FRVGI.

[88] The original suggestion was that of T. J. Luce. For the 'conflict' of obverses see, for example, Sydenham, *CRR*, pp. 111, 113 f., 116 ff.

[89] Piso's die-marking system did no more than show in what order the dies, obverse and reverse respectively, were used: no systematic correlations between the obverses and the reverses are apparent. Cf. Crawford, *Papers of the Brit. Sch. at Rome* 1966, p. 20.

[90] See Crawford, *NC* 1964, p. 141 f.

[91] A form of Priapus; cf. *BMCRR* i, p. 286, note 2.

[92] See Crawford's important analysis in *NC* 1964, pp. 148 ff., superseding such earlier views as those of Sydenham, *CRR*, pp. 123 ff.

[93] Cf. Crawford, *NC* 1964, p. 143 f.; *BMCRR* i, p. 314, note 2.

[94] The lituus and jug refer to the auguries which Metellus, as *imperator*, would take before battle : cf. *BMCRR* ii, p. 357, note 2.

[95] Some of these coins have been assigned to a mint in Greece in the light of Plutarch's statement (*Lucullus*, 2) that Lucullus operated a mint in the Peloponnese on Sulla's behalf during his campaign to recover Athens in 86. Grueber long since observed (*BMCRR* ii, p. 459, note 1) that Lucullus would have produced *Athenian*-style coins —a view now generally accepted : cf. M. Thompson, *The New Style Silver Coinage of Athens*, p. 425.

[96] That is, 'twice acclaimed *imperator* by his army'—at Chaeronea and Orchomenus ? The coarse technique of this issue may indicate Italian rather than Roman mintage.

[97] Proclaimed *dictator* in November 82, Sulla held a triumph in January 81, assuming the additional name *Felix*; and the Senate decreed a gilded equestrian statue in Rome to celebrate these honours.

[98] Cf. Pliny, *NH* 33. 46; *BMCRR* i, p. xlii; Mattingly, *RC²*, p. 20; Sydenham, *CRR*, p. xliv.

[99] See Crawford, *Papers of the Brit. Sch. at Rome* 1966, p. 19.

[100] Cf. Cicero, *De officiis* 3.20,80; *BMCRR* i, p. xlii.

[101] Cf. Sydenham, *CRR*, pp. 125-166.

[102] Cf. Buttrey, *Amer. Journ. Arch.* 71, pp. 184 ff.

[103] Crawford, *RRCH*, Table XIII (p. 28 f.).

[104] Opinions on the mintage of this denarial series have been various and perplexing. Sydenham (*CRR*) was content, upon subjectively assessed grounds of style and fabric, to assign certain issues to an 'auxiliary Italian mint' or to 'Italian provincial mints', without benefit of name. Mattingly, *RC²*, p. 21 f., postulated 'a mint in northern Italy, perhaps Pisa', as well as Lanuvium and Praeneste, in both cases upon grounds of type-content. It must be emphasized once more (see above, p. 55) that there is no evidence of any positive kind whatever that

the Senate of Rome at any time organized or tolerated the production of coinage elsewhere than at Rome itself. The only exceptions—and they were still of great rarity—comprised cases where a special distribution had to be made by a general in the field : in such cases the metal could be derived from the spoils of warfare.

[105] Lentulus' gold is discussed, not very helpfully, in *BMCRR* ii, p. 360, note 1, and that of Pompey, with discernment, in *BMCRR* ii, pp. 464 ff., note 1. Pompey was saluted as 'Magnus' by Sulla after warfare in Africa in 81, and he subsequently used this honorific adjective as a part of his name. He celebrated triumphs in 81, 71 and 61; and the proconsulship was conferred on him for foreign campaigns in 77 and 67. The issue of special gold, struck for distribution to his officers abroad to herald his triumph in 61, would have been a not uncharacteristic Pompeian method of advertising his now great military eminence in the face of Caesar's rising—and radical—political ambitions at Rome.

[106] Cf. Sydenham, *CRR*, nos. 937, 1029-33.

[107] Caesar's Gallic booty, and his action (Plutarch, *Caesar*, 35; Appian, *Bell. Civ.* ii, 41) in laying hands on the contents of the treasury at Rome, enabled him to pay out the equivalent of 125 denarii each to his legionaries and over 18 denarii each to the citizens of Rome. See also Pliny, *NH* 33. 17.

[108] Cf. *BMCRR* i, p. 505 f., note 1 *ad fin.*

IV. THE END OF THE ROMAN REPUBLIC, 48-27 B.C.

[109] As before, the sequence and relative chronology of undated or undatable issues of Rome is that given on the basis of hoard evidence by Crawford, *RRCH*, Table XIV, p. 30 f.

[110] Sydenham, *CRR*, no. 1027.

[111] Sydenham, *CRR*, no. 1022.

[112] Cf. Suetonius, *Div. Iul.* 6; *BMCRR* i, p. 542 f., note 1.

[113] Sydenham, *CRR*, nos. 1035-40.

[114] See Grant, *FITA*, pp. 7 ff., and E. R. Caley, *Orichalcum and Related Ancient Alloys.*

[115] Grant, *FITA*, pp. 13 ff., has attributed another series of orichalcum coins (struck at Thessalonica ?) to Caesar *c.* 45 B.C. : these bear a portrait which he argued to be Caesar's, though this seems to be by no means sure.

[116] Suetonius, *Div. Iul.* 41. Caesar introduced some of his own slaves into the mint; cf. Suetonius, *Div. Iul.* 76.

[117] Cicero, *Phil.* ii. 34.87.

[118] xliv 4; see Grant, *FITA*, p. 15 f.

[119] The chronology and arrangement of Caesar's coinage in 44 have been widely disputed. Alföldi's 'Studien über Caesars Monarchie' in *K. Humanistiska Vetenskapssamfundets i Lund Arsberattelse* 1952-3, i, relied upon the recognition as a royal diadem of what is, upon a unique coin, almost certainly a die-flaw or a die-defacement by the lituus behind the head. A clearer sequence is that of Kraay in *NC* 1955, pp. 18 ff. Alföldi has made other and important die-studies of the series, showing the intensity of production : see *Schweizer Münzblätter* 1969, pp. 1 ff., and *Schweiz. Numismat. Rundschau* 1968, pp. 51 ff., 85 ff. For the types as a whole see Sydenham, *CRR*, nos. 1055 ff., though not analytically arranged.

[120] Some of his coins bear the formula IIII VIR PRI FL — ? *primus flavit* : see Pink, *The Triumviri Monetales*, p. 61, and Sydenham, *CRR*, nos. 1088 f.

[121] For the composition of this *collegium* see Buttrey, *The Triumviral Portrait Gold of the Quattuorviri Monetales of 42 B.C.*

[122] Whose reverses use the personal and punning type of a calf (*vitulus*).

[123] Sydenham, *CRR*, nos. 1287-1315.

[124] These coins are specifically mentioned by Dio Cassius xlvii. 25.

[125] On capturing Rhodes, Cassius acquired booty and war-indemnity amounting to 8500 talents. The rose of Rhodes is to be seen on some of his coins.

[126] Sydenham, *CRR*, nos. 1344-51.

127 Sydenham, *CRR*, nos. 1156 ff.

128 This issue was repeated in 42 with A XL.

129 Sydenham, *CRR*, nos. 1316-36.

130 Thus, equestrian statues set up s(enatus) c(onsulto) and POPVLI IVSSV : Sydenham, *CRR*, nos. 1316-19.

131 L. Antonius' occupation of Perugia may be reflected in the gold and silver struck with *obv.* M ANTONIVS IMP III VIR R P C, head of Antony, and *rev.* PIETAS COS, standing figure of Pietas. (There are variants.) The legend on the *rev.* should probably stand for *pietas consulis*, i.e. the family loyalty shown by the consul Lucius Antonius in protecting the interests of his brother Marcus, the Triumvir, against Octavian. See Sydenham, *CRR*, nos. 1171-4; also Liegle, *Zeitschr. f. Num.* 1932, pp. 59 ff., suggesting mintage at Praeneste.

132 Sydenham, *CRR*, nos. 1329-34. For the designation of Octavian (and Antony) to consulships some years in advance, cf. Appian, *Bell. Civ.* v.73 and Dio Cassius xlviii.35, together with *BMCRR* ii, p. 414, note 1.

133 By Mattingly, *NC* 1946, pp. 91 ff., on the strength of Servius' commentary on Vergil, *Aen.* vii. 684-5 ('...Antonius, Augusti (i.e. Octaviani) sorore contempta, postquam Cleopatram duxit uxorem, monetam eius (sc. Cleopatrae) nomine in Anagnia civitate iussit feriri'.). See also Mattingly, *RC*², p. 23. Mattingly himself was fully aware of the extraordinary position that would have been created by Antony's striking coins of Cleopatra in Italy. He was not so fully aware of the fact that Antonian denarii and aurei coined in the East would not have been anomalous : they were, after all, primarily for the payment of *Italian* soldiers and sailors.

134 Cf. *BMCRR* ii, p. 502 f., note 2; Sutherland-Olcay-Merrington, *The Cistophori of Augustus*, pp. 86-8.

135 'Cistophoric' because, during its long previous history in Asia, the tetradrachm had shown a representation of the sacred *cista* or chest of Dionysus : this appears, between its guardian snakes, on Antony's pieces too.

136 The grammar of these legends is not easy : cf. *BMCRR* ii, p. 525 f., note 2. 'Antoni' and 'Cleopatrae' seem to be genitives. 'Queen of Kings' is a natural variation of 'King of Kings' : *filiorum regum* could mean 'and of her sons who are Kings' or 'and of the sons of Kings'.

137 Sulla's aurei stood at 1/30 of a pound (nearly 11 g.), Pompey's at 1/36 (*c.* 9 g.), and Caesar's at 1/40 (just over 8 g.) The aurei of Antony and Octavian preserved this last weight-standard after Caesar's death.

138 Sydenham, *CRR*, nos. 1059, 1080.

139 Sydenham, *CRR*, nos. 1255-70. An introductory As (Sydenham no. 1254) is said to be of copper, the rest of bronze (*BMCRR* ii, p. 501, note 1).

140 Grant, *FITA*, pp. 43 ff., where it is argued that uniformity of style suggests a single mint, possibly Tarentum, where Antony's fresh reconciliation with Octavian took place.

141 Grant, *FITA*, pp. 46 ff., where Puteoli is suggested on rather tenuous grounds.

142 Sydenham, *CRR*, nos. 1271-4.

143 For these *aes* coinages see Sydenham, *CRR*, nos. 1275-8, and pp. 214 f.; also Grant, *FITA*, pp. 50 ff.

144 For Antony's silver fineness cf. Pliny *NH* 33. 46 ('miscuit denario .... ferrum'); and for the survival of this coinage cf. (for Britain alone) Sutherland, *Coinage and Currency in Roman Britain*, pp. 20, 27, 31, 37 f. : the phenomenon was widespread elsewhere too.

145 Some numerals are expressed in alternative ways : thus VIIII and IX, XIIII and XIV, XVIIII and XIX. Sometimes a legionary number is found without and also with a distinguishing name : thus XII and XII ANTIQVAE, XVII and XVII CLASSICAE, XVIII and XVIII LVBICAE. Coins marked with legionary numbers above XXIV (running down to XXX) have aroused question. See Sydenham, *CRR*, nos. 1212-53.

146 Cf. *BMCRR* ii, pp. 535 ff. (29-37 B.C., eastern mintage); *BMCRE* i, pp. 97 ff. (31-29 B.C., eastern mintage). For more accurate dating cf. Crawford, *RRCH*, Table XVII (p. 34 f.).

147 First understood by K. Kraft, *Zur Münzprägung des Augustus* (Sitzungberichte der Wissensch. Gesellsch. an der J. W. Goethe-Universität Frankfurt/Main, 7 (1968), no. 5), pp. 206 ff.

148 Cf. Dio Cassius lii. 41.

149 See Seltman, *GC²*, pl. 50, 4.

150 See Sutherland-Olcay-Merrington, *The Cistophori of Augustus*, pp. 85 ff.

151 Lepidus, the third of the original three Triumvirs, had long since retired into privacy, though he still retained the sacred office of *pontifex maximus*, for which Octavian (as Augustus) had to wait until Lepidus' death in 12 B.C.

V. THE REFORMED COINAGE OF AUGUSTUS AND ITS DEVELOPMENT DOWN TO NERO, 27 B.C.-A.D. 68

152 The authority for coinage under Augustus has been much discussed. The old view of a planned division (gold and silver to the emperor, *aes* to the Senate; cf. *CAH* x, p. 198, and *BMCRE* i, pp. xv ff.) was followed by the suggestion that Augustus, while controlling gold and silver directly, prompted major *aes* issues through his effective control of business in the Senate (cf. Grant, *FITA, passim*). This suggestion has been weakened by the arguments of K. Kraft (*Jahrbuch für Num. und Geldgesch.* 1962, pp. 7 ff.) and Sutherland (*Revue Num.* 1965, pp. 99 ff.): see also Sutherland, *The Emperor and the Coinage* (forthcoming). It is reasonably clear that Augustus' authority was absolute over all coinage within the empire.

153 Cf. Grant, *SMACA*, pp. 1-20.

154 For example, Augustus' cistophoric tetradrachms struck in the province of Asia used to be regarded as a minor, if interesting, coinage. A study of it now shows that it was produced from certainly not less (and

probably a good many more) than 355 obverse and 568 reverse dies within a span of ten years : see Sutherland-Olcay-Merrington, *The Cistophori of Augustus*.

155 See Sutherland, *Gold*, pp. 93-4.

156 Carisius provides the last example of the usage, so common during the Republic, whereby a legate signed coinage on behalf of the supreme commander.

157 Cf. O. Gil Farrés, *La moneda hispánica en la edad antigua*, p. 396.

158 For circulation, and explanation of the reverse type, see Grant, *SMACA*, pp. 18 ff., 119 f.; for the chronology of the series, C. M. Kraay, *NC* 1955, pp. 75 ff., against Grant, *FITA*, pp. 70 ff.

159 Attribution to Caesaraugusta and Patricia : *BMCRE* i, pp. cviii ff., following Laffranchi. Essential distinctions analysed : Sutherland, *NC* 1945, pp. 58 ff. Urban *aes* coinages of Spain : A. Vives y Escudero, *La moneda hispánica*, and Grant, *NC* 1949, pp. 93 ff. Die found at Nîmes : P. Le Gentilhomme, *Revue Num.* 1946, proc., p. ii. Mint-attribution to Gaul may be forthcoming in a study by T. R. Volk.

160 Expressly defined, QVOD VIAE MVN(itae) SVNT.

161 Occasionally *quattuorviri*, colleges of four. No *collegium* coined all *aes* denominations. In some cases a *collegium* coined in gold or silver (see below) as well as in *aes* : in others they coined in precious metal only, without any *aes*, according to currency-demand. Their precise sequence and chronology is uncertain, depending largely on the known dates in their later careers : see the summary of conflicting views in A. S. Robertson, *Roman Imperial Coins in the Hunter Cabinet* i, pp. xxxii ff. The outside limits of their activity (in all metals) are *c.* 23 and *c.* 4 B.C. For the mint of Rome itself see R. A. G. Carson in *ERCHM*, pp. 227 ff.

162 For the abundance and wide circulation of this *aes* see Grant in *ERCHM*, pp. 96 ff., and *SMACA*, p. 16 f.; also Kraay in *ERCHM*, pp. 113 ff., where the countermarking of Augustus' *aes* by subsequent

emperors is fully discussed. For the significance of the s c, see the references to Kraft and Sutherland in note 152 above.

163 Cf. Meriwether Stuart, *Amer. Journ. of Arch.* 1939, pp. 601 ff.; J. M. C. Toynbee, *ERCHM*, pp. 205 ff. Some eastern portrait-variants of Augustus are discussed in Sutherland, *et al.*, *The Cistophori of Augustus*, pp. 109 ff.

164 Discussed by Sutherland in *NC* 1943, pp. 40 ff.

165 See Sutherland, *NC* 1952, pp. 139 ff., against H. R. W. Smith, *Problems Historical and Numismatic in the Reign of Augustus*.

166 Cf. the references in note 165. Basic evidence for Augustan coinage at Lyons from *c.* 15 B.C. lies in an argument stretching backwards from Strabo iv.3, 2 (of A.D. 18) through intermediate *aes* showing the great Altar of Lyons and starting after 12 B.C.

167 After Lepidus (see note 151 above) had died in 12 B.C.

168 For the wide distribution of 'Altar' *aes* see Grant, *SMACA*, p. 20; and for the possibility of a variety of mints see J.-B. Giard in *Revue Num.* 1967, pp. 119 ff.; 1968, pp. 76 ff.

169 See H. Mattingly's remarks in *NC* 1963, p. 255 f.

170 For the tetradrachms see note 154 above; for other Pergamene issues, Sutherland, *Revue Num.* forthcoming.

171 For c(ommune) A(siae)—not c(aesaris) A(uctoritate)—cf. Sutherland in *Revue Num.* 1965, pp. 99 ff.

172 J. G. Milne, *Catalogue of Alexandrian Coins*, pp. xv, 1.

173 Perhaps emphasizing the combined standing of Tiberius (as *pontifex maximus*) and Livia (Augustus' widow and Tiberius' mother) in the cult of Augustus. See also Sutherland, *CRIP*, p. 84 f.

174 See Sutherland, *CRIP*, pp. 79 ff., where the influence of the powerful praetorian prefect Sejanus is suggested. The 'Divus Augustus Pater' coinages: Sutherland, *NC* 1941, pp. 97 ff.; the 'Clementiae-Moderationi' coins, *id.*, *JRS* 1938, pp. 129 ff.

175 Grant's contention (*FITA*, p. 44 f., n. 11, pp. 31 ff.) that Tiberius' TR.POT. XXIIII (and Drusus' parallel TR.POT. II or ITER(um)) do not date these coins to A.D. 22-3 can be disproved : cf. Sutherland, *CRIP*, pp. 191 ff.

176 The difficult chronology of the 'Agrippa' coins is examined by S. Jameson in *NC* 1966, pp. 95 ff.

177 H. Mattingly's arguments in *BMCRE* i, p. cxlii f., can be expanded. He observed the change from bare to laureate head, and from looser to neater lettering, in the course of gold and silver of A.D. 37-8 (with TR P). There were changes also in the forms of the head, nose, and (most important) eye. Rome was the mint for gold and silver under Nero, in all probability (Carson in *ERCHM*, p. 231) : no evidence for transference from Lyons to Rome can be adduced for Claudius; and thus the internal changes of detail in the coins of Gaius argue for transference in 37-8. It should be noted that, although there is not any strict parallelism of *type* between Gaius' gold and silver and Gaius' *aes*, there is a strong parallelism of *concept* such as would have been natural if all imperial coinage was centralized at Rome.

178 Cf. Sutherland, *CRIP*, pp. 105 ff.

179 Cf. *BMCRE* i, p. cxlv; Sutherland, *CRIP*, pp. 109, 114; and, for the omission of s c, Kraft in *Jahrb. f. Num. und Geldgesch.* 1962, pp. 13 ff., with Sutherland in *Revue Num.* 1965, p. 106 f.

180 Cf. Grant, *NC* 1949, pp. 93 ff.

181 *BMCRE* i, p. lviii f.; H. Mattingly, *RC²*, p. 130 f.

182 See A. Momigliano's brilliant *Claudius : the emperor and his achievement*.

183 During which there were intermissions in 42/3, 45/6, 47/8 and (probably) 48/9.

184 See Grant, *Univ. Edinburgh Journal* 1949, pp. 229 ff., and *RAI*, pp. 74 ff.; also J. M. C. Toynbee in *ERCHM*, pp. 205 ff.

185 Cf. Kraay, *Gazette num. suisse* 1952, p. 53 f., emphasizing the fact that the abundant imitations of Claudian *aes* are mainly modelled on prototypes without P P.

186 Extremely rare sestertii with *obv.* portrait of

Britannicus (*BMCRE* i, p. 196, no. 226) are now recognized as being of Flavian date; cf. *BMCRE* ii, p. lxxviii.

[187] Cf. Milne, *op. cit.*, p. 3 f.

[188] The Lyons 'altar' issue of quadrantes *c.* 41 simply celebrated the fiftieth birthday of the emperor who was born on the day the altar was dedicated : it was very small.

[189] Cf. Sutherland, *CRIP*, p. 197, for references.

[190] Cf. *BMCRE* i, p. xliv f.; Mattingly, *RC²*, p. 132.

[191] Cf. Sutherland, *CRIP*, p. 152 f.; Mattingly, *RC²*, p. 107.

[192] Cf. Pliny, *NH* 33. 3, 13; *BMCRE* i, pp. xliv ff.; Mattingly, *RC²*, pp. 122 ff.; Sutherland, *CRIP*, pp. 199 ff.; West, *Gold and Silver Coin Standards in the Roman Empire* (American Num. Soc. Notes and Monographs, no. 94). A very slow decline in weight from reign to reign is due probably to the reluctance of any one emperor to issue coins heavier than the norm of what was already (partly worn) in circulation.

[193] For the differences between *aes* of Rome and Lyons, cf. *BMCRE* i, p. clxxxii; for analysis of distribution (Asses), Grant in *NC* 1955, pp. 21 ff., 1957, p. 229 f. A fully detailed catalogue of both series will exist in D. W. MacDowall's *Western Aes Coinages of Nero* (American Num. Soc. Numismatic Studies, forthcoming).

[194] The temple was certainly closed in 66—the 300th anniversary of its first such closure (Grant, *Univ. Edinburgh Journal* 1949, p. 239); but the coins suggest anticipation from 64 : cf. Sutherland, *CRIP*, p. 166.

[195] Cf. *BMCRE* i, p. cxliii; MacDowall, *op. cit.*

[196] Mint-organization itself may also have become more systematic. The existence of the *tresviri* under Augustus suggests three working sections (*officinae*) of the mint of Rome then (and cf. the triple-type series of 'cistophori' at Ephesus and Pergamum : Sutherland, *et al.*, *The Cistophori of Augustus*). Under Nero the operation of *officinae* (three ? six ?) is to be traced clearly; cf. MacDowall, *op. cit.*

VI. DISSOLUTION AND THE NEW IMPERIAL DYNASTIES : THE FLAVIANS, TRAJAN, AND THE ANTONINES, A.D. 68-192

[197] *BMCRE* i, p. clxxxvii.

[198] Cf. Kraay in *NC* 1949, pp. 129 ff.; Mattingly in *NC* 1954, pp. 32 ff.

[199] Cf. Kraay, *The Aes Coinage of Galba* with p. 47 on the 'posthumous' theory as against Mattingly in *BMCRE* i, pp. ccxii ff., and ii, p. lviii. Kraay's analysis of the internal arrangement of Galba's *aes* was successfully modified by MacDowall in *NC* 1957, pp. 269 ff.

[200] Cf. *BMCRE* i, p. ccxvi; Kraay, *The Aes Coinage of Galba*, pp. 39 ff.

[201] Only very seldom did Roman practice favour the demonetization of the coinage of a former and fallen *princeps* : the formidable difficulty of calling in such coinage was doubtless the reason. Numerous forgeries of Othonian *aes* exist, usually distinguishable as cast pieces of the last 200 years or so.

[202] Cf. Kraay in *NC* 1952, pp. 78 ff.

[203] Suetonius, *Div. Vesp.* 16, where the sum is calculated in sestertii—the accountancy-unit of the time.

[204] *BMCRE* ii, pp. liii ff.; Mattingly, *RC²*, p. 110 f.

[205] *Silvae* iii, 3.

[206] *BMCRE* i, pp. 196 ff.; ii, pp. 252, 351 ff.

[207] Herzfelder in *NC* 1936, pp. 1 ff.

[208] *RIC* ii, pp. 24 f., 81.

[209] *RIC* ii, pp. 247, 274.

[210] *RIC* iii, pp. 28 f., 98 ff.

[211] *RIC* ii, pp. 33 ff., 41 ff., 85 ff., 95 ff., 121 f., 135 ff.

[212] *RIC* ii, pp. 141 ff.; cf. Mattingly in *NC* 1920, pp. 179 ff.

[213] *RIC* ii, pp. 302 ff.

[214] *RIC* ii, pp. 376 ff., 445 ff.

[215] Mattingly in *NC* 1939, pp. 21 ff.

[216] N. A. Mouchmov, *Le trésor numismatique de Réka-Devnia* (Sofia, 1934).

[217] See, e.g. the use made of the Dorchester hoard material by Mattingly in *RIC* iv(3),

pp. 3 ff. See also Carson in *BMCRE* vi, pp. 43-5.

218 MacDowall, *The Western Aes Coinages of Nero* (forthcoming); P. V. Hill, *The Dating and Arrangement of the Undated Coins of Rome, A.D. 98-148*, p. 3; R. A. G. Carson, *BMCRE* vi, p. 7, and in *ERCHM*, pp. 233 ff.

219 Carson, *BMCRE* vi, p. 41; Hill, *op. cit.*, p. 4.

220 Cf. Sellwood in *NC* 1963, pp. 217 ff.; Sutherland, *et al.*, *The Cistophori of Augustus*, pp. 105 ff.

221 Sutherland, *et al.*, *The Cistophori of Augustus*, p. 119 f., with references.

222 C. C. Vermeule, *Some Notes on Ancient Dies and Coining Methods*.

223 These opinions are at variance with those of Mattingly, who wrote in *BMCRE* iii, p. liv, 'the portraiture of Trajan is treated with loving interest—sometimes with close attention to his strongly individualized features, sometimes more ideally, as the type of the best of Emperors'. However, in dealing with Hadrianic coin-portraiture, he could also write (*ibid.* p. cxiii) of 'the stately dullness that hangs about so much of Trajan's coinage'.

224 J. M. C. Toynbee, *The Hadrianic School: a Chapter in the History of Greek Art*.

225 Cf. *BMCRE* iv, pp. clxxviii, clxxxii f.

226 The ancient generic name for these pieces—if any existed—is unknown. For the narrow borderline between normal coins and 'medallions' cf. Grant in *ERCHM*, pp. 96 ff.

227 Cf. J. M. C. Toynbee, *Roman Medallions* (American Num. Soc. Num. Studies no. 5), especially pp. 24 ff., 28 ff., 127 ff.

228 That is, as the inheritor of the Roman tradition founded by Aeneas when fleeing from Troy to Italy with the figure of Pallas.

229 For the social, religious, and political importance of these 'personified' qualities, including Victoria especially, cf. Mattingly in *Harvard Theol. Review* 1937, pp. 103 ff.; Charlesworth in *Harvard Theol. Review* 1936, pp. 107 ff.; and Gagé in *Mélanges d'arch. et d'hist. de l'école fr. de Rome* 1932, pp. 61 ff.

230 For example, *Imp. Caes Nerva Traian Aug Germ/P M Tr P Cos III P P*.

231 Dio Cassius lxviii. 15.

232 Cf. *BMCRE* iii, pp. lxxxvi ff.; J. M. C. Toynbee in *Archaeological Journal* xcix, pp. 33 ff.

233 On which Hadrian came to abandon the radiate crown as the distinguishing mark of dupondii, of which the yellow brass was evidently held to be sufficient identification. It is possible that Hadrian disliked the heavy splendour of the radiate crown.

234 *BMCRE* iii, p. cxxxi with note 3.

235 The 'Britannia' smaller *aes* is of noticeably poor technique and fabric, and the fact that it is relatively common in Britain and distinctly uncommon elsewhere has led to the view not only that it was produced for Antoninus' forces in Britain but that it was actually struck in Britain; cf. M. Todd in *NC* 1966, pp. 147 ff.

236 Cf. L. C. West, *Gold and Silver Standards in the Roman Empire*.

VII. INFLATION, DECENTRALIZATION, AND REFORM: FROM THE SEVERI TO DIOCLETIAN, A.D. 193-305

237 For the more detailed history of these years cf. H. M. D. Parker, *A History of the Roman World from A.D. 138-337*, pp. 55 ff.

238 *Chronogr. of A.D. 354* (*Chron. Min.* i, p. 147).

239 Cf. West, *op. cit.*, p. 114 f.; *BMCRE* v, p. xx f. Calculation of the total bulk of Severus' coinage is a task for the future; but Mr C. L. Clay's die-analysis of the early *aes* shows, within a small span of years, and for one metal alone, that it must have been very large.

240 Cf. *BMCRE* v, pp. cii, cvii f., cxiv f., cxvii f., cxxi f.

241 The long and detailed introduction by H. Mattingly to *BMCRE* v is indispensable for the understanding of the subtle intricacies of the Severan coinage.

242 Cf. *BMCRE* v, p. xvii f.

243 Cf. *BMCRE* v, p. xviii, for the view, sometimes held, that the antoninianus = 1 1/2 or even 1 1/4 denarii. R.A.G. Carson in *BMCRE* vi, p. 19 f., followed Mattingly in the equation 1 antoninianus = 2 denarii. Note that, apart from all other major expenses or inflationary pressures at this time, the army was costing much more. Severus had increased the soldiers' pay from the figure of increase granted by Commodus, and a further rise under Caracalla is possible : Caracalla's enfranchisement of all subjects in the Roman empire (and with higher taxes) would at best only hold an even balance. Cf. Parker, *op. cit.*, p. 97 f.

244 As with the coinage of the Severi, full reference must be made to *BMCRE* v for detailed analysis.

245 See *BMCRE* vi, pp. 83 ff., for the limited series of eastern denarii, closely similar in their unpolished style to the eastern issues under the Severi.

246 Except for the sestertii, which often show an angular trimming which had first become obvious under Marcus Aurelius. Cf. *RIC* i, pp. 18 ff.

247 Cf. R. A. G. Carson in *BMCRE* vi, pp. 16 ff.

248 Cf. Carson, *BMCRE* vi, pp. 40 ff.

249 It may be remarked, in passing, that the art of the medallion, although still very high, by now showed a conception markedly different from that of the time of Hadrian, Antoninus Pius, and (sometimes) Commodus. In the second century, medallions were true (if small) *objets d'art* : their obverses, with imperial names and titles, might cleave to the conventions of coinage, but their reverses (often with no inscription at all) showed a power of free design which owed its inspiration not to coinage but to sculpture and relief. In the third century and later, medallions became and remained much more coin-like, however beautiful their workmanship might be. Cf. J. M. C. Toynbee, *Roman Medallions* (Amer. Num. Soc. Num. Studies, no. 5), plates xl-xlix.

250 A proliferating literature surrounds the complex question of imperial inflation, whether of prices or currency. The briefer comments of A. H. M. Jones in *ERCHM*, pp. 25 ff., should be read with his detailed treatment in *Econ. Hist. Review* 1953, pp. 313 ff. : those of H. Mattingly in *RC²* pp. 124 ff., with his paper in *Studies.....in honor of Allan Chester Johnson*, pp. 275 ff. The most recent examination, and in great depth, is that of J.-P. Callu, *La politique monétaire des empereurs romains de 283 à 311* (Paris, 1969). The quantitative and denominational pattern of coin-distribution in northern and central Italy, Gaul, and Britain is the subject of current study by R. Reece.

251 Note the appearance of the *officina* number, II. Philip's silver coins (not the gold or the *aes*) were marked from I to VI, or (in Greek numerals) from A to Z. *Officina* numbers were not to become a regular feature of imperial coinage for some few years to come. The first great exercise in the distribution of unmarked *officinae* preceding the marked issues was based on type-frequencies : cf. H. Mattingly, *NC* 1939, pp. 1 ff.

252 Cf. H. Mattingly in *NC* 1924, pp. 210 ff., and in *RIC* iv(3), pp. 113, 117 f. It is remarkable to find Commodus included among the 'good' emperors.

253 *RIC* iv(3), pp. 104 ff. It is not possible in this short sketch to discuss the very brief coinages of these and some other later usurpers.

254 The aurei of Uranius were once suspect, but recent work has authenticated them; cf. R. Delbrück in *NC* 1948, pp. 11 ff., and H. Mattingly in *RIC* iv(3), pp. 203 ff.

255 The coinage of the Gallic empire is complex and difficult. P. H. Webb's treatment in *RIC* v(2), pp. 310 ff., has been superseded by such basic studies as that of G. Elmer in *Bonner Jahrbuch* 1941, pp. 108 ff., and by a mass of subsequent work : special mention should be made of J. Lafaurie, *Bull. de la soc. franç. de num.* 1963, pp. 279 ff., and P. Bastien, *Le monnayage en bronze de Postume*. See also Callu, *op. cit.*, and *A Survey of Num-*

ismatic Research (Intern. Num. Congress, Copenhagen, 1967), p. 180 f.

256 Cf. R. A. G. Carson in *Congr. Internat. de Num., Paris 1953, Actes*, pp. 259 ff., and especially p. 267 f.

257 For a brief survey of third-century mint extension see H. Mattingly, *RC²*, pp. 115 ff.

258 For the date see *RIC* vi, p. 1 f.

259 The arguments against the equivalence T = Tarraco (in Spain) are summarized by H. Mattingly, *RC²*, p. 118.

260 Cf. H. Mattingly, *RC²*, pp. 126 ff.

261 It must be emphasized that the interpretation is still far from certain. Under Tacitus (275-6), Carus (282-3), and Carinus (283-4) antoniniani are found with x.i or i.a, i.e. 10 = 1, suggesting that the worth of the antoninianus was then halved. And only twenty years later, in 301, xx.i (or xxi) certainly signified, not that the unit contained two denarii, but that it contained 20 denarii: the significance of the numeral notation had by then completely changed (cf. K. T. Erim, J. Reynolds and M. Crawford in *JRS* 1971, pp. 171 ff.).

262 See *CAH* xii, p. 300. Ancient authors connected this with the bad quality of what they produced.

263 P. H. Webb's treatment in *RIC* v(2), pp. 204 ff., though now in need of revision, is still a good general source of material.

264 P. H. Webb, *RIC* v(2), pp. 426 ff. Later and more acute analysis has been supplied by R. A. G. Carson in *Journ. Brit. Archaeol. Assoc.* 1958, pp. 33 ff., and in *Mints, Dies and Currency* (Essays in memory of Albert Baldwin), pp. 57 ff.

265 A Vergilian echo; see *Aen.* ii.282.

266 P. H. Webb in *RIC* v(2), pp. 558 ff.

267 The two latter with either *Victoria Sarmatica, Virtus Militum,* or *Providentia Augg.* For the use of the term *argenteus* under Diocletian cf. Erim-Reynolds-Crawford, *JRS* 1971, pp. 171 ff.

268 For the 'reformed' coinage of Diocletian see *RIC* vi, passim; and, for 294 as the date of the reform, *RIC* vi, p. 1 f. The range of denominations and their weights are de-

scribed in *RIC* vi, pp. 93 ff. For the general tenor of the types employed, see Sutherland in *ERCHM*, pp. 174 ff. For the Arras hoard see J. Babelon and A. Duquenoy in *Aréthuse* 1924, pp. 45 ff., and P. Bastien in *Bull. de la soc. acad. des Antiquaires de la Morinie* 1959, pp. 1 ff. Since the publication of *RIC* vi in 1967 Bastien has contributed a great deal of excellent work in the further analysis and chronology of the Diocletianic issues.

269 Cf. Sutherland in *Schweiz. Münzblätter* 1962, pp. 73 ff.

270 Cf. Sutherland in *JRS* 1963, pp. 14 ff.

271 See Erim-Reynolds-Crawford, *JRS* 1971, pp. 171 ff., for new epigraphical evidence of the 'geminata potentia' of coins in 301. If they are correct in interpreting 'xx.i' folles of *c.* 301 as expressing the equivalence 1 follis = 20 denarii (i.e. the 'denarii communes' of the period), with its implication of a previous rate equal to 10 denarii, the interpretation in *RIC* vi, p. 98 (cf. *JRS* 1961, pp. 94 ff.), as 1 follis = 20 sestertii would have to be abandoned.

272 It must of course be remembered that an overvalued or inflated currency is usually the concomitant of a price inflation of a kind that Diocletian's price edict sought (vainly) to cure by legislation.

VIII. THE FINAL STAGE: FROM CONSTANTINE I TO ROMULUS AUGUSTULUS

273 For details of this period see H. M. D. Parker, *op. cit.*, pp. 240 ff.; Sutherland, *RIC* vi, pp. 25 ff.; Bruun, *RIC* vii, pp. 64 ff. Younger sons of Constantine were made Caesar in due course—Constantius II in 324 and Constans in 333. Delmatius and Hanniballianus, nephews of Constantine, received brief honour between 335 and their deaths in 337.

274 See *RIC* vi, pp. 88 ff.; vii, pp. 13 ff.

275 Above, p. 253.

276 *RIC* vi, pp. 100 ff., vii, pp. 8 ff. These

'reduced' folles perhaps contained 1 or 2 per cent of silver : cf. *RIC* vii, pp. 79 ff. The chronology of the weight-reduction between 307 and 313, worked out in some detail in *RIC* vi *passim*, has been further refined by the comparative measurement of the ever-smaller dies which were used—a method cleverly employed by L. H. Cope and P. Bastien.

277 London ceased to coin *c.* 325. Alexandria was converted by Diocletian from a Greek to a Latin-language mint *c.* 294 (*RIC* vi, p. 645). Carthage coined only *c.* 296-311, and Ostia only *c.* 308-13 (for Maxentius). Serdica closed in 314. The mint of Arles was established in 313, and Sirmium in 320 (until 325-6). Ticinum ceased coinage *c.* 326-7. Constantinople opened in 326. The major mints of Lyons, Trier, Aquileia, Rome, Siscia, Thessalonica, Heraclea, Nicomedia, Cyzicus, Antioch, and Alexandria were busy more or less throughout the period of the Tetrarchy and Constantine, though Aquileia underwent a temporary closure in the 320s.

278 For mint-control see *RIC* vi, pp. 105 ff.; vii, pp. 13 ff. Instructions for gold coinage involved a closer degree of direct control.

279 Diocletian, the first 'Jovian', had controlled the east : Galerius, Licinius, and Maximinus were nominees in succession. The 'Herculian' succession of Constantine was explicit on western types, though not so conspicuously.

280 Cf. H. M. D. Parker, *op. cit.*, pp. 299 ff.

281 The celebration of quinquennial vows for future imperial success combined with thanksgiving for past success was by now regularly reflected on imperial coinage : cf. *RIC* vi, pp. 19 ff.; vii, pp. 56 ff.

282 Constantine's ambivalent attitude to Christianity—perhaps less an outright conversion (though he recognized the Church) than a gradual move away from the pagan gods towards the one God—is well reflected in his coinage : cf. *RIC* vii, pp. 61 ff. The Christogram (☧) appears on a few coins, usually in a subordinate position, and very

occasionally on the emperor's helmet. The type with *labarum* (chrism on standard) and serpent, with the significant legend *Spes Public*, is the only purely and overtly Christian type; and even this could have been interpreted simply as Constantine overcoming Licinius in 324. Nevertheless it was in the Christogram that Constantine had seen his augury of victory in defeating Maxentius in 312.

283 Cf. P. Grierson in *ERCHM*, pp. 240 ff.

284 'Radiate' copies have been the subject of controversy, and (cf. Mattingly, *RC²*, p. 227, n. 3) there is still some room for argument. See, in general, Sutherland in *Dark Age Britain* (ed. D. B. Harden), pp. 3 ff., and J.P.C. Kent in *Proc. Third Congress of Roman Frontier Studies* (1957), pp. 61 ff.

285 Cf. J. P. C. Kent in *ERCHM*, pp. 190 ff., for the connection between increased precious-metal coinage and increased imperial insistence upon tax-payment in precious metal in the fourth century.

286 These smaller and larger silver coins are now often termed (without any total authority) 'siliquae' and 'miliarensia'.

287 The monetary system of this period is no less obscure than that of the Tetrarchy : cf. Mattingly, *RC²*, p. 220 f. Publication of J. P. C. Kent's *RIC* viii (337-64) is keenly awaited.

288 The pattern of *aes* coinage from Constantine onwards (down to 498) is clearly presented in *Late Roman Bronze Coinage* (P. V. Hill, J. P. C. Kent and R. A. G. Carson). Kent's *RIC* viii (forthcoming) will cover the years 337-64 in detail in all metals; J. W. E. Pearce's *RIC* ix covered all metals for the years 364-95.

289 That is, 'Victoriae Dominorum Augustorumque Nostrorum'.

290 Cf. Mattingly in *NC* 1933, pp. 2 ff., and in *RC²*, p. 236, where he suggested Vergilian echoes in the choice of these designs. For the chronological sequence of these types cf. *LRBC*, p. 41, and J. P. C. Kent in *NC* 1967, pp. 83 ff.

291 The great increase in the volume of silver

coined after Constantine poses the question of where increased silver sources had been obtained. In the later fourth century the silver of south-west Britain certainly seems to have been more busily mined. Doubtless other sources were, earlier on, more systematically exploited elsewhere.

292 Cf. Mattingly, *RC²*, p. 254 f.

293 For interesting recent work on this subject see M. H. L. Pirenne, *Optics, Painting, and Photography*.

294 Julian preserved the later monetary system of Constantius II—solidus with half and third, and heavy and light silver 'miliarensia' (of 1/60 and 1/72 of a pound) with 2 g. silver 'siliqua'. His *aes* ultimately comprised pieces of 8.5 and 3 g. The chronology of his coinage is discussed by J. P. C. Kent in *NC* 1959, pp. 109 ff., and the significance of the bull type on *aes* by Kent in *NC* 1954, p. 216 f., where references to Apis are discounted in favour of the symbolism of the bull as leader of the herd.

295 Cf. Pearce, *RIC* ix, p. 1 f.

296 The latest detailed treatment is that of Pearce in *RIC* ix, with some modifications in Hill-Kent-Carson, *LRBC*, especially pp. 41 ff.

297 Cf. *RIC* ix, pp. xxvi ff. The solidus stood at *c*. 4.5 g., and was of very pure gold: its fractions were the half and (at 1.7 g.) the 1 1/2 scripulum, which gave way under Theodosius to the one-third-solidus of *c*. 1.5 g. Heavy miliarensia weighed 1/60, and light 1/72, of a pound of silver; and siliquae 1/144 of a pound (*c*. 1.9 g.).

298 See for example *RIC* ix, p. 58 f.

299 Cf. *RIC* ix, p. 183.

300 See (for Britain) Sutherland, *Coinage and Currency in Roman Britain*, pp. 82 ff., 97; also *Reports of the Research Committee of the Society of Antiquaries of London* ix (Lydney Park), pp. 112 ff. Such copies were presumably among the 'pecuniae vetitae' of the Theodosian Code.

301 Pearce (*RIC* ix, p. xl) considered the Roman defeat by the Goths at Adrianople in 378 as the 'greatest blow to Roman arms since Cannae'.

302 This famous reverse passed into the repertoire of great types and lasted through the Byzantine period, being echoed even in such series as that of the Anglo-Saxon kings in England: cf. Sutherland, *English Coinage, 600-1900*, pls. 2, no. 6, and 12, no. 113.

303 Toynbee, *op. cit.* p. 117 f.

304 See above, note 285.

305 Metal-purity in the western mints was apparently the responsibility of a special *comes*: thus, at Mediolanum (Milan) for example, solidi could be fully marked M(*e*)D(*iolanum*) COMOB. See in general *RIC* ix, p. xxxv.

306 Cf. A. Alföldi, *A Festival of Isis at Rome under the Christian Emperors of the Fourth Century*. It is difficult to assign a deliberately anti-Christian quality or purpose to the puzzling and interesting group of fourth-century 'contorniates'—large *aes* pieces (certainly not coins), usually with hammered-up edges, often cast and partly engraved, and with types in general alluding to athletic contests and to great figures of the past: cf. A. Alföldi, *Die Kontorniaten: ein verkanntes Propagandamittel der stadtrömischen heidnischen Aristokratie in ihrem Kampfe gegen das christliche Kaisertum*, and Toynbee, *op. cit.*, pp. 234 ff.

SELECT BIBLIOGRAPHY

Listed below are those main books which have been most useful in the preparation of the present volume, and from which access can be gained to such fuller bibliographies as that, for example, in H. Mattingly's *Roman Coins*. Substantive works alone have been listed : certain other substantive works are mentioned, when appropriate, in the footnotes, where there are also to be found references to the many important articles on special subjects, included in a wide variety of journals, which are indispensable for fuller study.

Abbreviations

Callu, J.-P. *La politique monétaire des empereurs romains de 283 à 311*, Paris, 1969.

Cambridge Ancient History.   *CAH*

Carson, R. A. G., and Suther-   *ERCHM* land, C. H. V. (editors). *Essays in Roman Coinage presented to Harold Mattingly*, Oxford, 1956.

Crawford, M. *Roman Repub-*   *RRCH* *lican Coin Hoards*, London, 1969.

— *Roman Republican Coinage*, 2 vols., Cambridge, forthcoming.

Gil y Farrés, O. *La moneda hispánica en la edad antigua*, Madrid, 1966.

Grant, M. *From Imperium to*   *FITA* *Auctoritas*, Cambridge, 1946.

— *The Six Main Aes Coinages*   *SMACA* *of Augustus*, Edinburgh, 1953.

— *Roman Anniversary Issues*,   *RAI* Cambridge, 1950.

Grueber, H. A. *Coins of the*   *BMCRR* *Roman Republic in the British Museum*, 3 vols., London, 1910.

Hill, P. V., Kent, J. P. C., and   *LRBC* Carson, R. A. G. *Late Ro-man Bronze Coinage*, London, 1960.

Jenkins, G. K. *Ancient Greek*   *AGC* *Coins*, London, 1972.

Journal of Roman Studies.   *JRS*

Kraay, C. M. *The Aes Coinage of Galba*, New York, 1956.

MacDowall, D. W. *The Western Aes Coin-ages of Nero*, New York, forthcoming.

Mattingly, H. *Roman Coins*   *RC²* (2nd edition), London, 1960.

Mattingly, H., and Carson,   *BMCRE* R. A. G. *Coins of the Roman Empire in the British Museum*, 6 vols., London, 1923.

Mattingly, H., Sydenham, E. A., and others. *The Roman Imperial Coinage*, 8 vols., London, 1923. — RIC

Milne, J. G. *Catalogue of Alexandrian Coins in the Ashmolean Museum* (2nd edition), Oxford, 1971.

Mouchmov, N. A. *Le trésor numismatique de Réka-Devnia*, Sofia, 1934.

Museum Notes (American Numismatic Society). — ANSMN

Numismatic Chronicle. — NC

Pink, K. *The Triumviri Monetales and the Structure of the Coinage of the Roman Republic*, New York, 1952.

Pliny. *Natural History.* — NH

Robertson, A. S. *Roman Imperial Coins in the Hunter Coin Cabinet*, 2 vols., Oxford, 1962, 1971.

Seltman, C. T. *Greek Coins* (2nd edition), London, 1955. — GC²

Smith, H. R. W. *Problems Historical and Numismatic in the Reign of Augustus*, Berkeley, 1951.

Sutherland, C. H. V. *Coinage and Currency in Roman Britain*, London, 1937.

Sutherland, C. H. V. *Coinage in Roman Imperial Policy, 31 B.C.–A.D. 68*, London, 1951. — CRIP

Sutherland, C. H. V., Kraay, C. M., and Levick, B. *Ashmolean Museum, Oxford: Catalogue of Roman Coins, Augustus*, Oxford, forthcoming.

Sutherland, C. H. V., with Olcay, N., and Merrington, K. E. *The Cistophori of Augustus*, London, 1970.

Sydenham, E. A. *The Coinage of the Roman Republic*, London, 1952. — CRR

Thomsen, R. *Early Roman Coinage*, 3 vols., Copenhagen, 1957–61. — ERC

Toynbee, J. M. C. *Roman Medallions*, New York, 1944.

Vermeule, C. C. *Some Notes on Ancient Dies and Coining Methods*, London, 1954.

Vives y Escudero, A. *La moneda hispánica*, 4 vols., Madrid, 1924–6.

West, L. C. *Gold and Silver Coin Standards in the Roman Empire*, New York, 1941.

GLOSSARY

AES
Bronze; but used by loose convention to mean also coins of copper and brass.

AES GRAVE
Circular cast bronze coins.

AES RUDE
Unworked lumps of bronze, of irregular weight.

AES SIGNATUM
Bronze cast in bar form, with moulded designs.

ANTONINIANUS
Base silver coin, with radiate portrait, introduced (probably as a double denarius) by Caracalla.

AQUILA
The eagle surmounting a legionary standard.

AS
Originally a cast bronze coin of one Roman pound (12 unciae), and later a token coin of copper under the empire.

AUGUR
Priestly interpreter of heavenly omens.

AUREUS
(properly DENARIUS AUREUS)
Gold coin, in the earlier empire worth 25 denarii.

BIGA
Chariot drawn by two horses or other beasts.

BIGATUS
Silver coin of the Republic, with biga reverse.

BILLON
Alloy of base silver.

CISTA MYSTICA
Sacred Dionysiac basket with serpent emerging or entwined.

CISTOPHORUS
Originally a silver Asiatic tetradrachm, with *cista mystica* type, and later an imperial denomination worth 3 denarii.

CONGIARIUM
Public distribution of food.

DECUSSIS
10-As piece.

DENARIUS
Silver coin equivalent in value originally to
10 (later to 16) Asses.

DIDRACHM
2-drachma piece.

DIE
Tool for striking coins, engraved with the
design in negative.

DRACHMA
A coin expressing the normal Greek unit
of reckoning, varying in weight from mint
to mint.

DUPONDIUS
2-As piece.

FLAN
The circular piece of metal which, impressed
with types, forms a coin.

FOLLIS
Copper coin, with slight silver content,
introduced by Diocletian.

LITUUS
Augur's curved wand.

MILIARENSE
Larger imperial silver coin of the 4th century, of heavier and lighter weight (1/72
and 1/60 of a pound).

MONETALES (IIIVIRI A.A.A.F.F.)
The annual *collegium* of three junior officials
in charge of the mint of Rome.

OBVERSE
The front and principal side of a coin (e.g.
that on which the main design, generally
the portrait, is placed), struck from the
'anvil' or fixed die.

OFFICINA
A working-section within a mint.

ORICHALCUM
Brass.

QUADRANS
One quarter of an As, originally of 3 unciae.

QUADRIGA
A four-horse chariot.

QUADRIGATUS
Silver coin of the Republic, with quadriga
reverse.

QUARTUNCIA
Quarter-uncia.

QUINARIUS
Half-denarius.

REVERSE
The back side of a coin, struck from the
punch or loose die.

SEMIS
Half-As, originally of 6 unciae.

SEMUNCIA
Half-uncia.

SERRATUS
Republican denarius with notched edges.

SESTERTIUS
Quarter-denarius; ultimately a brass coin worth 4 Asses.

SEXTANS
One sixth of an As, originally of 2 unciae.

SILIQUA
Smaller imperial silver coin of the 4th century, latterly 1/144 of a pound.

SOLIDUS
Gold coin of Constantinian origin, lighter (at 1/72 of a pound) than the preceding aureus (1/45 of a pound from Nero, and 1/60 under the Tetrarchy).

TALENT
Greek weight-unit of 6000 drachmae.

TETRARCHY
Administrative system of empire instituted by Diocletian, with two Augusti and two Caesars.

TRESSIS
3-As piece.

TRESVIRI A.A.A.F.F.
See under MONETALES.

TRIBUNICIA POTESTAS
The power exercised by the tribunes of the people, and later by the emperor.

TRIENS
One third of an As, originally of 4 unciae.

UNCIA
One twelfth of an As.

VICTORIATUS
Silver coin of the Republic, with Victoria reverse.

INDEX

Mithradates, king of Pontus 74, 78-9
Moneyers *see Tresviri monetales*
Monograms on Republican coins 54, 56
Morgantina hoard 46-7
Multiples 206, 253, 261, 274
Munda, battle of 94
Mylae, battle of 39

Naples *see* Neapolis
Narbo 69, 287
Naulochus, battle of 103, 112, 145
Neapolis 14, 20
Nemausus 138, 291
Nepotian 268
Nero 158 ff., 179, 189, 208
Nerva 198, 207
Nicomedia 254, 275
Nîmes *see* Nemausus
Numa 17

Obryzum aurum 274
Octavia (sister of Octavian) 113-4, 117
Octavia (daughter of Claudius I) 159
Octavian (*see also* Augustus) 101-3, 112-3, 118-20, 129
Officinae 147, 182, 188, 224-5, 233, 243, 252-3, 262, 293, 295
'Optimus Princeps' 198, 207-8, 212
Orichalcum 95, 117; in Augustus' monetary system 139; in Nero's monetary reform 168
Oscan inscriptions 73-4, 288
Ostia 41, 297
—, port of 158, 168
Otacilia Severa 232
Otho 173-5

Pacatian 232
Palmyra 243
Parthia 112, 138, 140, 146-7, 212, 215-6, 225

Patricia *(colonia)* 138, 291
Patrician families, influence on Republican types 61, 68, 78
Paula, Julia *see* Julia Paula
Pecunia 17
Pergamum 114, 146-7, 158
Perseus of Macedon 54, 68
Pertinax 215-6
Pescennius Niger 215-6
Pharsalus, battle of 88
Philip I and II 232, 242
Philip II of Macedon 13
Philippi, battle of 102-3
Plated coins (*see also* Counterfeiting) 69, 80, 158
Plautilla 216-7
Pliny (the Elder) 17, 19, 27, 40, 45-6, 80, 159
Plotina 208
Pompey the Great 86-8, 94, 103, 289
Pompey, Cnaeus 93-4
Pompey, Sextus 93-4, 103, 112, 118
Pomponius 19
Poppaea 159
'Populares', influence on Republican types 68
Portraiture, Republican 79, 86, 94-6; of Octavian 119; imperial 189, 198-9, 208, 224, 232-3, 243, 252, 261-2, 275, 276, 292, 294
Postumus 232-3
Privernum 87
Probus 243
'Prow' bronze 33, 40-1, 60; types later varied 70
Pupienus 225, 232
Pyrrhus of Epirus 19, 26, 36

'Quadrigati' 40-1, 46
Quinarius (silver) 46-7, 77
Quintillus 242

The text of this book, the four-colour offset illustrations and the jacket were printed by the Imprimerie Paul Attinger S.A., Neuchâtel.—The heliogravure reproductions were executed by Roto-Sadag S.A., Geneva.—Photolithos by Atesa, Geneva. —The binding is by Clerc & Cie S.A., Lausanne.—Layout and design by André Rosselet.—Editorial: Dominique Guisan.— Production: Suzanne Meister.

Printed in Switzerland